Humans at Work

*The Art and Practice of Creating
the Hybrid Workplace*

Anna Tavis and Stela Lupushor

KoganPage

First published in Great Britain and the United States in 2022 by Kogan Page Limited

2nd Floor, 45 Gee Street	8 W 38th Street, Suite 902	4737/23 Ansari Road
London	New York, NY 10018	Daryaganj
EC1V 3RS	USA	New Delhi 110002
United Kingdom		India

www.koganpage.com

Kogan Page books are printed on paper from sustainable forests.

© Anna Tavis and Stela Lupushor, 2022

The right of Anna Tavis and Stela Lupushor to be identified as the authors of this work has been asserted by them in accordance with the Copyright, Designs and Patents Act 1988.

ISBNs

Hardback	978 1 3986 0426 1
Paperback	978 1 3986 0423 0
Ebook	978 1 3986 0424 7

British Library Cataloging-in-Publication Data

A CIP record for this book is available from the British Library.

Library of Congress Cataloging-in-Publication Data

Names: Tavis, Anna, author. | Lupushor, Stela, author.
Title: Humans at work: the art and practice of creating the hybrid
   workplace / Anna Tavis and Stela Lupushor.
Description: London, United Kingdom; New York, NY: Kogan Page, 2022. |
   Includes bibliographical references and index.
Identifiers: LCCN 2021056358 (print) | LCCN 2021056359 (ebook) | ISBN
   9781398604230 (paperback) | ISBN 9781398604261 (hardback) | ISBN
   9781398604247 (ebook)
Subjects: LCSH: Work environment. | Manpower planning. | Strategic
   planning.
Classification: LCC HD7261 .T38 2022 (print) | LCC HD7261 (ebook) | DDC
   658.3/8–dc23/eng/20220106
LC record available at https://lccn.loc.gov/2021056358
LC ebook record available at https://lccn.loc.gov/2021056359

Typeset by Integra Software Services, Pondicherry
Print production managed by Jellyfish
Printed and bound by CPI Group (UK) Ltd, Croydon CR0 4YY

PRAISE FOR *HUMANS AT WORK*

Humans at Work meets today's moment. Too often, organizations adopt mechanistic approaches to living, dynamic, human organizations. Anna Tavis and Stela Lupushor inject the human element into an intuitive yet clear and systematic framework for any organization seeking alignment with the people that are its business.
Dr Michael N. Bazigos, Senior Partner and Global Managing Director of Accenture Strategy's Talent and Organizational Analytics business

Anna Tavis and Stela Lupushor continue to be at the forefront of the future of work. The social contract and world of work is shifting at earthquake levels of magnitude and intensity. Their research and new ways of thinking help us accelerate our understanding of these shifts and solutions that can help our organizations survive this phenomenon and become more fit for human beings and performance.
Wendy Branche, Vice President and Head of Global Talent Management, Visa

Despite everything we know about humans at work, the undeniable fact is that work is simply not working for many people. This timely book, by two of the leading experts in the field, shows us why there has never been a better time to apply the key lessons from the science of human resources management and organizational psychology, as well as the growing field of people analytics, to help every human thrive at work. A book that every organization needs to study in detail.
Dr Tomas Chamorro-Premuzic, Chief Innovation Officer at ManpowerGroup and Professor of Business Psychology at Columbia University and University College London

Humans at Work is a must-read for anyone who's struggling with the effects of the Covid-19 pandemic and the myriad of other forces changing in fundamental ways how people work and how organizations need to organize and manage to deliver value-added products and services. Anna Tavis and Stela Lupushor have synthesized this complex and ever-changing environment into a cogent guidebook and playbook full of significant insights and benefits for readers.
Michael Dulworth, CEO, Executive Networks

If the "great reassessment" taught us anything, it is the willingness to listen and to meet people where they are. At Mastercard, this is central to our DQ or Decency Quotient. Anna Tavis and Stela Lupushor show how empathy can be a force multiplier in our organizations that, when done in an authentic way, can build a winning culture that our people and stakeholders will trust and value.
Michael Fraccaro, Chief People Officer, Mastercard

At this time of intense change, the voices of deep thinkers like Anna Tavis and Stela Lupushor are crucial. *Humans at Work* adds significant insight about empathy and technology into this evolving debate about the future of work.
Dr Lynda Gratton, Professor of Management Practice at London Business School and author of *Redesigning Work*

Humans at Work explains how to both consider and, crucially, apply technology and analytics in the workplace with the human purpose in mind. In the book, Anna Tavis and Stela Lupushor provide a timely reminder that our tools, frameworks, and technologies should have the ultimate purpose of restoring the workplace to its human-centric design. The four parts of *Humans at Work* explore the origins and the evolution of the 4Ws of "work"—work, workforce, workplace, and worth. The book's extensive appendix helps translate these concepts into practical tools that can be applied in the day-to-day work of human resources teams. *Humans at Work* is an indispensable guide for any HR leader or professional looking to ensure that their work has a positive impact on their firm and, more importantly, the people who work for it.

David Green, co-author of *Excellence in People Analytics*, Managing Partner of Insight222, and host of the *Digital HR Leaders* podcast

Humans at Work is the book, roadmap, and manifesto we have been waiting for. After years of handwringing on the "future of work," and the "middle skills gap," *Humans at Work* takes us back to the necessary fundamentals that the largest and truest successes—for businesses, workers, and in our personal lives—happen when we take a radically honest approach to what we do and why we do it. Thank you for this wonderful work that finally makes sense and brings order to the crashing levels of noise and dissonance on the "work, workforce, workplace, and worth" conversation.

Angie Kamath, Dean, NYU School of Professional Studies

Workplaces are now subject to a new "social contract," where the needs of "humans" are transcending the safety of pay and benefits to experiences of purpose for themselves and their communities. A must-read for anyone involved with defining "work," this book showcases the expertise of two convincing analysts.

Rajamma Krishnamurthy, Senior Director HR Technology, Microsoft

In this thought-provoking book, Anna Tavis and Stela Lupushor challenge our thinking about how to design work and the workplace to create value for humanity at large. Well researched and evidence-based, yet filled with practical frameworks and advice, this is a must-read for future-minded business leaders and HR leaders alike. The authors compel us to choose empathy, trust, and impact on others to design workplaces that benefit all stakeholders.

Michaela Schoberova, Worldwide Director for People, Organization and Leadership Development, Colgate-Palmolive

Many leaders recognize that we are lacking the skills needed for the future of our workforce. Stela Lupushor and Anna Tavis have outlined a practical user guide and model through which to consider the relevant aspects of the new world of work and how to optimize the relationship and outcomes for both companies and the workforce. I look forward to further exploring and engaging in this journey.

Zane Zumbahlen, Chief Human Resources and Talent Officer, Cancer Treatment Centers of America

To all the humans at work.

CONTENTS

List of Figures xiii
About the Authors xv
Preface xix
Foreword by Peter Cappelli xxiii

Introduction 1

PART ONE
Work

01 What Is Work? 7

Introduction: Evolution of Work 7
The Rise of the No-Collar Economy 8
Work and Its Boundaries 10
Work and Leisure 11
Work and Health 14
Work and Mental Health 16
Work and Mindfulness 18
Work and Coaching and Mentoring 19
Reclaiming the Humanity of Work 21
Endnotes 21

02 Jobs vs Work 27

The "Work" Is Not Working 27
Swapping Skills for Jobs Is Too Little Too Late 28
Beware of Exponential Growth 30
Are We Heading Towards a Post-Work Society? 35
Endnotes 36

03 How Work Is Measured: Productivity vs Impact 39

Why Measurements Matter 39
Has Measuring Become Monitoring? 42
Does Pursuit of Productivity Still Make Sense? 44
The Productivity Race is Lost, Long Live Impact 45
How Impact Can Overtake Productivity as a Success Measure
   of Work 49
The Impact Journey Starts with an Audit 50
Endnotes 52

PART TWO
Workforce

04 Human-Centered Work Design: Humans vs Workforce 57

The Evolutionary Case for a Human-Centered Approach 57
A New Way of Looking at Our Relationship with
   Technology 58
Institutional Speedbumps 60
Business Turns to Human-Centric Solutions 61
Human-Centricity Takes Center Stage 63
How Performance Management Became the Battleground for
   HCD 64
How Humans Reclaim the Workplace 66
Endnotes 67

05 Designing for Inclusion: Empathy as a Superpower 69

Discovering Empathy 69
Anti-Empathy Backlash 72
Empathy by Design 77
Let Empathy Not Numbers Drive Inclusion 80
Artificial Empathy (AE) 82
The Future of Empathy 83
Endnotes 83

06 From Customers to Employees: Employees Are the New Customers 87

"They're Not Employees, They're People" 87
Customer Experience Sets the Stage 91
Employees Are the New Customers 95
Towards the Worker-Centered Economy 97
Endnotes 98

PART THREE
Workplace

07 Where Work Happens 103

The Return of the Hybrid Workplace 103
Why Working From Home Is Not the Answer 105
The Future of Work Is Hybrid 107
Co-working Spaces Re-enter the Scene with a Vengeance 109
Taking Work to People Rather Than People to Work 110
Endnotes 113

08 Work at Scale: Organizations as Platforms 115

The Platforms Have Arrived 115
Talent Platforms Break Through the Firewall 116
Key Talent Marketplace Players 119
How Platforms Are Changing People Practices 121
Why Industrial Leadership No Longer Works 122
Organizational Considerations for Implementing Platforms 126
Endnotes 127

PART FOUR
Worth

09 Why Work? The Rise of Employee Experience 131

The Turnover Tsunami 131
Defining Work 133
Employee Experience: What Took So Long? 134

Employee Experience Is Not About the Tools 137
The Search for the Meaning of Work 140
Endnotes 142

10 Work Reputation as Experience 145

Four Historical Stages of Reputation 145
Reputation and its Discontents 146
Reputation as Honor 148
Reputation as an Asset 150
Reputation as Currency 152
Reputation as Experience 155
Endnotes 158

Conclusion 161

What Is a Manifesto? 161
Why a Manifesto? 162
Humans at Work Manifesto 162
Endnotes 164

Appendices
1: (4+3) Ws Framework 165
2: Work 167
3: Workforce 171
4: Workplace 177
5: Worth 183
6: Worker Journey 191
7: Work Experience Design 201
8: WorkTech 209
Glossary 221
Index 225

LIST OF FIGURES

Figure I.1   (4+3) Ws Framework 2
Figure 1.1   Hard Work 8
Figure 2.1   Work Is Not Working 28
Figure 3.1   Measuring Work 40
Figure 4.1   Fusion of Humans and Machines 58
Figure 5.1   Empathy 70
Figure 5.2   Empathy Map 79
Figure 6.1   From Customer Experience to Workforce Experience 92
Figure 7.1   The Stages of the Hybrid Workplace 108
Figure 9.1   Work: Push vs Pull 133
Figure 10.1   Evolution of Reputation 146
Figure 10.2   Everyone is a Dog on the Internet 147
Figure 11.1   Humans at Work Manifesto 162
Figure A.1   (4+3) Ws Framework 165
Figure A.2   Work 169
Figure A.3   Workforce 174
Figure A.4   Workplace 178
Figure A.5   Worth 184
Figure A.6   Worker Journey 193
Figure A.7   Work Experience Design 203
Figure A.8   WorkTech 210

ABOUT THE AUTHORS

Anna Tavis

Dr Anna Tavis is Professor and Academic Director of the Human Capital Management Department at NYU School of Professional Studies, Senior Fellow with The Conference Board, and the Academic in Residence with Executive Networks. Dr Tavis has been named on the Thinkers50 Radar for 2020.

Dr Tavis is a former Executive Editor of *People+Strategy* journal and is an Associate Editor of Workforce Solutions Review. She publishes regularly in the business media and has been quoted by *The Washington Post*, *Bloomberg*, *The Human Resources Executive*, and *Training* magazine. Her *Harvard Business Review* articles with Peter Cappelli, "HR Goes Agile"[1] (2018) and "The Performance Management Revolution" (2016), were reprinted in HBR's Must Reads (2016 and 2018), Definitive Management Ideas of the Year[2] (2016 and 2018) and in *Agile: The insights you need from Harvard Business Review*[3] (2020). Dr Tavis co-edited two volumes of essays, *Point Counterpoint (2012) and Point Counterpoint II (2017)*,[4] that are approved for HR professional certification credit. Dr Tavis is a frequent presenter at international conferences on the topics of Future of Work, People Analytics and Technology, Employee Experience, and Intelligent Automation in the Workplace. Prior to joining the NYU faculty, Dr Tavis navigated a diverse global career in academia, business, and consulting. In academia, she was on the faculty at Williams College, Fairfield University and Columbia University. In business, Dr Tavis was the Head of Motorola's EMEA OD function based in London, Nokia's Global Head of Talent Management based in Helsinki, Chief Learning Officer with United Technologies Corp based in Hartford, CT, and Global Head of Talent and Organizational Development with AIG Investments based in NYC. Dr Tavis received her PhD in Comparative Literature from Princeton

University and an Executive MBA in International Business from the University of South Carolina.

Stela Lupushor

Stela is the founder of Reframe.Work Inc., a consulting firm advising clients on how to innovate and develop a workforce strategy that creates a resilient, inclusive, and accessible workplace through the use of technology, human-centered design, and future thinking. She is also the Program Director, Strategic Workforce Planning and Talent Management Councils as well as the Human Capital Analytics Institute Senior Fellow shaping the research agenda of The Conference Board—a member-driven think tank that produces economic indicators (such as Consumer Confidence Index™) and research, organizes conferences, and brings together peer networks. Stela is also the founder of amazing.community, a non-profit organization extending the work horizon for women, empowering them to thrive in the workplace of the future. Most recently, Stela led the people analytics functions at Fidelity Investments and TIAA, where she developed analytics capabilities and enabled data-driven workforce decision making. Previously, Stela led the HR Strategy and Social Analytics function at IBM where she built their "future of work" strategy. She brought to these initiatives her consulting experience from Price Waterhouse, PwC Consulting, and IBM Global Business Services. Stela is the co-founder of the Strategic HR Analytics Meet-up, bringing together over 2,400 members in the NYC area to shape community thinking around people analytics. She has been recognized as one of the Top 100 HR Influencers, Top 40 Global Influencers in HR Tech, and was the judge for MIT's Inclusive Innovation Challenge and MIT Solve (marketplace for social impact and social entrepreneurship, connecting startups with the funding and resources to solve global challenges). Stela teaches Digital Workplace Design at NYU. She holds a diploma in Mathematics and Computer Science, speaks English, Romanian, and Russian, has a patent pending for a social sentiment analysis tool, and is a sought-after speaker on the topics of People Analytics and the Future of Work.

Endnotes

1 Cappelli, P and Tavis, A (2018) HR goes agile, *Harvard Business Review*, **96** (2), pp 47–53

2 Harvard Business, ed (2018) *HBR's 10 Must Reads 2018: The definitive management ideas of the year from Harvard Business Review*, Boston, MA: Harvard Business Review Press

3 Harvard Business Review (2020) *Agile: The insights you need from Harvard Business Review*, Boston, MA: Harvard Business Review Press

4 Tavis, A, Vosburgh, RM, Gubman, E (2012) *Point Counterpoint: New Perspectives on People and Strategy,* Chicago, IL: Society For Human Resource Management; Vosburgh, RM, Tavis, A and Sokol, M (2017) *Point Counterpoint II: New Perspectives on People and Strategy*, Chicago, IL: Society For Human Resource Management

PREFACE

The Humans at Work Revolution Is Here

In December 2015 the term "Fourth Industrial Revolution"[1] was officially coined by Klaus Schwab in the publication *Foreign Affairs*. Since then, it has shaped the agenda of many forums and entered the vocabulary of global leaders. The so-called "cyber-physical systems" underpinning this revolution combine human and technical capabilities in ways that create new markets, a dynamic competitive landscape, and new ways to generate value.

The impact of this revolution is showing up in the form of accelerated digitization, growing wealth inequality, and major restructuring of traditional value chains. Scientific discoveries and technological innovation permeate all parts of contemporary life and work. Organizations are taking advantage of technology to automate routine work, speed up lengthy production cycles, transform the interactions between humans and machines, create vast amounts of data leading to sophisticated insights, and deliver "delightful" experiences for consumers. These changes have benefited many: shareholders who have seen significant returns from the new crop of companies, consumers who are expecting and receiving increasingly frictionless and personalized experiences, corporate executives with outsized compensation packages,[2] and investors and stock markets encouraging short-termism and financial engineering[3] to manipulate earnings. These changes also come with downsides such as loss of privacy, decay of trust in institutions, health and environmental crises, and erosion of social contracts.[4]

These positive and negative outcomes are referred to by economists as "externalities."[5] *Moral hazard* is an externality that leads to decisions that maximize benefits for some at the expense of others without any consequences (think toxic waste and pollution, congestion and high noise, economically devastated neighborhoods). One of the big moral hazards of the Fourth Industrial Revolution is labor market externalities.[6] Workers are continuously expected to do more with less, and faster. They are monitored and quantified as organizations become obsessed with efficiency and shorter production cycles. Growing rates of precarious employment,[7] constant risk of job displacement, pay insecurity, as well as shrinking corporate benefits and social welfare programs—all creating new segments of society at or below poverty level. All these factors combined with growing rates of insecurity, anxiety, and inequality in the workplace lead to physical and mental health deterioration and general challenges to human wellbeing.

If this trend were to be reversed, we could be at the precipice of a new kind of revolution—where cyber-physical systems are restructured and transformed around the human, to benefit the human and elevate human conditions for everyone.

We want to call this, accordingly, the "Humans at Work" revolution.

While the term "revolution" implies a sudden and forceful change of social systems and structures, the Fourth Industrial Revolution did not hold those characteristics, nor should the subsequent revolutions. Societal restructuring comes with a mix of small and large shifts in social awareness and focus.[8] Industries and sectors are continuously being reshaped. Innovations, scientific discoveries, and "black swan" events create major points of pivot, forcing companies to adapt, evolve or perish. Few such disruptions happen overnight and unexpectedly. There is usually a slow progression of events, papers, patents, developments, projects—all constituting weak signals[9] that point to the evolving nature of these disruptions and the building up of momentum.[10] A weak signal is a "seemingly random or disconnected piece of information that at first appears to be background noise but can be recognized as part of a significant pattern by viewing it through a different frame or connecting it with other pieces of information."[11]

We—as representatives of both research and practitioner worlds—have been detecting the signals that point to a big transformative surge impacting the world of work. It includes not only how people work, how work is defined, who is considered workforce, and the value individuals get from work, but also the infrastructural elements organizations need to put in place to support these changes. We describe it here with the formula (4+3) Ws. This formula represents four core elements—work, workforce, workplace, worth—and three enabling elements—worker journey, work experience design, and WorkTech. By examining each of these elements from both historical and present-day perspectives we are offering a solution to how to break down and reassemble the *puzzle* of work.

In the book, we examine each element in the (4+3) Ws formula from an evolutional viewpoint and in the Appendices we explain and expand on the current and technical side of each element. We asked ourselves the following questions: What is this W? How did we get here? What's the issue today? Why does it matter? We illustrate our perspective with historical examples, company case studies, and contemporary research to support our point of view.

We use the body of the book to set the broader context to current thinking about the urgent issues associated with Work, Workplace, Workforce and Worth. We look for inspiration to the classics and marvel at how relevant their wisdom remains today. When it comes to being human, history and culture keep iterating, adding new tools and giving rise to the future.

Technology has always had a disproportionate impact in how society organizes itself and how companies operate and create value. As consumers, we have lived through remarkable changes to our experience of using technology; the same transformation is now coming to the world of work. Technology cannot be stopped from advancing and taking over human tasks, and we try to communicate a sense of urgency for humans to take charge. As humans, we have to be the mindful stewards of the unfolding tech revolution in the workplace.

The "Humans at Work" Revolution is here. This book gives you both a deeper historical framework and a set of practical approaches to help navigate your organizational transformation independently, with your humans in mind. Collectively, we can make the world of work *work* for everyone.

Endnotes

1 Davis, N (2016) What is the Fourth Industrial Revolution? World Economic Forum, https://www.weforum.org/agenda/2016/01/what-is-the-fourth-industrial-revolution/ (archived at https://perma.cc/L9NN-5RNY)

2 Mishel, L and Wolfe, J (2019) CEO compensation has grown 940% since 1978, Economic Policy Institute, https://www.epi.org/publication/ceo-compensation-2018/ (archived at https://perma.cc/3ADN-EMNH)

3 Dharan, BG, Creekmore, JH, and Jones, JH (2003) Earnings management with accruals and financial engineering, https://www.semanticscholar.org/paper/Earnings-Management-with-Accruals-and-Financial-Creekmore-Jones/203da35dc92c9cf16113748044cec3ce7379f3ed (archived at https://perma.cc/U78U-N8WR)

4 D'Agostino, F, Gaus, D, and Thrasher, J (2021) Contemporary approaches to the social contract, *Stanford Encyclopedia of Philosophy*, https://plato.stanford.edu/entries/contractarianism-contemporary/ (archived at https://perma.cc/5QD4-VELE)

5 Helbling, T (2020) Externalities: Prices do not capture all costs, *Finance & Development*, International Monetary Fund, https://www.imf.org/external/pubs/ft/fandd/basics/external.htm (archived at https://perma.cc/N9ZX-5VAR)

6 Acemoglu, D (2014) Labor Economics, 14.661, Lectures 1 and 2: Labor Market Externalities, MIT (lecture slides)

7 International Labor Rights Forum (nd) Companies worldwide are shirking their legal obligations to workers by replacing permanent jobs with contract and temporary work, https://laborrights.org/issues/precarious-work (archived at https://perma.cc/3JJ3-P5D6)

8 Figura, A and Wascher, W (2008) The causes and consequences of economic restructuring: Evidence from the early 21st century, Board of Governors of the Federal Reserve System, https://www.federalreserve.gov/pubs/feds/2008/200841/200841pap.pdf (archived at https://perma.cc/8EYY-R4L3)

9 Kaivo-Oja, J (2012) Weak signals analysis, knowledge management theory and systemic socio-cultural transitions, *Futures*, 44 (3), pp 206–17

10 Green, D (2016) *How Change Happens*, Oxford University Press

11 Schoemaker, PJH and Day, GS (2009) How to make sense of weak signals, *MIT Sloan Management Review*, https://sloanreview.mit.edu/article/how-to-make-sense-of-weak-signals/ (archived at https://perma.cc/RDR9-8UQL)

FOREWORD

The legal theorist and social commentator William Blackstone, writing in the 1700s, noted that employment was one of the three fundamental relationships in life, behind only parent and child and marriage.[1] This is because it is very complicated, loaded with conflicts of interest but also mutual obligations and responsibilities. Especially for employees, the outcomes affect all aspects of their life and, in turn, society.

The United States has had a distinctive and, by world standards, a reasonably peculiar view of employment, one that is weaker on obligations by the employer and that gives them greater power to look after the employer's interests. It is rooted in a kind of free-market notion of individualism and the assumption that the employer and individual employees are on more of an equal footing than reality actually suggests.[2] In that context, employers have exercised more power over employees than in most any other society. What they do with that power is the question.

Along with the industrial revolution came an effort to get employees and their work to adapt to the logic of production systems, machinery in particular, most notably in the form of scientific management. The pushback against the extremes of scientific management has continued ever since.

By the 1950s, management scholar Douglas McGregor articulated the two worldviews that divided the governance of the workplace. The first was this scientific management notion of bending workers to the productive process and making optimization of that process the goal. The second began with the Human Relations movement rooted in the 1930s and its belief that humans had fundamental needs that, if met, could actually make production and employers more successful. In other words, backing off efforts to optimize production and pay attention to those needs was actually the best way to optimize production. In McGregor's famous phrase, the former became known as Theory X and the latter as Theory Y.[3]

That tug-of-war between the two has been playing out ever since. By the 1980s, the accumulation of research on these human needs and the effects on workplace outcomes was so large that Harvard Professor Richard Walton essentially declared Theory Y the winner.[4] In the past 10 years or so, the growing belief that there was but one measure to optimize—shareholder value—and the rise of data science and its optimization-based algorithms represented a strong push in the other direction. By my accounting, Theory X was once again winning.[5]

Humans at Work represents a counter-reformation, though, pointing out that we have neglected the human aspects in modern management, that this is costing us a lot in terms of damage to people, employees in particular, and finally that these costs are big enough that any employer worried about the success of their organization should be taking this issue seriously. The book outlines what should be done.

The issue, of course, is that employers hold all the marbles in determining what happens at work. Why should they care? Stock market values have been booming, and in Washington and state capitals, business lobbyists are largely in control of the agenda, snuffing out most efforts to reel in their power. Is this just a "feel good" demand, that employers should care about other things as well, such as the welfare of employees? Nothing is likely to happen, at least in the short run, unless employers are persuaded to think differently about the way they manage their employees.

Yet there are some reasons for thinking that the pendulum in society is swinging in another direction, one that employers like everyone else can't help but notice. One aspect of this is that what we have been teaching in colleges and universities has slowly begun to change. The simple view of economics taught in the 1980s, that people are basically rational, the way to get them to behave is with financial incentives, that markets solve most problems, and that optimization ideas are best for expanding resources, has slowly given way to a more sophisticated understanding. Behavioral economics, the application of cognitive psychology to economic problems, demonstrated that we can understand and explain how people make decisions that systematically deviate from rationality. Empirical evidence on incentives shows the many ways that they go wrong and the situations where they do not push people in appropriate directions. Market failures of various kinds are seen as common rather than anomalies.

On the social front, a number of problems that have their roots in the workplace have received so much attention as to push even the most traditional organization to take them seriously. The best-known of these is now diversity and inclusion, and the pressures to improve outcomes in this area have now moved inside the business community. The best example is companies demanding that their vendors demonstrate good diversity outcomes as a condition for winning "requests for proposals." Next on the list has been "social impact," the ability to show success in product markets in reducing the negative externalities that Anna and Stela describe. The most important of these so far have been around global warming and pollution. The list is expanding, though, as employees in many organizations push their leaders to make decisions that improve people's lives.

The Covid-19 pandemic has brought attention to the treatment of employees, especially the need to address mental health issues associated with working in the stressful pandemic period and the possible benefits of allowing more time to work from home. We could be on the cusp of getting to the core issue: how we actually think about and manage our employees.

Peter Cappelli
George W. Taylor Professor of Management
Director, Center for Human Resources, Wharton School of Business,
University of Pennsylvania

Endnotes

1 Blackstone, W (2009) Chapter 14, On Master and Servant, In *Commentaries on the Laws of England, Book the First*, ed Linda Cantoni, The Bookworm, https://www.gutenberg.org/files/30802/30802-h/30802-h.htm (archived at https://perma.cc/4LPU-UXBM)

2 The obvious example is at-will employment where the assumption is that an employee quitting is an equivalent act to an employer dismissing an employee. Feinman, JM (1976) The development of the employment at will rule, *The American Journal of Legal History*, 20 (2), pp 118–35

3 McGregor, D (1957) An uneasy look at performance appraisals, *Harvard Business Review*

4 Walton, R (1985) From control to commitment, *Harvard Business Review*

5 Cappelli, P (2020) Stop overengineering people management, *Harvard Business Review*

Introduction

How to Navigate This Book

The organizing principles for the book are built around the framework we refer to as the (4+3) Ws Framework.

The book is structured in four parts, focusing on the first 4Ws—Work, Workforce, Workplace, and Worth. We dive into the historical evolution of these elements and the factors that have impacted their development to the modern day. We provide stories and case studies that illustrate our argument for bringing the humans and their experience back to the center of work. We show that our current experience with work is not necessarily new (plenty of history to learn from). What's new is the pace of the technology evolution that is changing how humans relate and interact, how they learn and lead. Human norms and biases are readily codified into the algorithms that in turn replace human decision making. We find ourselves at a unique moment in human history where what we do next will impact the evolution of humanity at large.

The book contains a detailed appendix that includes supporting explanations of the (4+3) Ws Framework.

Part One: Work

In Part One of the book, we explore how the concept of work has been evolving through the ages and why today's model of work finds itself in flux. We explore the parallel paths between human work and

FIGURE I.1   (4+3) Ws Framework

"tools and methods" and illustrate how and why "human" and "tool" development became interdependent. We examine the detrimental impact of work without boundaries on human health and wellbeing and call for making work holistic and human-centered again. In subsequent chapters, we show how the traditional construct of work as jobs is no longer valid. We track the shifts from traditional administrative systems to universal work design, from productivity to impact, and from streamlined global supply chains to platforms and networks. We also discuss the changes in how success is measured and how the measurement systems are moving from capturing effort/efficiency/effectiveness towards a broader impact-driven thinking.

Part Two: Workforce

In Part Two we focus on the complexity of the relationship between the workforce and the workplace environment. We build the case for the use of human-centric design in creating the right environment for workers. Underlying this human-centric lens is the importance of elevating empathy as a workplace value both in building human relationships and creating technology. We see the role of Human Resources evolving to become Employee Experience and Workforce Relationship Management functions, akin to the evolution we saw in marketing and Customer Experience Management.

Part Three: Workplace

In Part Three we explore the evolving concept of the workplace that is inclusive of the physical workspace and the digital work environment.

Increasingly, the workplace is a hybrid intersection and integration of both. Intentional design choices need to be made at these intersections to ensure the worker experience is not diminished at the expense of cost, efficiency, and automation.

Part Four: Worth

In Part Four we focus on the evolving dynamics of the value exchange between workers and their employers. We show how organizations are recognizing a more complex set of motives and drivers for employee engagement and diversifying their approaches to rewards. Workplace experience, social bonds, personal and professional growth, decision autonomy, and brand affiliation serve as powerful portfolio employment benefits. Figuring out how to personalize and deliver individual benefits to employees will be the key challenge for 21st-century organizations. The purpose is to maximize the value of work relationships for both the individual workers and their employers. Powered by social media and transparency, reputation building through work creates the next generation of rewards from work that remains to be better managed and leveraged by both sides.

Conclusion

We conclude the exploration of the Work × Workforce × Workplace × Worth with a "Humans at Work" Manifesto that we offer to workplace designers, HR practitioners, technologists, and leaders as a guide to transform the work environment for current and future generations.

Appendices

The Appendix contains eight sections, the first one providing an overview of the entire (4+3) Ws Framework and the other seven dedicated to each of the W constructs in the framework. In each section we provide contextual background for the W construct in focus, the framework itself, a detailed description of the framework elements, and instructions on how to apply them in practice. The following are the appendix sections:

1 (4+3) Ws Framework

2 Work

3 Workforce

4 Workplace

5 Worth

6 Worker Journey

7 Work Experience Design

8 WorkTech

Modern scientific, technological, design, and human consciousness advancements are creating the perfect conditions for all of us to reimagine our relationships with work.

PART ONE

Work

01

What Is Work?

Introduction: Evolution of Work

At dawn, when you have trouble getting out of bed, tell yourself: "I
have to go to work—as a human being. What do I have to complain of,
if I'm going to do what I was born for—the things I was brought into
the world to do? Or is *this* what I was created for? To huddle under the
blankets and stay warm." (Marcus Aurelius, *Meditations*[1])

To the Roman emperor and stoic philosopher (161–180 AD), work
was the essence of human existence. From the slavery-based Roman
state to Newtonian mechanics, Keynesian economics to today's digital
workplace and quantum computing to the Metaverse of tomorrow—
humans evolved through their work by innovating and developing
smarter tools. Yet often, whenever the future of work is being discussed
today, it disproportionately credits tools and technology for humanity's progress. Workers traditionally appear to be mere accessories to
technology, valued for their skills and rewarded for the products they
deliver.

The Covid-19 pandemic stopped humanity in its tracks and forced
the focus onto the humans at work amid the public health crisis. Work
moved to people's homes along with the technology devices and tools.
The essential workers became the most vulnerable, left to serve the rest
of humanity who were safe in their home offices. As much as the
pandemic is being credited with the acceleration of technology adoption, it has been an even greater catalyst in changing human behavior
at work. There is no going back for the humans. Work needs to continue
to adapt to put humans at its center.

FIGURE 1.1   Hard Work

The Rise of the No-Collar Economy

For the most part of the last century work was metaphorically described in terms of the color of the shirts worn at work. There were "blue collar" workers who could be easily spotted wearing durable and affordable clothing that did not stain easily and was customarily made of blue denim or cambric cloth.[2] The "white collar" worker was a term coined in the 1930s by US writer Upton Sinclair to describe clerical, administrative, and managerial office work. There were attempts at applying other "collar" colors to signal belonging to certain professions, but none had the lasting usage of their blue/white-collar equivalents.

In November 2016, Ginni Rometty, then CEO of IBM, wrote an open letter to the US president urging his support for the introduction of the "new collar jobs" in technology that required skills in data, artificial intelligence, computing, and cyber security.[3] IBM supported the idea of creating career pathways for talented high school graduates to become trained in technology jobs and bypass college, creating opportunities for successful careers while rejecting traditional recruitment channels.

In 2020, the pandemic caused the largest ever global workplace disruption. Covid-19 put the final nail in the proverbial coffin of the white-collar economy. Overnight, office workers were sent home, abandoning cubicles and corner offices alike and putting an end to the century of the office dress code culture. What came to replace the "white-collar" etiquette was the essential "Zoom shirt"—the one that hangs camera-ready on the back of the chair only to be used when the video call is on.[4] An informal poll by LinkedIn confirmed that at least 42 percent of the online workers owned the "Zoom shirt."[5] As uncertainty remains about the right on-screen decorum, experimentation with "workleisure" attire[6] continues and technology is stepping in to help.

By contrast, the blue-collar economy turned out to be even more essential and, for the moment, irreplaceable. Given the high human cost of not having technology alternatives immediately available, the pandemic became just as much of an accelerator for essential jobs automation and adoption of robotics as it was for the "Zoom shirt." With automation as an ultimate target, transformation of those essential jobs is now coming at a much greater speed. As per the 2020 World Economic Forum *Future of Jobs Report*, "43% of businesses reported that they were about to reduce their workforce due to technology integration, 41% plan to expand their use of contractors for task-specialized work, and 34% plan to expand their workforce due to technology integration."[7] Yet, despite fears, Robotic Process Automation (RPA) does not spell blue-collar job elimination but rather provides an ability to transform those jobs to a new level of collaboration between the humans and the machines. The loss of jobs that are destined to disappear by 2030 such as cashier, travel agent, and bank teller will be counterbalanced by those in healthcare, social work, coaching, and others for which demand will continue to grow.

Work clothing is coming full circle to close the gap between white- and blue-collar work attire and become an all-performance, technology-smart, human-centric wardrobe.[8] The pandemic accelerated the departure of fashion from the look to the function, focusing on enhancing human performance enabled through technology via the clothes people wear. Truly integrated smart performance clothing was first adopted in sports but did not stop there. Smart textiles technology is coming to the mainstream, evolving from smart yoga pants designed by companies such as WearableX to the collaboration between Google and Levi Strauss, creating the new tech-enabled denim "Jacquard" Trucker Jacket.[9] The jacket functions as an alert system, enabling one to answer or locate one's phone, play music, or use maps.

The relationship between workers and their clothing is changing as experiments with sensor-enabled apparel continue and new designs are added to provide more control, variety, and choice. As per technology analysts, the global smart clothing market is set to grow from $1.9 billion in 2019 to over $5.9 billion in 2024.[10] By fusing clothing and smart technology, work apparel is transformed from being an accessory to work to becoming the source of physical and intellectual capability, performance, and learning all in one. The evolution of workplace clothing is one of the facets of the profound transformation happening in the workplace today.

Work and Its Boundaries

"Freedom comes from understanding the limits of our power... By accepting life's limits and inevitabilities and working with them rather than fighting them, we become free" (Epictetus).[11] The ancient Stoics were among the first to recognize the importance of setting boundaries and thus achieving freedom and control over the unpredictability of life.

Day-to-day boundaries are invisible yet they provide structure and a sense of control over uncertainty; they help manage energy, prioritize tasks, and maintain mental and physical health. Boundaries define social roles and become embedded in our sense of who we are.[12]

An abrupt dislocation from the *office* routine and setting up a new *work from home* regime brought out a new appreciation for setting personal boundaries around the work day. Working, parenting, housekeeping, and caregiving roles all rolled into one long day. Frequent trips from the computer to the kitchen replaced catching up with co-workers at the water cooler. Periodic checking on kids' virtual school stood in for the lunchtime trip to the gym. Weekdays merged into weekends. The new pandemic normal felt like a loss of professional identity for many. The "always on" culture fit for robots has proven to be destructive in the longer term for humans at work. The tech world serving the workplace had to adjust fast. Tech solutions providers divided up into those who were set to exploit this addictive propensity of users to be "always on" and those who set out to create "speed bumps" along the way.

Apple CEO Tim Cook, in his address to European regulators in early 2021, summed up this new responsible tech best: "We believe that ethical technology is technology that works for you. It's technology that helps you sleep, not keeps you up. It tells you when you've had enough. It gives you space to create or draw or write or learn, not refresh just one more time."[13]

In 2018, Apple launched a series of digital wellness apps for all its iOS users to help them manage their time in more productive ways. Along with enhanced features such as "Do not disturb" that allow pre-programming of breaks, sleep time, notification delivery, as well as control over children's screen time and access, Apple devices are offering enhanced reporting for time and activity spent on the screen and a detailed breakdown on how that time is being used and which notifications need to be canceled.

Setting boundaries for children's use of devices is just as important for working parents as controlling their own screen time. Parents' ability to create allowances and turn on the "downtime" option is just as important as the ability to limit certain app categories while keeping on critical functions, such as books. Use could be blocked altogether at bedtime. All these controls are available from parents' own devices and create the vital boundaries that are necessary for the family to function in the work-from-home environment and beyond.[14]

As the pandemic proved humans to be vulnerable, smart technology showed how these vulnerabilities could be supported.

Work and Leisure

"... insofar as work and leisure are both good, work is extrinsically good, while leisure is intrinsically good."[15] Aristotle saw work as just one facet of the human condition, implying that there could be no good work without leisure. The Greek philosopher perceived work and leisure as equally important in the pursuit of human flourishing. Aristotle cautioned that if work is "accompanied by toil and strain... we should be careful to use amusement at the right time, dispensing it as a remedy to the ills of work."[16]

Labor economists agree. Thinking about "work" as employment/ unemployment only is convenient but reductive and leads to a distortion of the true context of the human relationship with work.[17] People make different choices across cultures and throughout history, prioritizing between work, leisure, and sleep. The activities one chooses determine the relevant definition of work for the place and time.

It is not surprising that it was leisure and sleep that continued to lose out to work in the years preceding the pandemic. Aristotelian equilibrium was crushed under the overwhelming primacy of work for most of the working population. Jeffrey Pfeffer's *Dying for a Paycheck*[18]—by now a contemporary classic—named the phenomenon of "the relentless tyranny" of corporate employment and shined critical light on the workers' condition of major concern. The 24/7 "always-on economy" breaks the day-to-day rhythm of life in favor of less leisure and more work. The phenomenon of the "Sunday Blues" has been covered extensively in business literature. A study by Monster.com found that eight out of ten workers reported feeling anxious at the end of the weekend and almost half were saying that they had really bad "melancholy."[19]

The pandemic blurred the boundaries between work and leisure altogether. In the first few weeks of the shutdown, the "rallying around the flag" effect kicked in productivity increases, to everyone's surprise, and indirectly created a false "we can do it all" bravado effect.

As the lockdowns stretched to over a year and schools remained closed, the concept of leisure all but disappeared from everyday vocabulary and from people's everyday lives. In September 2020, a Harvard study of 3 million adults working from home showed what everyone already suspected—people felt overwhelmed.[20] The days got longer and there were more meetings to attend; the boundaries between work and leisure were erased, with the predictable outcome of increased levels of depression, burn-out, and, tragically, addiction and suicides. According to a CDC study of over 3,000 adults, close to 40 percent of the US population reported struggling with mental health issues and substance abuse.[21] The imbalance disproportionately affected mid-career women workers who had to leave their employers to take care of school-age children at home, thus being dealt the most major setback to gender equality in a generation.[22]

All challenges notwithstanding, there was a silver lining to the pandemic. The workplace would be the right place to look for an upside. The pandemic not only exposed workplace vulnerabilities, it accelerated the adoption of innovative practices that would have normally taken a decade to implement. One area where innovation was particularly needed was wellness and wellbeing in the workplace. In the wake of collective burnout and general Covid fatigue, employers looked for new solutions to lessen the stress of boundaryless working.

The scientific foundations for the new approach to human decision making under uncertainty were developed a few decades earlier by Daniel Kahneman and Amos Tversky, the founders of Behavioral Economics.[23] Richard Thaler, another Nobel Prize-winning economist, introduced the concept of "the nudge" and "choice architecture." Thaler argued that to incentivize people to make certain decisions, choices needed to be prompted, not imposed; there needed to be plenty of room allowed for workers to choose their own paths towards the solution they would accept:

> A nudge... is any aspect of the choice architecture that alters people's behavior in a predictable way without forbidding any options or significantly changing their economic incentives. To count as a mere nudge, the intervention must be easy and cheap to avoid. Nudges are not mandates. Putting fruit at eye level counts as a nudge. Banning junk food does not.[24]

These new design approaches were especially relevant in the pandemic when help was needed to curb employees' addictive and unhealthy work habits. Left to monitor themselves in the work-from-home setting, many employees overworked, skipped breaks, and developed other addictive work behaviors. To address this need, the next generation of digital tools was designed and widely deployed to help guide employees' wellness and leisure choices.[25] As we learned along the way, not all such well-intentioned innovations delivered. When workdays became a series of starts and stops and the flow of work was arbitrarily interrupted, employees found themselves more exhausted at the end of the day and without the sense of accomplishment of big goals.

However, there were undisputed successes as well. Take the eponymous "The Nudge," an SMS subscription service whose mission is to pull workers away from their screens and "make tools that help you watch more sunsets, try new workouts, and sip wine with friends. In other words, be your best self in your precious free time."[26] The idea behind The Nudge is to create a counterpoint to the screen-dependent lifestyle that is based on overdependence on digital tools: "Most tech companies are empowering us to be lazy: To binge TV rather than see a concert, post a comment rather than call, or scroll social media rather than talk to our roomie."[27] By providing their planned leisure services in the major cities—San Francisco, New York, Austin, Seattle—The Nudge is aspiring to help users break away from the tyranny of the screens because, in the Aristotelian sense, "Free time is the most important part of our lives." Decisions about how we spend our leisure, according to Aristotle, "create what we see in the mirror every day."

Work and Health

The pandemic has forever changed the relationship between work and health. Once a near taboo, employees' overall health became management's everyday concern. No matter the seniority or rank, no one was exempt from health risks in a pandemic. Most companies reorganized quickly the need to increase their level of commitment and preparedness. Analytics and reporting teams were tasked to produce daily reports on the state of health among the employees globally, custom built from location to location. The benefits teams were ensuring continuation of health coverage for laid-off and furloughed employees, and new extended leave policies were considered. Significant investments had to be made in retrofitting and upgrading offices and, ultimately, top-level decisions had to be made on the safety and desirability of returning to the office. Workforce healthcare management became a much larger part of overall people operations and had to be overseen by the most senior leadership teams.

Many organizations appointed their first chief medical officer (CMO) to the senior executive team, thus placing employee health focus in the center of operational decision making.

According to the workforce recruitment platform ZipRecruiter, the exponential growth in CMO hiring signals a policy and culture pivot across all industry sectors. In late 2021, there were more than 58,000 open CMO jobs in the United States, with 2,700 in the greater New York City area alone. The average salary for those appointments ranges from $200,000 to $300,000, with the top package bringing over $400,000 *per year*.[28] In addition to the new healthcare governance in place, organizations needed to achieve greater reach and scale. Companies saw the accelerated adoption of new digital healthcare technology solutions.

The first industry to launch a digital health passport was the International Air Transport Association (IATA), an industry group of about 290 airlines in 120 countries.[29] Their digital health app was designed to collect, access, and update information on the health and vaccination status of passengers. The digital tool brought efficiency to the already developed protocols of global vaccination documentation and health checks that were quickly becoming a requirement for travel and work around the world.[30]

Reaching beyond travel is Clear, the biometric health pass app that made conference attendance and other public gatherings possible through the tool's ability to integrate data on testing, vaccines, and health risk assessments.[31]

The overall global digital health market is one of the fastest-growing segments of the economy, projected to reach $500 billion by 2025. It is driven by the largest healthcare crisis in a century that not only prompted innovation but also accelerated general population behavior change.[32]

The workplace adoption of digital healthcare tools has advanced in parallel with the broader medical technology market. The goal for organizations is not to take over employee healthcare management—even though such models and experiments have existed.[33] Privacy considerations and the constraints on data transparency and accessibility at work make such adoption much more complex. One thing is clear—the workplace will continue to be the center for many healthcare decisions and workplace benefits portfolios will have to continue to evolve.

Work and Mental Health

'It is not events that disturb people, but their judgements concerning them,' wrote Epictetus, reflecting on the uniquely human root causes of illness.[34]

A silent and no less destructive second pandemic ran its course parallel to the Covid-19 health crisis. Mental health, depression, anxiety, and stress represented an even greater and far-reaching fallout from the extended periods of isolation, distance learning, and remote work. The World Health Organization defined mental health as more than a lack of clinical mental disorders: "a state of well-being in which the individual realizes his or her own abilities, can cope with the normal stresses of life, can work productively and fruitfully, and is able to make a contribution to his or her community."[35] It is the effect on productivity and employee contribution that concerns businesses directly.

The data is most telling of the harmful impact of the pandemic on an individual's ability to cope. About four in ten US adults experienced symptoms of anxiety or depression, up from one in ten prior to the pandemic. Other symptoms such as loss of sleep, eating disorders, substance abuse, or worsening chronic conditions represented a concerning deterioration in employees' health. Annually, according to the WHO report, depression and anxiety alone contribute to about $1 trillion in losses. For every $1 spent by employers on mental health care, there is a return of $4 in productivity improvement.[36]

Although employers had been generally paying attention to mental health issues at work before the pandemic, the issues had been handled in confidence, privately and often out of sight of the employer. Organizations have always prioritized general wellness and physical fitness. Gym memberships, corporate athletic challenges, golf outings, or fundraisers involving competitions were much more on the employers' radar and were easier to support than dealing with the causes of mental illness. The scale and the duration of the pandemic thrust mental health into the open, raising concerns about the mental state of employees working remotely and often in social isolation. Reports of burnout, stress, anxiety, prolonged loneliness, and potential for serious mental illness continued to raise concerns. Employers had to step up, create more transparency, remove the stigma, and offer resources for a better support system for all employees.

Platforms providing mental health support services grew exponentially during the pandemic. There are currently over 300,000 mental health mobile apps worldwide.[37] A few of the leading platforms used by major employers include BetterHelp[38] and Talkspace.[39] The services range from psychiatric evaluations and medication management to therapies delivered in a confidential manner in the privacy of the employee's computer or mobile phone. As insurance companies and individuals begin to accept telemedicine, online platforms will continue to expand and offer specialist support not available to millions of workers before. The employers are actively contributing by signing up their organizations and making these services broadly available to employees.

Work and Mindfulness

"Do you not realize that when once you have let your mind go wandering, it is no longer in your power to recall it, to bring it back to what is right, to self-respect, to moderation?" (Epictetus).[40]

The ancient wisdom and mental practices of the East were slow in coming to the pragmatic and extrinsically oriented West. Mindfulness practices have taken off and have been in circulation among the broader population since the 1960s; it took the global lockdown for businesses to recognize and accept mindfulness or "secular spirituality" as an effective way to counter the harmful effects of stress, anxiety, and depression. The story of how companies embraced mindfulness is closely linked to the evolution of technology and innovation. Technology got humans to the state of "always on," but it also offered help with the way out.

"Secular spirituality" was notably embraced by Steve Jobs. The iconic tech entrepreneur opened the tech world to alternative management approaches in contrast to the "greed is king" mantra. Jobs' biographer Walter Isaacson quotes Jobs' explanation of how he sought insight and inspiration:

> If you just sit and observe, you will see how restless your mind is. If you try to calm it, it only makes it worse, but over time it does calm, and when it does, there's room to hear more subtle things—that's when your intuition starts to blossom, and you start to see things more clearly and be in the present more. Your mind just slows down, and you see a tremendous expanse in the moment. You see so much more than you could see before.[41]

Steve Jobs was followed by a long list of CEOs who credit their success to a regular meditation practice, including Jeff Weiner (LinkedIn), Ray Dalio (Bridgewater), Marc Benioff (Salesforce), Bill Gates (Microsoft), and many others. The question of how to share the powerful practice with thousands of global employees has been answered by the meditation and mindfulness app Headspace.[42]

CASE STUDY
Headspace

Behind the rise of Headspace is the personal story of co-founders Andy Puddicombe[43] and Richard Pierson.[44] Puddicombe, an ordained Tibetan monk, partnered with Richard Pierson, an established advertiser, to found a training company for corporate clients, teaching the Eastern art of meditation to solve workplace problems. The app was developed from this training to promote meditation globally. Since its founding in 2010, meditation teaching and guidance through Headspace is now available to over 2 million people around the world; over 600 businesses have partnered with Headspace to offer free apps to their employees.[45] The app took off fast, growing among knowledge workers and adopted by companies as a benefit to their workforce.

Mindfulness needs to be recognized as critical to the future of work—no less critical than the technology full stack. As the succession of visionary entrepreneurs and thought leaders proposes, the future of work cannot be achieved without changing the way our human brain works.

Work and Coaching and Mentoring

"Only the educated are free."[46] Those words belong to Epictetus, who was born a slave 2,000 years ago. Freed by his wealthy owner, he took to learning and was mentored by his teacher, Musonius Rufus, to become the foremost Stoic philosopher of his time. In today's terms, Epictetus's career from slave to one of the most revered ancient philosophers was accelerated by his learning and the mentorship of his prominent teacher.

Coaching and mentoring date back to ancient Greece but in the pandemic this highly personalized support service went through an unprecedented expansion and adoption across the broadest segments of the workforce.

Traditionally, executive coaching and leadership development services were reserved for the top leaders and high-potential employees.

Coaching was a privilege and a perk, supporting the succession pool or staving off high-profile derailment. At the start of the 21st century, organizations accelerated towards agile working and distributed decision making. The demand for coaching and development support grew exponentially as the workplace became remote and distributed due to the pandemic. The need for a more personalized professional support at a time when most managers and co-workers were distant and unavailable created an even greater opportunity for online coaching services to fill the gap.

A new generation of technology services sprang up dedicated to supporting the broadest populations of employees at all organizational levels. BetterUp, Bravely, and Ezra in coaching and Imperative and Everwise in mentoring services are among hundreds in this fast-growing, multibillion-dollar industry. Growing at a rate of close to 7 percent per year, online coaching services are experiencing great demand and market expansion. According to the International Coaching Federation, online coaching represents close to a third of all coaching services and is the fastest-growing segment of all such services. At the same time, the share of traditional one-on-one coaching is continuing to decline.[47]

New technology helped "democratize" delivery of these highly sought-after online coaching and mentorship services.

The ability of these services to blend behavioral science, the latest AI technology, and personal human interaction in any place and at any time is a compelling proposition for widely spread-out remote workers. Meeting companies' diversity goals is of particular focus for Bravely, one such fast-growing coaching startup. In the words of Toby Hervey, a co-founder of Bravely:

> Because we're going to different levels of the organization—more junior employees, folks who are earlier in their career, different teams than those that traditionally get coaching—we're reaching more women, more people of color, more LGBTQ-identifying folks, and intersections of those identities.[48]

Companies can now expand the offering of these highly personalized coaching services to all members of their organizations. The benefits will come back in the form of better performance, engagement, and belonging of their diverse and distributed employees.

Reclaiming the Humanity of Work

The often-quoted maxim "One cannot step twice into the same river," attributed to the Greek philosopher Heraclitus, describes a world that is always changing and is never the same. The workplace is no exception. In the last few centuries historical transformations were tracked against technological changes and were named after stages in technology development. Industrial, Technological, and Digital Revolutions came and went, and we are still analyzing their long-term impact on human beings and our lives. It is time to name the next revolution after Humans and radically reimagine how we connect with technology in the workplace. As work has moved away from the office, so has the center of the workplace community. Technology has intervened to bridge the gap and help reconnect and restore humanity at work. John Goulding, founder of the workplace collaboration startup Workvivo, said it best when describing the main challenge of the 21st-century workplace as the optimal human experience: "It's obvious there's a battle to be won for the center of the digital workplace. We're here to capture the heartbeat of an organization, not its pulses."[49]

Endnotes

1   Ackeren, MV (2012) *Marcus Aurelius' Meditations*, New York: Oxford University Press

2   Wickman, F (2012)Working man's blues: Why do we call manual laborers blue collar? *Slate*, https://slate.com/business/2012/05/blue-collar-white-collar-why-do-we-use-these-terms.html (archived at https://perma.cc/6QC2-J53L)

3   Lovelace Jr, B (2016) IBM CEO Rometty in letter to Trump: Help secure 'new collar' IT jobs, CNBC, https://www.cnbc.com/2016/11/15/ibm-ceo-rometty-in-letter-to-trump-help-secure-new-collar-it-jobs.html (archived at https://perma.cc/RH33-QR7B)

4   Stein, J (2020) The video call is starting: Time to put on your Zoom shirt, *New York Times*, https://www.nytimes.com/2020/06/29/business/zoom-shirt.html (archived at https://perma.cc/JH5L-RS8K)

5   Yeomans, C (2020) So, who else owns a Zoom shirt? *LinkedIn*, https://www.linkedin.com/news/story/so-who-else-owns-a-zoom-shirt-4899860/ (archived at https://perma.cc/M9WK-2W6P)

6   Friedman, V (2020) Behold, 'Workleisure': What will we wear come fall? *New York Times*, https://www.nytimes.com/2020/08/20/style/work-from-home-clothes.html (archived at https://perma.cc/GCJ8-AQ8L)

7   Russo, A (2020) Recession and Automation changes our future of work, but there are jobs coming, report says, *World Economic Forum*, https://www.weforum.org/press/2020/10/recession-and-automation-changes-our-future-of-work-but-there-are-jobs-coming-report-says-52c5162fce/ (archived at https://perma.cc/57L4-WGLU)

8   Stephenson, B (2021) 7 best smart clothes 2021, *Lifewire*, https://www.lifewire.com/best-smart-clothes-4176104 (archived at https://perma.cc/9EUF-ZXHB)

9   Bohn, D (2019) Google Levi Project Jacquard is available on new Levi's jackets, *The Verge*, https://www.theverge.com/2019/9/30/20888909/google-levi-project-jacquard-available-trucker-sherpa-jackets-price-design (archived at https://perma.cc/S6EE-NF63)

10 Van Hooijdonk, R (2020) Top 10 smart clothes provide a glimpse of what people will wear in the future [blog], https://blog.richardvanhooijdonk.com/en/top-10-smart-clothes-provide-glimpse-of-what-people-will-wear-in-the-future/ (archived at https://perma.cc/E3R3-7QLD)

11 The Daily Stoic (nd) Maximize your potential: The Stoic life in accordance with nature, https://dailystoic.com/stoicism-nature/ (archived at https://perma.cc/7497-KD4N)

12 Ebert, P and Freibichler, W (2017) Nudge management: Applying behavioral science to increase knowledge worker productivity, *Journal of Organization Design* (Aarhus), **6** (1), pp 1–6

13 Asher Hamilton, I (2021) Tim Cook took a swipe at Facebook after Mark Zuckerberg accused Apple of misleading users, *Business Insider*, https://www.businessinsider.com/tim-cook-takes-swipe-at-facebook-social-catastrophe-2021-1#:~:text=Tim%20Cook%20took%20a%20swipe,accused%20Apple%20of%20misleading%20users&text=Apple%20CEO%20Tim%20Cook%20made,sell%20user%20data%20to%20advertisers (archived at https://perma.cc/3DPP-FUUC)

14 Perez, S (2018) Apple unveils a new set of 'digital wellness' features for better managing screen time, *TechCrunch*, https://techcrunch.com/2018/06/04/apple-unveils-a-new-set-of-digital-wellness-features-for-better-managing-screen-time/#:~:text=At%20its%20Worldwide%20Developer%20Conference,device%20usage%20for%20their%20children (archived at https://perma.cc/GCN2-4BC9)

15 Höffe, O (2010) Aristotle's "Nicomachean ethics," Leiden, Boston, MA: Brill
16 Taub, T (nd) Aristotle on Work vs. Leisure, Harvard blog: The Noble Leisure
    Project, https://blogs.harvard.edu/nobleleisure/aristotle-on-work-vs-leisure/
    (archived at https://perma.cc/2L6A-6UDE)
17 Blanchard, O (2006) The many dimensions of work, leisure, and employment:
    Thoughts at the end of the conference, Comments on the papers presented at
    the Rodolfo DeBenedetti conference on "Are Europeans lazy or are Americans
    crazy?" Portovenere, June
18 Pfeffer, J (2018) *Dying for a Paycheck: How modern management harms
    employee health and company performance—and what we can do about it*,
    New York: HarperBusiness
19 Feintzeig, R (2013) Got a case of the Mondays? Blame the Sunday blues, *Wall
    Street Journal*, https://www.wsj.com/articles/BL-ATWORKB-1381 (archived at
    https://perma.cc/9WA6-K7DM)
20 DeFilippis, E et al (2020) Collaborating during Coronavirus: The impact of
    COVID-19 on the nature of work (No. 21-006), https://www.hbs.edu/faculty/
    Pages/item.aspx?num=58440 (archived at https://perma.cc/3XFV-WPCJ)
21 Czeisler, M et al (2020) Mental health, substance use, and suicidal ideation
    during the COVID-19 pandemic, https://www.cdc.gov/mmwr/volumes/69/wr/
    mm6932a1.htm (archived at https://perma.cc/6EUZ-JPNK)
22 McKinsey Insights (2021) Seven charts that show COVID-19 impact on
    women's employment, Insights, https://www.mckinsey.com/featured-insights/
    diversity-and-inclusion/seven-charts-that-show-covid-19s-impact-on-womens-
    employment (archived at https://perma.cc/52MR-XCEC)
23 Tversky, A and Kahneman, D (2005) *Judgment Under Uncertainty: Heuristics
    and biases*, Psychology Press, pp. 167–77
24 Thaler, RH and Sunstein, CR (2009) *Nudge: Improving decisions about
    health, wealth, and happiness*, Revised and expanded edition, New York:
    Penguin Books
25 Ebert, P and Freibichler, W (2017) Nudge management: Applying behavioral
    science to increase knowledge worker productivity, *Journal of Organization
    Design* (Aarhus), 6 (1), pp 1–6
26 The Nudge, https://www.nudgetext.com/ (archived at https://perma.cc/
    BGJ3-HAUY)
27 Ibid.
28 Ziprecruiter.com (archived at https://perma.cc/Z8TZ-NT23)
29 International Air Transport Association (IATA), https://www.iata.org/
    (archived at https://perma.cc/AHS6-XQLM)
30 Gilchrist, K (2021) Quarantine-free travel may be one step closer with new
    travel industry app, *CNBC*, https://crytonic.com/quarantine-free-travel-may-
    be-one-step-closer-with-new-travel-industry-app/ (archived at https://perma.cc/
    P8C6-9JND)

31 Pike, A (2021) See how this new technology can streamline health screenings at live events, *BizBash*, https://www.connectmeetings.com/corporate/news/ see-how-this-new-technology-can-streamline-health-screenings-at-live-events (archived at https://perma.cc/T6CW-YVRT)

32 Statista (nd) Medical technology, https://www.statista.com/markets/412/ topic/453/medical-technology/#overview (archived at https://perma.cc/ TY6N-LTCK)

33 Son, H (2021) Haven, the Amazon-Berkshire-JPMorgan venture to disrupt health care, is disbanding after 3 years, *CNBC*, https://www.cnbc.com/ 2021/01/04/haven-the-amazon-berkshire-jpmorgan-venture-to-disrupt-healthcare-is-disbanding-after-3-years.html (archived at https://perma.cc/ 84DF-N9M3)

34 Dobbin, R (2008) *Epictetus: Discourses and Selected Writings,* 1st edition, London: Penguin Classics

35 World Health Organization (2018) Mental health: Strengthening our response, https://www.who.int/news-room/fact-sheets/detail/mental-health-strengthening-our-response (archived at https://perma.cc/6UFA-VHXH)

36 World Health Organization (2021) Mental health: Prevention guidelines, https://www.who.int/health-topics/mental-health#tab=tab_1 (archived at https://perma.cc/7T2G-R453)

37 MarketWatch (2021) Mental health apps market size 2021, https://www. marketwatch.com/press-release/mental-health-apps-market-report-size-2021-by-top-countries-data-industry-analysis-by-regions-revenue-share-development-tendencies-and-forecast-to-2027-2021-08-02 (archived at https:// perma.cc/37AF-JMC5)

38 https://www.betterhelp.com/ (archived at https://perma.cc/6R43-PA4K)

39 https://www.talkspace.com/ (archived at https://perma.cc/UX8E-8PEJ)

40 Epictetus (2000) *Discourses, 4:12*, South Bend: Infomotions, Inc.

41 Isaacson, W (2015) *Steve Jobs*, New York: Simon & Schuster Paperbacks

42 https://www.headspace.com/ (archived at https://perma.cc/QGJ4-9A5T)

43 https://www.headspace.com/about-us (archived at https://perma.cc/WWJ7-2AF5)

44 The Entrepreneurs (2020) Richard Pierson, Monocle Radio, https://monocle. com/radio/shows/the-entrepreneurs/394/ (archived at https://perma.cc/ KMB8-6F6W)

45 Curry, D (2021) Headspace revenue and usage statistics, *Business of Apps*, https://www.businessofapps.com/data/headspace-statistics/ (archived at https:// perma.cc/4PR3-9YC5)

46 Epictetus (2000) *Discourses*, 2.1.21-23a, South Bend: Infomotions, Inc.

47 Willis, R (2021) 3 Trends that will shape the future of coaching, International Coaching Federation, https://coachingfederation.org/blog/3-trends-that-will-shape-the-future-of-coaching (archived at https://perma.cc/MF64-2YGV)

48 Glover, E (2021) Career coaching app Bravely raises $15 m amid the changing world of work, *BuiltIn NYC*, https://www.builtinnyc.com/2021/08/24/bravely-raises-15m-series-a-hiring (archived at https://perma.cc/32JF-MU6Q)

49 Azevedo, MA (2021) Inside Workvivo's plans to take on Microsoft in the employee experience space, *TechCrunch*, https://techcrunch.com/2021/03/04/inside-workvivos-plans-to-take-on-microsoft-in-the-employee-experience-space/ (archived at https://perma.cc/B25X-QE9B)

02

Jobs vs Work

The "Work" Is Not Working

Most humans today cannot imagine life without work. In the developed world, work runs through every aspect of adult life. Employability defines education choices, determines credit scores, and predicts healthcare and quality of life outcomes. Political rhetoric centers on job creation and minimum wage; politicians portray the plight of "hardworking families" as their primary concern. Corporations strive for round-the-clock employee engagement and productivity. The gig economy evangelists sell the myth of 24/7 work without benefits as workers' liberation. Digital technology erases boundaries between work, rest, and leisure in favor of work. The cities are designed around workday schedules and the flow of commuters and workers in and out of urban centers. As the pandemic pushed employees into their homes, work also overtook kitchens, bedrooms, and even closets to accommodate makeshift offices in people's homes.

Joanna Biggs summed up the hegemony of work in developed economies in the following way: "Work is... how we give our lives meaning when religion, party politics and community fall away."[1] *Workism* is the term coined to describe the belief in the centrality of work in people's lives, not just as a means of earning a living.[2] Some may argue that there are cultures that have figured out a better balance between work and quality of life. Denmark and Sweden often come up as the exemplars of possible solutions. Regrettably, these are exceptions rather than rules. The American dream still holds

FIGURE 2.1 Work Is Not Working

a strong fascination for so many around the world and over-promotes achievement of material rewards through hard work. Furthermore, Americans tend to view "leisure with ambivalence and at times guilt, disdain those who do not work and see the work ethic as a key element to what it means to be an American."[3] Crisis at work often shows up as crisis at home for way too many workers. Questions persist as to whether the current level of work can be sustained in its most toxic form.

Many agree that "work" as we know it today is not working. Not "jobs" alone but the entire culture of work built in the last century cannot be sustained and is becoming particularly vulnerable in the face of relentless social, political, and economic changes. As is the case with all ideologies, there is an expiration date on the all-consuming work ethic and the society that is based on it. New solutions are not only needed, they are long overdue. The biggest and most widely acknowledged threat to the work-obsessed society is the acceleration of automation. What are the new ways that can help transition the current psychological contract of work to the next levels of work experience and engagement?

Swapping Skills for Jobs Is Too Little Too Late

"All models are wrong, but some are useful" is a famous adage attributed to statistician George Box.[4]

A whole new generation of *"Future of Work"* theorists, academicians, and consultants has emerged and flourished, promising to fix the looming "end of work" crisis. Amidst the enormity of the challenge, multiple scenarios, have been put forward and successfully advanced. The "Work Without Jobs" approach gets perhaps most of the industry and academic attention today. This workforce planning method advocates replacing "jobs" with "skills." It argues that traditional workplace structures and practices based on jobs are outdated and must be replaced with ones based on modular, easily replaceable clusters of skills.[5] Embedded in this workforce planning methodology are the scenarios that require 1) creation of universal skills taxonomies, 2) an audit of skills to assess their relevance and obsolescence, and 3) retraining, substitution, or augmentation of skills with "bots" to continuously respond to the changing skills requirements. The "Work Without Jobs" skills-based solution promises to set up an agile system of continuous renewal ahead of automation and skills obsolescence. Compatibility and adjacency of skills are of particular relevance in keeping up with the pace of change. Due to the uneven pace of automation and skills replacement there is an opportunity to transition workers from certain sectors in the economy to others; repurpose the skills from the area that is disappearing to another one that is in high demand. A classic example of such adjacent skills transition is hospitality workers trained in customer service whose skills are compatible and easily transferable to the caregiving sectors such as general healthcare, elder care, and similar caregiving occupations. The overall outcome resembles a Lego-like construct of work anchored in projects or "gigs" requiring a specialized assembly of skills to be applied on a just-in-time basis. The skills solution to the challenges of workplace automation is a winning model today due to its operational clarity. At a closer look, we cannot be complacent, thinking that the skills-based model of work would solve the bigger challenge of the displacement of work's purpose, the shifting social context, and the need to rediscover work's broader meaning.

As an example, the changing gender roles in the workplace at large are receiving a lot of attention. Much has been written about women's careers and their growing contribution to the economy. During the pandemic, reporting was focused on the outflow of women from the workforce. However, a few unspoken workforce paradoxes are not getting their fair share of attention in "*Future of Work*" discussions. There is an increasing number of "working age American men" leaving the workforce. The fact that close to 20 percent of the "prime working-age" males in the United States are unemployed is one of those mysteries that cannot be solved through reskilling alone.[6] The skills as a solution argument points out the mismatch between the demand for certain skills and their available supply on the job market. The catch is that the demand for traditionally male-dominated blue-collar service jobs is not being automated nor is it shrinking. It is growing at a faster rate. Electricians, plumbers, and builders are in high demand, while mid-level office jobs are being automated and disappearing. "It is well past time for America to recognize the collapse of work for men as the grave ill that it truly is," writes Nicholas Eberstadt, a labor economist, calling the phenomenon "a quiet catastrophe."[7] It is not a question of skills training alone. There needs to be a broader cultural shift that would destigmatize traditional service jobs such as nursing and teaching. The skills conversation at large needs to be accompanied by the broader cultural transitions in the social context of jobs.

Actionable and expedient, the skills model of work is a case of a one-sided solution for a societal evolutional challenge. The task of reskilling whole segments of the working population in new technologies is critically important but woefully insufficient. It is critical to not only break down jobs into skills but also to elevate the conversation from jobs to the greater context of work and its greater social and economic purpose to meet the challenges of the coming economy.

Beware of Exponential Growth

A simple mathematical miscalculation known as the "exponential growth bias" explains why the Covid-19 pandemic presented such an insurmountable challenge to the enforcement of public health policies. The Coronavirus was spreading exponentially around the globe. At the same time, the familiar way of thinking about its dangers was "linear," distrustful of medical guidance to immediately lock down and socially distance. Within just a few weeks, the pandemic grew to become a global health catastrophe with dire consequences.

The limits of intuitive human ability to comprehend exponential growth have been documented throughout the millennia. One such parable came from India, where the legendary Sissa ibn Dahir, the alleged inventor of the game of chess, was asked by the ruler how he wanted to be awarded for his invention. Sissa wanted one grain of wheat to be placed on the first square and then double the amount placed in each subsequent square. The ruler laughed at the humble request until he was informed by his treasury that they had run out of wheat supplies in the entire land. The total amount of grains in the last 64th square would have been 18,446,744,073,709,551,615, weighing about 1,199,000,000,000 tons. In total, it was more than two billion times as many grains as there were on the first half of the chessboard.[8]

The lesson of this parable is that much like the ancient ruler and his court, most humans are hard-wired to think linearly and are not prepared for the consequences of exponential events.

The urgency to think differently about work is perhaps the most important message to sound today. While we are still responding to the digital transformation as a dominant trend, the next-generation technologies such as artificial intelligence (AI), augmented and virtual reality (AR, VR), biotech, nanotech, digital fabrication, and robotics are joining the workforce in greater numbers every day. Just like those grains on the chessboard, the first signs of AI takeover are slowly beginning to show everywhere in our personal and professional lives. Recruitment ads, learning tips, and behavioral nudges are being served to workers to make work easier and more scalable. The exponential changes will occur fast and will catch most humans by surprise. Thinking of the future of work in exponential terms is what is required of business leaders today. It cannot come fast enough. Exponential technologies require exponential thinking about the workplace where humans must face their own future and be prepared for it.

We chose two exponentially growing companies—Amazon and Patagonia—to illustrate the diversity and complexity of decisions that companies must make when confronting the future. The two approaches to work, jobs, and the workers could not be more diametrically opposed. The fast-accelerating Amazon is committed to the path of maximum productivity and efficiency through advanced automation. Amazon's culture is a race between humanity and technology. Patagonia, the independent outdoor clothing retail brand, does not sell on Amazon. The company embraces a regenerative business model and is using its "business to protect nature." A closer look at the two business models is a study of divergent paths. Both are focused on the future but choosing different focus. It is a study in contrast between the skills and the values.

CASE STUDY

Will Technology Fail Humans? Hard Lessons From Amazon

Amidst the layoffs and furloughs of the pandemic, Amazon defied the trend as a business success story. The company increased its global workforce during the pandemic to over 1.2 million, the equivalent of the population of Dallas, TX. Amazon was adding close to 1,500 employees a day and rose to number five in the ranks of Fortune's largest employers. That number did not include close to 500,000 delivery drivers and over 100,000 seasonal workers for the holiday rush. On average, the company received close to 400,000 applications a day and was second only to Walmart, which was still leading the world with 2.2 million employees.[9]

It is hard to imagine that the same technological prowess that works magic with logistics and customer service would fail the very people who do the work at Amazon's 110 US and 185 global fulfillment centers. The warning signals about the company burning through workers at an alarming attrition rate of 150 percent per year first started to be leaked in the media. *The New York Times* ran a series of stories describing a relentless mechanistic, skills-based approach to managing workers.[10] The company squashed a series of unionization efforts in Amazon's warehouses including the largest such attempt in Alabama.[11] As more information emerged about the Amazon work culture, it challenged organization management to confront some fundamental questions about the dark side of turning people into automatons. Even if we can steer towards ubiquitous automation, should we?

Amazon's people management model relies heavily on metrics, apps, chatbots, sensors, and devices tracking every minute and every movement of a warehouse worker on their shifts. The algorithms intentionally minimize human contact and maximize productivity. A note left by an employee on the internal feedback board is revealing: "It is very important that area managers understand that associates are more than just numbers. We are human beings. We are not tools used to make their daily/weekly goals and rates."[12]

A telling observation by one of the company's former executives in the interviews with *The New York Times* reveals that the warehouse employee churn may be intentional. It stemmed from Jeff Bezos' belief that long-tenured workers become "entrenched." It signals, according to Bezos, "a march to mediocrity."[13] The size of the company mattered as well. The larger the company grew, the more it was about scale and speed and the harder it became to worry about its culture and workers' experiences. In the end, it became a *numbers game* and employees became lost in the bowels of the warehouse.

Amazon's story is especially instructive. It is proof that managing people by collecting employee data, automating all processes (including people processes), remoting working, and optimizing for efficiency could actually work if efficiency and productivity were the sought-after outcomes. In the end, Amazon's business grew by 200 percent in the pandemic's first year alone.[14] The question to ask is whether the long-term consequences of managing people as machines are fully understood. What should be the role of the people function in the automation scenario that we see at Amazon? Focusing on skills, setting up data teams, investing in new tech, and automating processes are a given. What other obligations does a company have to treat employees with care and respect? Should a company care for *employee experience* or should the focus be on skills and productivity alone? Is paying minimum wage and benefits all that an employer needs to worry about to earn the loyalty of their employees? Amazon's overwhelming market success and the volume of job applications they receive force these questions into the open. Patagonia might as well offer some answers.

CASE STUDY

Patagonia Is "A Cause, Disguised as a Company"

Dean Carter, Patagonia's head of HR, likes to share the story of how he was hired at Patagonia and how he first met with the company's legendary founder and first CEO, Yvon Chouinard.[15] Carter was invited to go surfing with the CEO before any discussion of business took place. The experience was as much of an "un-interview" as Patagonia itself, which is often branded as an "un-company." "Let My People Go Surfing" was the philosophy described in Chouinard's book of the same name. Surfing or other outdoor sports breaks was exactly what all employees did as a normal part of the workday.[16] The company was set up to accommodate such a schedule as long as work got done by the end of the day.

Patagonia's employee-centric culture long pre-dates the current obsession with employee experience. Its investment in people has paid significant dividends in business, in brand reputation, and in customer and employee loyalty. The company ranks at the top of multiple "Best Places to Work" lists, with the employees giving its culture a 91 percent approval score compared with an average of 59 percent among US companies in general. Employee turnover rate is a low 4 percent compared with 13 percent on average in the retail and consumer product sectors.

Patagonia today is committed to *regenerative people practices* as an extension of the company's adoption of an overall *regenerative business model*. Regenerative business models originated with regenerative agriculture and today go beyond sustainability initiatives; they encompass all aspects of running a business including supply chain, operations, and people practices. As a recognition of its success, Patagonia was named the United Nations Champion of the Earth in 2019. The company's achievements would not be possible if its employees were not primary contributors to its entire ecosystem—its community, industry, and resources. As Chouinard writes in *Let My People Go Surfing*:

> Much like a plant only thrives if its soil provides the necessary nutrients, an employee's potential and behavior are best cultivated in a healthy work environment. All parts of the system work in unison to support life and growth.[17]

A brief overview of some core people practices shows just how much Patagonia can achieve high performance by connecting with employees' humanity first.

To start with recruitment, Patagonia tells the story of its business in a transparent and authentic way. The company is clear about its mission from the start—"we're in business to save our home planet." The first question they ask interviewees is, "What drew you here?"

- Recruiters read job applications "bottom up," starting with hobbies and extracurricular activities such as volunteering, service, and environmental activism that are considered an asset to getting hired. According to Dean Carter, they want to find people "who care about something beyond themselves."[18]

- Patagonia is looking for *culture add, not culture fit* to diversify the culture. Referrals are encouraged as community and fresh perspectives are sought after.

The benefits that Patagonia offers to all employees go beyond health insurance and onsite childcare; they also provide 60-day paid internships with an environmental activist group and pay bail to employees who are arrested during peaceful protests.

Patagonia's culture is built on trust and equity. To allow for free information flow, they do not have more than 100 people at once in one location. Designed on the open plan model with no one in individual offices, managers are always visible and easily approachable. The best parking places go to people with the most fuel-efficient cars. Everything about Patagonia's culture and people encourages working towards a common cause of saving the planet. To get there they follow their company's values, one of which tells them not to be bound by convention. By not following convention, they arrive at a very different vision of the world, unique among their peers in the retail business. They are a company that remains private by design.

Are We Heading Towards a Post-Work Society?

Nearly 4 million Americans quit their jobs in April 2021 according to an official US Labor Department statistic.[19] Hundreds swapped their matchbox city apartments for converted vans to live and work on the road, crisscrossing the country.[20] The pandemic years of 2020–21 saw the largest workers' exodus on record, pushing the rate of job leavers to 2.7 percent of all those employed. While some departures were planned, most could be explained by the lingering pandemic and concerns about safety. For the majority, the recess into their homes was an opportunity to reassess what work really means and how they wanted to spend the rest of their lives.

The conversation regarding the need for a radical change in the most fundamental of human relationships—the relationship with work—is finally happening in earnest. The cases of Amazon and Patagonia offer two opposite scenarios of where companies can choose to go to achieve their objectives. One is taking the strategy of maximum focus on skills, efficiencies, and around-the-clock productivity powered by automation. The other is focused on regenerative strategy by creating space for its workers to bring the whole of themselves, contribute to the good of the larger community, and blend work and play in one place. Both are successful from the current marketplace perspective in which success is measured by hours and dollars. Yet the set of human outcomes and impacts on their workers could not be more different. If sustainability and regeneration are accounted for, there are clear winners and losers. What would it take to have a multidimensional measure of business success? For that shift to happen, the new philosophy of life and work needs to be embraced. In the words of C.G. Jung, "Every transformation demands as its precondition 'the ending of a world'—the collapse of an old philosophy of life."[21] We can see that the collapse of the old philosophy of life and work has arrived.

Outside the extreme working cultures of the US and the UK, the developed economies in Europe have already started pulling away from the relentless work ethic and from the philosophy that work is the only way to live. Patagonia is proving that blending work and life is not only nice to have but it is achievable and commercially successful. We anticipate that the debate about the nature of work, the role of skills and jobs, as well as the divergent views on work's purpose in life is just starting.

Endnotes

1 Beckett, A (2015) All day long: A portrait of Britain at work by Joanna Biggs – review, *Guardian*, https://www.theguardian.com/books/2015/mar/27/all-day-long-a-portrait-of-britain-at-work-joanna-biggs-review (archived at https://perma.cc/36D2-MJBU)

2 Thompson, D (2019) Workism is making Americans miserable, *The Atlantic*, https://www.theatlantic.com/ideas/archive/2019/02/religion-workism-making-americans-miserable/583441/ (archived at https://perma.cc/2RND-PR3S)

3 Huntington, SP (2004) *Who Are We? The challenges to America's national identity*, New York: Simon & Schuster

4   Box, GEP (1976) Science and statistics, *Journal of the American Statistical Association*, **71** (356), pp 791–99

5   Jesuthasan, R and Boudreau, J (2021) Work without jobs, *MIT Sloan Management Review*, **62** (2), pp 1–5

6   Yarrow, A (2020) The male non-working class: A disquieting survey, *Milken Institute Review*, https://www.milkenreview.org/articles/the-male-non-working-class (archived at https://perma.cc/YH6H-PVTT)

7   The Week (2016) The mystery of America's missing male workers, https://theweek.com/articles/659245/mystery-americas-missing-male-workers (archived at https://perma.cc/7W9R-NW7P)

8   Macdonell, AA (1898) Art. XIII–the origin and early history of chess, *Journal of the Royal Asiatic Society*, **30** (1), pp 117–41

9   Weise, K (2020) Pushed by pandemic, Amazon goes on a hiring spree without equal, *New York Times*, https://www.nytimes.com/2020/11/27/technology/pushed-by-pandemic-amazon-goes-on-a-hiring-spree-without-equal.html (archived at https://perma.cc/QCG3-LPHH)

10 Kantor, J, Weise, K, and Ashford, G (2021) The Amazon that customers do not see, *New York Times*, https://www.nytimes.com/interactive/2021/06/15/us/amazon-workers.html (archived at https://perma.cc/W27A-DBCT)

11 Streitfeld, D (2021) How Amazon crushes the unions, *New York Times*, https://www.nytimes.com/2021/03/16/technology/amazon-unions-virginia.html (archived at https://perma.cc/7QZR-WYBZ)

12 Kantor, J, Weise, K, and Ashford, G (2021) The Amazon that customers do not see, *New York Times*, https://www.nytimes.com/interactive/2021/06/15/us/amazon-workers.html (archived at https://perma.cc/DU8J-YY4U)

13 Ibid.

14 Takefman, B (2021) Amazon profits increased nearly 200% since start of Covid-19 pandemic, *Research FDI*, https://researchfdi.com/amazon-covid-19-pandemic-profits/ (archived at https://perma.cc/VUT8-GDXY)

15 Carter, D (2019) Beyond stoked: The power of living values wildly, Talent Connect Conference, https://www.talentconnect2022.com/past-session/a-keynote-from-dean-carter (archived at https://perma.cc/L5QZ-K8YJ)

16 Chouinard, Y (2005) *Let My People Go Surfing*, New York Penguin Press

17 Sanford, C (nd) The regenerative business: Redesigning work & cultivating human potential, Growth Ensemble Podcast, https://growensemble.com/regenerative-business/ (archived at https://perma.cc/NZK5-7L7F)

18 Carter, D (2019) Beyond stoked: The power of living values wildly, Talent Connect Conference, https://www.talentconnect2022.com/past-session/a-keynote-from-dean-carter (archived at https://perma.cc/N8X4-XD88)

19 Liu, J (2021) 4 million people quit their jobs in April, sparked by confidence they can find better work, *CNBC*, https://www.cnbc.com/2021/06/09/4-million-people-quit-their-jobs-in-april-to-find-better-work.html (archived at https://perma.cc/HPK2-BX7Q)

20 Bomey, N (2021) #VanLife takes off during COVID-19 as Americans convert vans for a life on the road, *USA Today*, https://www.usatoday.com/story/money/cars/2021/02/17/van-life-coronavirus-pandemic-remote-work-mercedes-sprinter-van-life/4371726001/ (archived at https://perma.cc/8GTF-62VM)

21 Jung, CG and Franz, MV (1979) *Man and His Symbols*, London: Aldus Books

03

How Work Is Measured: Productivity vs Impact

Why Measurements Matter

"What gets measured gets managed" is perhaps one of the lines most wrongly attributed to the management guru Peter Drucker. Drucker never said any of that nor did he see management through the lens of measurement only.[1] The quote actually belongs to the academic V.F. Ridgway, who cautioned in the 1950s against unquestioning acceptance of numerical performance measurement assessments: "What gets measured gets managed—even when it is pointless to measure and manage it, and even if it harms the purpose of the organization to measure it."[2]

At the threshold of the 21st century, leading management thinkers from Drucker to Deming and Mintzberg cautioned against business's overreliance on numbers alone as accurate measurements of work. Quality guru W. Edwards Deming ranked "management by use only of visible figures, with little consideration of figures that are unknown or unknowable" as number five on his list of deadly management sins.[3] Henry Mintzberg, a leading management academic, advised managers that starting "from the premise that we can't measure what matters gives [managers] the best chance of realistically facing up to their challenge."[4] In 1990, Peter Drucker advised one of his executive clients that taking up a new role was first a personal decision. "It is the relationship with people, the development of mutual confidence,

FIGURE 3.1   Measuring Work

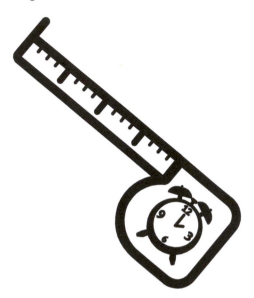

the identification of people, the creation of a community. This is something only you can do… It cannot be measured or easily defined. But it is not only a key function. It is one only you can perform."[5] By the end of the 20th century, questions about the accuracy of measurements of work were raised but not definitively answered. It was left for the internet generation to figure out what really matters when it comes to work.

The search for the "objective" and universal measure of work has been shaping economic systems since the start of this civilization. A brief retrospective into the evolution of measurements and measurement tools can offer a unique perspective on the relative interdependence between work, its tools, and the multiple ways of measuring work's outcomes. What it also proves is that data does not merely stand for objective reality but rather serves as molds in which ideas take shape. These same ideas impact our worldview and define what is considered accurate, equal, and truthful. The history of measurement systems shows how and why our data dependency developed, and what the data revolution may mean in the context of today's workplace.[6] At stake are the new ways of thinking about the workplace once the new context is established.

Civilization did not arrive at its first universal measurement system until the late 18th century, when the development of global trade and the subsequent Industrial Revolution drove the need for standardization. The remnants of the ancient measurement units are still with us, preserved in some of the terminology we still use today. Many of these terms came from human morphology such as the foot (feet), the pace, the pinch. There were as many measurements in circulation as there were locations and trades. In 1795, for example, France was known to have over 700 measuring systems, one almost for every profession.

Take the evolution of one such universal standard, the measurement of time. Time is universally considered today a uniquely global measure. Time dictates when we sleep, eat, work. However, as an abstract measure it can only be captured through specialized tools such as a sundial, an hourglass, a watch, or a digital device. Before modern time measurement tools were invented, people were able to distinguish times of day by tracking the movement of the sun and stars through the sky. The concept of a 24-hour day emerged in antiquity, but once dials were applied to the faces of clocks in the 14th century, people became able to distinguish minutes and seconds. Mechanical watches were invented in the 16th century and were mass manufactured in the 18th century to be replaced by the advent of quartz in the 20th century and the digital solar and motion interfaces that in the 21st century can deliver atomic levels of precision.

In the early 20th century, Albert Einstein famously challenged the certainty of time as a stable measure. Time, according to Einstein, was only one of the four interdependent dimensions of the universe. In its fourth dimension, time existed interdependent with space. Space provided the context in which time occurred. Einstein's colleague Kurt Gödel took the theory of relativity to the next level and produced a proof that in any universe described by quantum physics, time could not exist. The very idea that time could disappear into irrelevance was so radical for its time that it was suppressed until the 21st century. The book *A World Without Time* reclaimed Gödel's discovery and argued for the possibility of a world in which there was no time.[7] Such patterns of iterative disruption and reinvention persist throughout science, technology, and ultimately arrive in the workplace. The lesson to be learned from physics and natural sciences is that measurement tools and methods matter but they are relative.

Technology laws have become ubiquitous today, just like those of physics. There were no combustion engines and electricity 150 years ago, and the printed press was invented in the 15th century; life today is unimaginable without the smart phones that did not exist just 15 years ago. Gordon Moore, an American engineer, made his prediction in 1965 that the number of transistors per silicon chip would double every year. Moore's law today may just as well be technology's equivalent of Newtonian physics. The pace of technology innovation has accelerated exponentially, surpassing every single milestone and baseline set. Smart AI programs are already reading legal documents and providing basic medical advice. Innovation in AI is beginning to center on the most sacred of human abilities: thinking, reasoning, and creating. Predictive modeling is already being replaced with inference and at the end of the day there will be nothing artificial left in "artificial intelligence." All these systems are collecting data, measuring tangible and intangible outcomes, and learning faster than any human is capable of. The measurement systems of the latter half of the 21st century will be future focused and most likely be based on simulating, inferring, and predicting.[8]

The adoption of advanced sensing and inference technologies, the rise of people analytics, and the arrival of technologically and analytically equipped HR professionals create a new workplace capability to focus not only on what is being done but on how it is being done and measured. The measurement revolution in people management has already taken off and is transforming the workplace.

Has Measuring Become Monitoring?

When office workers logged into their company laptops remotely during the pandemic, each keystroke, each mouse movement and email could be tracked. Dedicated VPNs (virtual private networks) allowed employers to observe virtually everything employees were doing online.[9] Screenshots to check whether workers were paying full attention while online and monitors collecting biometric data could have been turned on if the employers so required. Productivity scoring algorithms made it possible to break down how efficient each individual employee, team or department unit was. Keystroke monitoring allowed administrators to see the aggregate of user-based behavior analytics.[10]

Employers are now able to aggregate enormous volumes of employee data. According to Gartner, about 30 percent of companies were already using employee monitoring outside traditional surveys in 2015, with anticipated growth to 80 percent in the coming decade.[11] In addition to technologies such as InterGuard software[12] specializing in employee monitoring, the accelerated adoption of Employee Experience Platforms and Talent Marketplace Platforms[13] allows unprecedented access and visibility into employee online behavior and sentiment.[14]

Ambient data today is the essential workplace infrastructure and the principal medium for measuring work. Gone are the days when managing schedules and workloads was the supervisor's responsibility and the annual employee surveys served as the way to figure out employees' satisfaction and engagement. Most companies today have replaced annual check-ins with ubiquitous monitoring technologies, from location tracking to the latest deep monitoring platforms.[15]

Collecting employee data serves at least three workplace goals, especially in a remote setting:

- companies seek to monitor risk, provide cyber security, and ensure compliance;
- data supports achieving productivity goals by helping individuals and teams with feedback to course-correct on projects and to stay productive;
- industrial-era compliance functions of monitoring and disciplining employees are delivered electronically.

The discussion of whether collecting employee data is about monitoring and disciplining employees or about helping individuals and teams to stay productive is complicated. In the meantime, there is no escaping the fact that both are happening, both are needed, and both will go hand in hand in the future. Today's organizations are well equipped not only to supervise and direct the workforce but to collect and analyze extensive personal information to best respond to employees' needs. By delivering the nudges and prompts to proactively intervene and assist their employees and teams with feedback, problem solving, ongoing learning, and even wellbeing at scale, technology is an inalienable part of the work process today. However, the downsides of this much access to employees' most private information are a cause for serious concern.

Management and employees often come down on the opposite sides of the workplace data monitoring debate. The big question is whether a compromise between employers and employees is possible and a middle ground achieved. Transparency, new guidelines, and regulations are long overdue, and organizations have a hard time coming up with adequate governance structures and necessary communication processes. Time is running out on the much-needed reorganization around technology and data monitoring in the new world of work.

Does Pursuit of Productivity Still Make Sense?

Productivity has been humanity's never-ending economic pursuit since before the Industrial Revolution. Commonly defined as a "ratio of output to input," productivity became the measure of workforce effectiveness and the leading performance goal.[16] Looking back at the last couple of centuries, the industry's single-minded obsession with productivity growth was understood to be delivering most value. Labor economists convinced the world that high productivity led to profitability for companies and greater prosperity for countries.[17] For most of modern history the workplace was defined by the relationship between labor and capital. Pursuit of productivity propelled by technological advances was the engine that brought about the Industrial Revolution and powered the three subsequent technological revolutions. The pursuit of faster, cheaper, and better ways of building products and delivering services offered the world unprecedented levels of prosperity and advancement. Yet going forward, humanity's relationship with work needs to be revisited and rebalanced if humans are to continue to flourish.

Mechanical tools surpassed human physical performance centuries ago. Today, humans are finding themselves competing for relevance and primacy in areas that have traditionally been considered uniquely human. Artificial intelligence is starting to outpace humanity in the most unique human faculties such as reasoning, creativity, and intuition. Singularity—defined as the ability of a smart machine to replace human brain function—is no longer the product of science fiction. Unlike anything experienced before, humans may soon find themselves displaced by intelligent technologies in development today.[18] Will it threaten the survival of human civilization, as the preeminent British physicist Stephen Hawking warned about and the futurist Ray Kurzweil predicted for the mid-21st century?[19]

The potential implications of such a dramatic societal, economic, and lifestyle shift by far outpace the current organizational efforts to counterbalance technology with strategic workforce planning, re-skilling, and jobs redesign. In addition to addressing jobs and skills development, the question may come down to changing work's primary focus and purpose. The question today should be whether efficiency, productivity, and growth remain the ultimate goal and measure of business and organization success. Should the current business mandate be replaced with one of greater social impact and long-term sustainability? What kinds of tensions would arise and how would they be resolved?

The Productivity Race Is Lost, Long Live Impact

It may be still too close to call, but humanity has all but lost its race for productivity to the machines. While work will always be vital to human wellbeing and flourishing, productivity will continue its slide down humanity's priority list. Productivity has all but become synonymous with technology. Technology prevails over humans in speed, efficiency, precision, and overall endurance. It is time for the humans to stop competing with the machines and to prioritize the critical human pursuit of purpose, sustainability, and impact.

The project of bringing technology and humanity together is as ancient as technology itself. The term "technology" came from the Greek *technē* meaning "art or craft" and *logos* meaning "word, speech." In other words, *technology* originally meant conversations about the arts and crafts that were the privilege of the most educated elite members of Greek society. Technology represented the highest forms of human expression. Through the centuries that followed, technology became "the means or activity by which man seeks to change or manipulate his environment,"[20] meaning handling more and more sophisticated tools and machines.

It was not until the mid-20th century that technology began to encompass processes and process management in addition to the handling of tools and machines. The term "Information Technology" was first introduced and recognized as an independent branch of technology in 1958. Two organizational psychologists, Harold J. Leavitt and Thomas L. Whisler, wrote an *HBR* article, "Management in the 1980s," in which they defined information technology as consisting of three categories: techniques for information processing, the application of statistical and mathematical methods to decision making, and simulation of higher-order thinking through computer programs.[21] Of significance was their foresight of the potential implications of these technologies for organizational structure, functions, span of control, and overall productivity: "Information technology promises fewer people to do more work." Inspired by the emerging field, the authors anticipated "revolutionary" changes in how organizations operate. Yet, productivity in the United States and other developed countries has not been keeping up with the exponential growth of computational power. The phenomenon became known as the "productivity paradox," ie the discrepancy between expanding technological capability and anemic productivity growth.[22]

The pandemic served as a dual catalyst of a special kind. Accelerated adoption of technology received most attention, but perhaps more important was the global experiment in changing human behavior at scale. The pandemic made the case for stronger alignment between two complementary pursuits: commitment to technological innovation and investment in people at work. Fast scaling of technology and adaptive human behavior went hand in hand to change how work gets done.

The pandemic left more questions than it gave answers. The purpose, the value, and the measure of work were at the top of the list. Could organizations abandon productivity and turn to impact as an ultimate measure of their performance? What would be the criteria to measure success going forward? Should there be numerical data to compare impact across industries and domains? How will the intangible assets be accounted for? What to make of impact that can be positive, negative, or neutral; how should it be understood?

A lot could be learned from a few innovative companies that lead the way, building their commercial success with impact first as their guiding principle. Patagonia, the outdoor clothing retailer, and Ben and Jerry's, the premium ice cream producer, are exactly the success stories to learn from when prioritizing social and environmental impact as a company's North Star.

CASE STUDY

Patagonia and Ben & Jerry's Journey to Impact

In November 2011, on the run-up to Christmas, the busiest shopping day in the United States, *The New York Times* ran a full-page ad urging shoppers, "Don't Buy This Jacket." Patagonia published its anti-consumerism ad educating consumers not to buy the jacket if they did not need it.[23] The ad explained the environmental cost of the jacket. The sales went up. As an article in *The New Yorker* magazine explained, "It is confounding to try to draw lines around when Patagonia's marketing encourages sales and when it discourages them."[24]

Patagonia is a 100 percent principle-based retail brand that reached its $1 billion valuation in 2018. The company is using its business to practice the stakeholder-first brand of capitalism; it sees business as a vehicle to "fulfill its commitment to employees, customers and to the planet." Success is measured by its achievement of two sets of goals: being purposeful and being profitable.

The company's compelling story brings more equity to its success than its profits. It accomplishes the goals it sets for its business in three interconnected ways:

- investing in and empowering its employees;
- being transparent about its actions and decisions;
- holding itself publicly accountable.[25]

When it comes to fair labor practices across its supply chain, Patagonia partners with third-party organizations such as Fair Trade USA and the MIT Sloan Sustainability Initiative. The company invests in educating employees through monthly mandatory seminars with athletes, artists, and activists to understand diverse aspects of the agenda and be better educated to take on the responsibility of internal monitoring for their commitments. Employees' opinions are listened to, internal audits and self-assessments are an ongoing practice, and external expertise is invited and valued. Most importantly, there is a commitment to authenticity in the culture Patagonia has built.

Ben and Jerry's got started at an abandoned gas station in Vermont in 1978. It is now a wholly owned subsidiary of Unilever. The company is pursuing one of the most aggressive environmental impact agendas focused on renewable energy, pricing of its carbon footprint, and auditing its entire supply chain for environmental standards. The first environmental wakeup call came when they found out that each pint of ice cream produced roughly 3.3 pounds of greenhouse gases.[26] Their science-based estimated goals are set high, with the environment as their primary consideration:

- 100 percent renewable energy by 2025;
- 40 percent greenhouse gas intensity reduction by 2025;
- 80 percent greenhouse gas intensity reduction by 2050.

Ben and Jerry's are transparent and public about their progress on the impact goals that they prioritize as much as their Product and Economic Mission. For the last 31 years their goals achievement was updated through the annual Social and Environmental Assessment Report (SEAR).[27]

The winning stories of Patagonia and Ben & Jerry's may seem to be exceptions rather than the rule today but they are persuasive and powerful examples. The business model that prioritizes impact and purpose over profits and yet comes out commercially successful and profitable offers new benchmarks and measurement and creates the much-needed context for whole-industry transformation to get started.

How Impact Can Overtake Productivity
as a Success Measure of Work

July 17, 2013 was the date the Delaware Governor signed into law benefit corporation legislation, making Delaware the 19th state to recognize *Benefit Corporation* as an alternative legal form of doing business. Delaware's recognition was a critical milestone, as it is the home to over a million businesses, including 50 percent of all publicly traded companies and 64 percent of the Fortune 500 list; it is the state most important for businesses seeking access to venture capital, private equity, and public capital markets.[28] Until the 21st century, corporate law did not recognize the legitimacy of any corporate purpose other than maximizing profits. The B-Corp movement recognizes the legitimacy of committing to a higher organizational purpose, accountability, and greater levels of transparency. It helps companies build longer-term trust with their stakeholders. It helps companies attract talent, offers more transparency, and delivers a better employee experience to a company's talent. It promises to both make money and make a difference.

The practice and methodology of measuring impact is beginning to take priority in the private sector. The worlds of philanthropy and not-for-profit organizations have always known the importance and challenges of measuring and communicating impact. "Claims about making a difference are no longer sufficient; evidence of how much difference you're making is now required," writes Alnoor Ebrahim, the leading academic authority on measuring impact and accountability in public sector organizations.[29] To understand and fully measure impact, voices of all stakeholder groups need to be acknowledged including employees, executives, board members, investors, and customers. All participants need to know what made a difference and how much; what worked and what needed to be changed and how to move forward.

As more private sector players are sharing the goals of not-for-profit organizations and aligning some of their priorities with broader societal and economic goals, a more comprehensive measurement system has been taking shape. The initial list of the impact goals has come together as a starting point for a more rigorous exploration:

- longer-term impact needs to be measured and interpreted as positive, neutral or negative;
- impact needs to be measured through data to be fully understood;
- data is just the start; the impact story behind the data needs to be told and shared;
- there are always two levels of impact—societal and institutional;
- individual organizations often cannot create societal-level impact;
- to achieve broader societal and economic impact, organizations need to work in tandem, to collaborate with each other.

The first step in the evolution of the workplace towards impact is the hardest. That first step is the impact audit.

The Impact Journey Starts with an Audit

Following the tragic events of the summer of 2020, racial equity and justice were thrust into the center of attention for both the business community and social justice organizations alike. The immediate business response to the events of George Floyd's murder and subsequent social unrest was universal and overwhelming. There was no getting away with well-intentioned statements of solidarity this time. The world was watching to see whether businesses would follow through with specific actions and if they were committed for the long term. A growing number of companies were breaking ranks with their corporate peers and moving to action on their own ahead of the curve. BlackRock, the world's largest asset manager, committed to launching a racial audit at the request of a shareholder. In a letter to employees, BlackRock announced that it would conduct an external review of how its diversity, equity, and inclusion policies impact stakeholders.

The first major US company to undergo such a third-party racial audit was Airbnb. In 2016, Airbnb partnered with Color of Change to launch a three-year review of the company's platform and their practices. Color of Change, the largest online justice organization in the US, issued a statement following the report's findings praising the leadership of Airbnb for their commitment and effort in becoming a pioneer among the peer companies for addressing structural biases in their operating model. The statement also noted that more work needed to be done in the areas of offline and community relations.[30]

Starbucks followed Airbnb after a 2018 incident at its Philadelphia store that started a national and global conversation about public displays of bias and its consequences. Global training was conducted in collaboration with the former US Attorney General Eric Holder. The company laid out a public set of commitments.[31]

In 2020, Facebook reluctantly conducted its own racial equity reviews and created internal teams to "examine how Black and minority users are affected by the company's algorithms as compared with white users."[32]

The position of the major financial institutions has also been changing since the summer of 2020. The measurement criteria for change are being defined and agreed upon. With them, CtW Investment Group responded to events by openly requesting major US financial organizations to launch racial equity audits to "identify, prioritize and remedy the adverse impacts of the bank's policies and practices on non-white stakeholders and communities of color."[33]

With BlackRock still being one of a few exceptions, most banks declined the external audit and chose instead to address these issues internally. Morgan Stanley, for example, shared internal plans for "an independent review of the global talent program, the creation of an Institute for Inclusion with an independent advisory board, and enhanced disclosures about the bank's diversity and inclusion efforts."[34]

The status of the racial audit shows that it is just the beginning of a much longer journey towards shifting priorities to what matters. The fact that major economic players are taking steps towards making systemic changes in the way they run their businesses marks an important transition to the realignment of business goals.

The new Human Capital disclosures issued by the US Securities and Exchange Commission (SEC) consolidate the trend that started in the private sector and has become the area of focus for major government regulations.[35] Momentum for environmental, social, and governance reporting is building across the globe and companies are moving from compliance to a proactive change of direction in their businesses. The trend is growing from introducing new measurements to embedding these new goals in the flow of work.[36]

Endnotes

1 Zak, P (2013) Measurement myopia, Drucker Institute, https://www.drucker. institute/thedx/measurement-myopia/ (archived at https://perma.cc/7B6A-UKRM)

2 Ridgway, V (1956) Dysfunctional consequences of performance measurements, *Administrative Science Quarterly*, 1 (2), pp 240–47

3 Deming, WE, Cahill, KE, and Allan, KL (2018) *Out of the Crisis*, Cambridge: The MIT Press

4 Mintzberg, H (1979) *The Structuring of Organizations: A synthesis of the research*, Englewood Cliffs, NJ: Prentice-Hall

5 Zak, P (2013) Measurement myopia, Drucker Institute, https://www.drucker. institute/thedx/measurement-myopia/ (archived at https://perma.cc/VKP6-ZBL9)

6 Lugli, E (2019) *The Making of Measure and the Promise of Sameness*, Chicago, London: The University of Chicago Press

7 Yourgrau, P (2005) *A World Without Time: The forgotten legacy of Gödel and Einstein*, 1st edition, New York: Basic Books

8 Vellante, D and Floyer, D (2021) A new era of innovation: Moore's Law is not dead and AI is ready to explode, *A Silicon Angle*, https://siliconangle.com/2021/04/10/new-era-innovation-moores-law-not-dead-ai-ready-explode/ (archived at https://perma.cc/9PC3-W5LE)

9 Kropp, B (2019) The future of employee monitoring, Gartner Human Resources, https://www.gartner.com/smarterwithgartner/the-future-of-employee-monitoring (archived at https://perma.cc/862V-KBJN)

10 For example, https://www.teramind.co/ (archived at https://perma.cc/XG3W-GZKS)

11 Kropp, B (2019) 5 changes HR leaders can expect to manage in 2019, Gartner Human Resources, https://www.gartner.com/smarterwithgartner/5-changes-hr-leaders-can-expect-to-manage-in-2019 (archived at https://perma.cc/4G34-TSYH)

12 https://www.interguardsoftware.com/ (archived at https://perma.cc/Z4SB-GPVE)

13 Bersin, J (2021) The employee experience platform: A new category arrives, https://joshbersin.com/2019/02/the-employee-experience-platform-a-new-category-arrives/ (archived at https://perma.cc/7TDB-A7LM)

14 Bersin, J (2020) Talent marketplace platforms explode into view, https://joshbersin.com/2020/07/talent-marketplace-platforms-explode-into-view/ (archived at https://perma.cc/8FAE-K9S9)

15 Marvin, R and Sevilla, G (2021) The best employee monitoring software for 2021, *PC Magazine*, https://in.pcmag.com/software/117679/the-best-employee-monitoring-software (archived at https://perma.cc/EK7G-P2N8)

16 Sickles, R and Zelenyuk, V (2019) *Measurement of Productivity and Efficiency Theory and Practice*, New York: Cambridge University Press

17 US Bureau of Labor Statistics (nd) Productivity 101, https://www.bls.gov/k12/productivity-101/ (archived at https://perma.cc/BEE7-57VP)

18 Schulze-Makuch, D (2020) Reaching the singularity may be humanity's greatest and last accomplishment, *Airspacemag*, https://www.airspacemag.com/daily-planet/reaching-singularity-may-be-humanitys-greatest-and-last-accomplishment-180974528/ (archived at https://perma.cc/W4QY-SKKF)

19 Cellan-Jones, R (2014) Stephen Hawking warns artificial intelligence could end mankind, *BBC News Tech*, https://www.bbc.com/news/technology-30290540 (archived at https://perma.cc/93EW-2JCB)

20 Buchanan, RA (2020) History of technology, *Encyclopedia Britannica*

21 Leavitt, HJ and Whisler, TL (1958) Management in the 1980s, *Harvard Business Review*, https://hbr.org/1958/11/management-in-the-1980s (archived at https://perma.cc/LKF5-TSGW)

22 Brynjolfsson, E (1993) The productivity paradox of information technology, Association for Computing Machinery, http://ccs.mit.edu/papers/CCSWP130/ccswp130.html (archived at https://perma.cc/PML3-5YTC)

23 Clarke, C (2017) Why Patagonia's off-the-wall advertising asks customers to think twice before buying its products, *The Drum*, https://www.thedrum.com/news/2017/02/22/why-patagonias-the-wall-advertising-asks-customers-think-twice-buying-its-products (archived at https://perma.cc/KPG5-UC69)

24 MacKinnon, JB (2015) Patagonia's anti-growth strategy, *New Yorker*, https://www.newyorker.com/business/currency/patagonias-anti-growth-strategy (archived at https://perma.cc/A4L7-RVYY)

25 Atlassian (2020) Patagonia's demand for ethical supply, https://www.atlassian.com/blog/podcast/teamistry/patagonias-demand-for-ethical-supply (archived at https://perma.cc/G7YT-DS8M)

26 Ben & Jerry's (2018) If it's melted, it is ruined, https://www.benjerry.com/whats-new/2016/endangered-pints (archived at https://perma.cc/N2XD-EMCP)

27   Ben & Jerry's (nd) Our SEAR reports, https://www.benjerry.com/about-us/
sear-reports (archived at https://perma.cc/KZG7-UVJE)

28   Coen Gilbert, J, Houlahan, B, and Kassoy, A (2013) Today marks a tipping
point in the evolution of capitalism, *Forbes*, https://www.forbes.com/sites/
skollworldforum/2013/07/17/today-marks-a-tipping-point-in-the-evolution-of-
capitalism/?sh=5f30cdb063a7 (archived at https://perma.cc/Y7P4-PM5Z)

29   Ebrahim, A (2013) Let's be realistic about measuring impact, *Harvard
Business Review*, https://hbr.org/2013/03/lets-be-realistic-about-measur.html
(archived at https://perma.cc/K9SN-F3G6)

30   Color of Change (2016) Progress report shows Airbnb is a model for big tech
collaboration with civil rights groups: Company must extend focus to offline
experience of black guests and hosts, https://colorofchange.org/press_release/
progress-report-shows-airbnb-is-a-model-for-big-tech-collaboration-with-civil-
rights-groups-company-must-extend-focus-to-offline-experience-of-black-
guests-and-hosts/ (archived at https://perma.cc/X8T4-B2AR)

31   Starbucks (nd) Racial equity—learn with us, https://stories.starbucks.com/
stories/racial-equity/ (archived at https://perma.cc/XXT4-5K62)

32   Seetharaman, D and Horwitz, J (2020) Facebook creates teams to study racial
bias, after previously limiting such efforts, *Wall Street Journal*, https://www.
wsj.com/articles/facebook-creates-teams-to-study-racial-bias-on-its-
platforms-11595362939 (archived at https://perma.cc/MWP7-NNR9)

33   SOC Investment Group (2021) Racial equity audit, https://www.
socinvestmentgroup.com/racial-equity-audit (archived at https://perma.cc/
K6BF-RXSY)

34   Morgan Stanley (2020) Annual report and 2021 notice of meeting & proxy
statement, https://www.morganstanley.com/about-us-ir/annual-reports
(archived at https://perma.cc/J5AF-Q8EU)

35   EY (2021) How to approach the SEC's new human capital disclosures: Year 1,
https://www.ey.com/en_us/assurance/accountinglink/how-to-approach-the-sec-
s-new-human-capital-disclosures (archived at https://perma.cc/S39G-ZWS2)

36   BlackRock (nd) Integrating the UN SDGs in investments, https://www.
blackrock.com/institutions/en-ch/insights/investment-actions/integrating-un-
sdgs-in-investments (archived at https://perma.cc/5LYQ-6B4G)

PART TWO

Workforce

04

Human-Centered Work Design: Humans vs Workforce

The Evolutionary Case for a Human-Centered Approach

"The point is not to be better robots than robots, but to have more human work than our ancestors—creative, caring, curious," commented labor historian Louis Hyman about the misplaced focus on the competition between the humans and the machines.[1] Super computers, powerful AI, and intelligent robotics have already arrived and are closer than ever to supplementing if not fully replacing human workers. As the production and transactional role of work gets outsourced to technology, human work needs to shift to deploying capabilities that remain singularly human. In that scenario, the future of work looks more and more like a hybrid compact between technology and humans. Yet, today's workplaces have been set up to serve the marketplace first and the workplace last. Any transition is bound to hit the speedbumps of the legacy organization systems. A broad rethinking and redesign of the workplace is due, and the humans need to step up and correct the imbalance.

A look back at the history of humans' relationship with their environment, its objects, and its creatures offers some helpful clues about how humans may ultimately relate to technology and why the focus on human-centricity is not only nice to have but imperative to adopt and the only *right* path forward.

FIGURE 4.1   Fusion of Humans and Machines

A New Way of Looking at Our Relationship with Technology

For centuries, human beings endowed inanimate objects and non-human creatures surrounding them with their own characteristics, behaviors, intentions, and emotions. Humans have worshipped gods in their own image, projected human-like qualities onto non-human creatures, and represented them in art and writing as having human-like attributes. To explain unknown phenomena, humans predictably reached out to the most familiar and closest available source: themselves. The practice known as anthropomorphism implies the attribution of human traits, emotions, and intentions by humans to their surroundings. Anthropomorphism is an inherent human bias towards personification of the world. The word "anthropomorphism," first used in the 1750s, came from the Greek *Anthropos* (human) and *morphe* (form) and became a recognized way for humans to explain the world around them. If one is looking for anthropomorphism, it can be found everywhere. It dominates children's language and literature and shows up everywhere, from literary classics such as Lewis

Carroll's *Alice's Adventures in Wonderland* (1865) and Rudyard Kipling's *The Jungle Book* (1894) to Walt Disney's Mickey Mouse and Donald Duck, Sesame Street characters, and more recently video games like the Super Mario Bros series in which the protagonists include turtle-like creatures with human qualities.

In the natural sciences, anthropomorphism was considered "unscientific" and subjective until the rise of the animal rights movement in the late 20th century.[2] Despite Charles Darwin's breakthrough discovery of evolutionary theory in *On the Origin of Species* (1859) and *The Descent of Man* (1871), animal studies were restricted to the study of ethology, the science of animal behavior, denying the existence of emotions in animals. The work of primatologists, especially Jane Goodall studying chimpanzees, brought attention to the emotional life of animals, and contributed to the change in perception and broader acceptance of empathy in the study of animals. Frans de Waal, a primatologist working at Emory University, wrote an article, "Are We in Anthropodenial?" (1997), stating that "as soon as we admit that we are far more like our relatives than like machines, then anthropodenial becomes impossible and anthropomorphism becomes inevitable and scientifically acceptable." He added an important insight, warning, "if we don't, we risk missing something fundamental, about animals and about us."[3] Human–animal interactions have evolved not only to the point of shifting social norms towards protecting animals but further towards creating laws and institutions that govern interactions between animals and humans while acknowledging the rights of animals.

It may appear to be far-fetched to look to the evolution of human relationships with animals as a historical precedent to how humans may eventually relate to intelligent automation. The question we should be asking is whether the anthropomorphic bias will work with computers the same way as it has worked with other neighbors in the ecosystem. Anthropomorphic language has already invaded computer vocabulary and has helped make technological complexity more accessible. A computer "reads" and "thinks," it could be "friendly," it "gets infected with viruses and bugs," it "needs rest, cleaning" etc. The machines are beginning to look and act more like humans while invading all aspects of work and life. One universal example of this phenomenon is the priority given to user experience (UX) as a design objective. UX makes human use of technology intuitive and optimal. By using smart personalization based on the customer's historical purchase patterns, Starbucks, for one, makes ordering online easy.

Alexa, the voice-based, AI-enabled digital assistant, can now recognize household voices and personalize its services.

Just like before, there is an ongoing debate among technologists and technology ethicists as to whether robots should be created in the human image at all. There are inventors like David Hanson, the creator of the android Sophia, the first robot to be awarded citizenship (by Saudi Arabia). They argue for the humanoid robots. On the other side of the argument, there are ethicists who specialize in AI and argue that human-like robots are a deception: "we can build lifelike bodies, but we cannot yet equip them with AI to match the expectations created by their appearance."[4] Behavioral scientists are joining with technologists to study the consequences of human empathy with the humanoid robots and its full implications.

The human relationship with technology is a two-way street. Technomorphia is a growing tendency to attribute technological qualities to human behavior. Among the most frequently used phrases that have entered everyday vocabulary are phrases such as "I need to reboot," "let us discuss offline," "I do not have the bandwidth," and many others. The human-machine vocabulary creates space for the new hybrid workplace, the hybrid between human and technology workers, no matter whether they work from home, the office, or any other space.

Institutional Speedbumps

When MIT president Dr Rafael Reif called on a team of the institute's researchers to figure out the impact of advancing technology on society and the workforce, he called it the defining issue of our time.[5] The purpose of the study was to explain imbalances in the economy caused by advancements in technology and to come up with policy recommendations to correct these imbalances. The resulting 92-page report, "The Work of the Future: Building Better Jobs in an Age of Intelligent Machines," delivered important insights regarding the changing workforce.[6] The researchers showed that the human return on investment (ROI) in technology investment was low, and that was the failure of social institutions and not technology per se. David Autor, MIT labor economist and one of the authors of the report, concluded that it was not that technology needed to get better or more middle-wage jobs needed to be automated. Instead, "we have worse institutions." It has been rightly predicted that automation will replace many jobs while creating others. Yet, embedding ever-advancing technology into traditional institutional structures would lead to even more dramatic disruption as organizations and institutions are not prepared to handle the change. The pandemic made the focus on reorganizing the workplace a priority. To prepare the workforce ahead of the coming technological change, organizations need to accept the sunk cost and reorganize for the hybrid workplace where technology and human workers are on the same team.

Business Turns to Human-Centric Solutions

Every spring, Larry Fink, the CEO of BlackRock, the world's largest asset manager, writes a letter to the CEOs of the portfolio companies. Fink's letter is a highly anticipated event and is one of the most definitive statements on the priorities for the global business. The letter not only outlines what BlackRock expects of its investment portfolio companies but sets strategy for the systemic changes expected throughout the investment industry and in the economy at large. Since 2019, Fink's letters have been calling for the reorientation of the US economy from shareholder first to stakeholders, from consumption to sustainability, and from exploitation of resources to exploration of opportunities and innovation.[7]

The loudest signal that corporate America is turning the corner and breaking away from four decades of the primacy of the "shareholder-first" doctrine came from the influential Business Roundtable, a group of 200 powerful US CEOs who speak for the leading global employers. Their 2019 statement superseded earlier declarations of corporate purpose and assured that the biggest US corporations are committed to serving the diverse pull of stakeholders including customers, employees, suppliers, communities, and ultimately the shareholders who provide the capital.

Jamie Dimon, then the chairman of Business Roundtable and chairman and CEO of JPMorgan Chase & Co, signed off on the statement, confirming that "Major employers are investing in their workers and communities because they know it is the only way to be successful over the long term."[8]

Within just a few months following the publication of Business Roundtable's statement of corporate purpose, the pandemic tested every company's commitment to their stakeholders; foremost— commitment to their employees. Concern and responsibility for the safety and general wellbeing of employees, coupled with a renewed commitment to equity and inclusion in the wake of the racial justice events of the summer of 2020, brought the new stakeholder purpose orientation into focus.

With the pandemic receding in the spring of 2021, Larry Fink's letter specifically emphasized the growing importance of an employee-centric focus for companies coming out of the pandemic and rebuilding for the future:

> A company that does not seek to benefit from the full spectrum of human talent is weaker for it—less likely to hire the best talent, less likely to reflect the needs of its customers and the communities where it operates, and less likely to outperform. While issues of race and ethnicity vary greatly across the world, *we expect companies in all countries to have a talent strategy that allows them to draw on the fullest set of talent possible.*"[9]

The focus on stakeholders reprioritizes what organizations value, who they pay attention to, and how they continue to grow. Early signs that the transition is already beginning to work were revealed in the special 2021 Edelman Annual Trust Barometer report. Edelman's global survey, taken across 28 countries and with over 33,000 respondents, showed that of the four key global institutions—business, government, NGOs, and the media—business was the one seen by the majority as the most competent and ethical.[10] To make this pivot permanent and continue to deliver, a new type of organization needs to be put in place. Human-centric design kicks into full gear.

Human-Centricity Takes Center Stage

We have seen how hard-wired humans are to put themselves at the center of their universe. Traditional workplaces were designed to be an exception to this rule: humanity had to be checked at the door when entering factories and office buildings. To remedy this centuries-old design flaw, new tools had to meet a dual goal: they needed to be effective and human-centric at the same time.

Human-centered design (HCD) methodology "jumped species" in the mid-20th century. It migrated from the creative arts and architecture to the business domains of industrial design, technology, and communications. David Kelley, the founder of the Design Thinking movement, recognized that design was an effective tool that could help reorganize the world according to human-centric principles. Kelley's mission was to demystify the complex creative process and make it scalable and accessible for everyday use. Kelley marveled at finding and activating the secret formula for creativity: "It is a radical notion, the idea that creativity can be summoned at will, with a process not unlike the scientific method. That contradicts what most people have always thought."[11] The approach not only demystified and standardized innovation, it made innovation predictable; it created a reliable road map that could be taught, learned, and could even guarantee successful outcomes.

David Kelley became the principal architect for making HCD methodology globally knowable and accessible to anyone willing to learn. He founded his consultancy IDEO in 1991 and later established Stanford d-school (2004) to teach the HCD methodology and assist organizations in developing their own internal expertise in human-centric design. IDEO gave rise to the design thinking movement;

consultancies and educational offerings sprang up everywhere in the world and become an industry of their own.

The fast-growing adoption of human-centered design raises questions about the legacy of traditional approaches to policy, governance, business culture, medical care, education, training, and pretty much every aspect of life and work. Practitioners of HCD soon discovered that the same principles could be applied to the design of emergency-room procedures, school curricula, as well as mobile phones and children's playgrounds. For the business sector, the real shift occurred with the changing focus from object design to organizational processes, transitioning from the application of HCD in designing user-friendly technology to building great customer services and ultimately to employee-centered human resource management practices. International HCD standards were established with the release of ISO standards in 2008, later updated in 2019. Known as ISO 9241-210:2019, these regulatory guidelines prove the point that the human-centric approach has taken center stage in industry and is now serving the mission of transforming organizations.[12]

How Performance Management Became the Battleground for HCD

The best proof that the human-centric design approach works is the central role it has played in the fundamental redesign of the performance management process across all industries in the last decade and a half. The performance management process has always served as the organizational highway that connects workforce with work. It has been often described as the Swiss army knife of workforce management. Goals, assessments, employee development, rewards, careers, and most of the employee life cycle converged onto companies' annual performance appraisal process. The crescendo of employee discontent with this legacy process became louder as the work itself became more distributed, project based, and collaborative.

When Diane Gherson, the SVP of HR at IBM at the time, decided to transform the HR function, the outdated performance management process stood in the way. Gherson was successful at convincing the company's senior leadership that making performance management more employee-centric would be an essential step in transforming the business. Instead of looking for "best practices" or hiring consultants, IBM HR engaged in the transformative internal journey and learned from within.

To prepare for the kick-off of the performance management redesign initiative, the IBM HR teams were all trained in the design thinking process, the methodology fully based on the core HCD principles. Discovery was perhaps the most labor- and time-intensive step in this new approach. It was also the most novel and counterintuitive for the specialist HR teams that had always relied on their expertise to develop solutions. In the case of performance management, the redesign team needed to listen, gather feedback and input from thousands of employees, and crowdsource ideas and recommendations through IBM's internal collaboration tools. HR managers volunteered to personally reach out to the most vocal critics. In the final design, all descending voices and opinions had to be acknowledged to include a variety of perspectives. Take the name of the redesigned process itself. It had to be crowdsourced and validated through employee input. When the newly redesigned performance management process was finally launched in February 2016, it was called the Checkpoint. IBM's checkpoint consisted of the frequent touchpoints between employees and their managers, the final year-end conversation, and a simple rating at the end. The employee-focused design was based on the premise that development comes first, the manager is the best coach, and evaluations are guidelines for improvement and career growth. The trust developed through the discovery and validation of the new design helped make the roll-out and implementation process seamless and effective.

IBM's example was creative and bold for its time. It set the precedent and developed a model to be later replicated by multiple organizations on their way to redesigning their own internal processes. Today, more than 50 percent of organizations have undertaken the performance management transformation journey. Most of these companies adopted human-centric design and ended up in a place where Human Resources have never been before: organization processes and systems designed for employees first rather than the convenience of the employer. The implications of the change are wide-ranging and go beyond individual organizations.

How Humans Reclaim the Workplace

Human-centric design is not a trend, it is how work needs to be done today. Its principles are deeply rooted in human psychology and embedded in the history of humanity. Rediscovered at the times of the economic recessions of the past few decades and enabled through the infusion of intelligent technologies and advanced analytics, HCD serves as the glue that connects today's workplaces and workforces with the future of work. What started as an experiment would end up as the norm. If flexible workplace arrangements stay and employee workplace experience becomes the first order of business, employers could successfully compete in the broader job market for those workers who fled their full-time jobs to join platforms on the promise of the autonomy and flexibility the gig economy had to offer. Employers can once again outcompete the platforms by introducing their own flexible arrangements, designed with the employee experience in mind. The same platforms that propelled the gig economy can now serve employers and help retain the talent they need.

"Uber is a symptom, not a cause," wrote Louis Hyman in one of the best historical studies of the origins and nature of temporary employment in the United States. Hyman's *Temp* unmasks Western society's glorification of the gig economy as a cure-all for the woes of full-time employment.[13] It is a compelling counterpoint to the almost unanimous consensus that "gig" employment is what the future of work will be.[14] The Covid-19 pandemic exposed the hypocrisy of the gig construct. Designed for the convenience of employers, the essential gig employees were left to fend for themselves, uninsured, unprotected, and exposed to the virus. The pandemic set off the next wave of layoffs and furloughs, further exposing the fragility of the gig work model. By contrast, the forced flexibility of working from home model during the pandemic proved to employers the advantages of giving up some control and allowing employees more choices in getting work done in their own way. Employee productivity went up in the first few months of the pandemic. The widely promoted idea that markets would be the answer to all social issues was quickly debunked by the pandemic reality. Thousands of traditional employers increased and invested in a much-needed transformation of their places of work with the employee experience in mind. Those employers that embrace an employee-centric workplace and strike a new and more sustainable compact with their workforce will effectively outcompete in the talent market for those very rare skills.

Endnotes

1 Hyman, L (2018) *Temp: How American work, American business, and the American dream became temporary*, New York: Viking

2 Ryder, RD (1998) *The Political Animal: The conquest of speciesism*, Jefferson, NC: McFarland & Company.

3 De Waal, F (1997) Are we in anthropodenial? *Discover*, https://www.discovermagazine.com/planet-earth/are-we-in-anthropodenial (archived at https://perma.cc/YJ87-UV2E)

4 Goodman, J (2018) Robotics roundtable: Should robots look like humans, or like machines? *Internet of Business*, https://internetofbusiness.com/should-robots-look-like-humans-or-like-machines/ (archived at https://perma.cc/M2EC-Q4B2)

5 Lohr, S (2020) Don't fear the robots, and other lessons from a study of the digital economy, *New York Times*, https://www.nytimes.com/2020/11/17/technology/digital-economy-technology-work-labor.html (archived at https://perma.cc/ZWA7-W8K8)

6 MIT (2020) The work of the future: Building better jobs in an age of intelligent machines, https://workofthefuture.mit.edu/research-post/the-work-of-the-future-building-better-jobs-in-an-age-of-intelligent-machines/ (archived at https://perma.cc/7KT9-S7LN)

7 The shareholder first ideology was famously sealed in an oft-quoted article by Chicago School economist Milton Friedman: "There is one and only one social responsibility of business—to use its resources and engage in activities designed to increase its profits so long as it stays within the rules of the game, which is to say, engages in open and free competition without deception or fraud" (Milton Friedman, "The Social Responsibility of Business is to Increase Its Profits." In *Ethical Theory and Business,* 8th edition, ed. Tom L Beauchamp, Norman E Bowie, and Denis G. Arnold, Hoboken, NJ: Pearson, 2009, p 55)

8 Business Roundtable (2019) Business Roundtable redefines the purpose of a corporation to promote "an economy that serves all Americans", https://www.businessroundtable.org/business-roundtable-redefines-the-purpose-of-a-corporation-to-promote-an-economy-that-serves-all-americans (archived at https://perma.cc/X3HX-NHCQ)

9 BlackRock (2021) Larry Fink's 2021 letter to CEOs, https://www.blackrock.com/corporate/investor-relations/larry-fink-ceo-letter (archived at https://perma.cc/FSR4-75RH)

10 Edelman's attention to trust was prompted by Francis Fukuyama's influential book *Trust: The social virtues and the creation of prosperity* (1996). Fukuyama predicted that only those societies that can cultivate high degrees of social trust in the next generation prosper, social capital may be as important as physical capital, and only those organizations with a high degree of social trust could compete in the new global economy

11 Tischler, L (2009) Ideo's David Kelley on "Design Thinking," *Fast Company*, https://www.fastcompany.com/1139331/ideos-david-kelley-design-thinking (archived at https://perma.cc/W3SX-BV86)

12 Human-centered design is an approach to interactive systems development that aims to make systems usable and useful by focusing on the users, their needs and requirements, and by applying human factors/ergonomics, and usability knowledge and techniques. This approach enhances effectiveness and efficiency, improves human wellbeing, user satisfaction, accessibility, and sustainability, and counteracts possible adverse effects of use on human health, safety, and performance (ISO 9241-210:2019, Ergonomics of human-system interaction Part 210: Human-centered design for interactive systems, https://www.iso.org/standard/77520.html) (archived at https://perma.cc/KN6D-XCNN)

13 Hyman, L (2018) *Temp: How American work, American business, and the American dream became temporary*, New York: Viking

14 Gitis, B et al (2017) The gig economy: Research and policy implications of regional, economic, and demographic trends, Aspen Institute, https://www.aspeninstitute.org/publications/the-gig-economy-research-and-policy-implications/ (archived at https://perma.cc/8DTX-DV92)

05

Designing for Inclusion:
Empathy as a Superpower

Discovering Empathy

Speaking at a commencement for Northwestern University's graduating class of 2006, then-senator Barack Obama called his address "Cultivating Empathy: The world does not just revolve around you."

> There's a lot of talk in this country about the federal deficit. But I think we should talk more about our empathy deficit—the ability to put ourselves in someone else's shoes, to see the world through those who are different from us—the child who's hungry, the laid-off steelworker, the immigrant woman cleaning your dorm room.[1]

Obama's interpretation of empathy as one's ability to step inside another's experience has become an accepted definition broadly used today in politics, business, and science. Ironically, present-day empathy means the opposite of the original meaning of the phenomenon when it first appeared in the English language in the early 20th century. As a term, empathy owes its origins to the development of psychology as a science in German universities in the 1920s. The word "empathy" was the English translation of the German word *Einfühlung* (literally "in-feeling"). In the early days of psychology, empathy was associated primarily with the arts and aesthetic endeavors, and implied projecting the observer's emotional state onto the object of their contemplation.[2] With the rise of social psychology around the time of the Second World War, empathy began to signify

FIGURE 5.1   Empathy

one's ability to make predictions about another's emotional state without mixing in one's own emotions. Today, the psychology of aesthetic perception has joined up with neuroscience to create the new discipline of neuroaesthetics. Neuroaesthetics deploys new tools to better explain the human capacity to collectively experience beauty. It takes the original concept of empathy back to its roots in the arts.[3]

Without using the exact word "empathy," the acknowledgment of the importance of such a phenomenon in social and economic life goes back to Adam Smith, the founder of modern economics, and his classic treatise *The Wealth of Nations*. Smith saw empathy as a "fellow feeling" conducive to a successful exchange between economic agents.[4] Early industrialist Henry Ford recognized the value of empathy in business when he noted that "if there is any one secret of success, it lies in the ability to get the other person's point of view and see things from his angle as well as your own."[5]

Yet, for most of the 20th century, the study of empathy was confined to the arts and to the evolving science of psychology. There was no place for empathy in mainstream 20th-century economics and business. Neoclassical economists were almost exclusively focused on the autonomous market actor—"homo economicus," an "economic man." The "economic man" was seen as a rational decision maker guided by self-interest and having full access to information to make the right choices.[6] In neoclassical economics, there was no reason for individuals to need or to want to put themselves in another person's place. The "economic man" cared primarily about maximizing his own profit and making decisions in pursuit of optimal utilitarian objectives. In summary, consumers maximized the utility of the transactions while the producers pursued maximum profit.

The development of game theory in economics in the second half of the 20th century and the evolving research in behavioral and neuroeconomics debunked the foundational premise of the utilitarian supply and demand model in favor of a more complex understanding of decision-making behavior among economic players. The concept of empathy factors prominently in the 21st-century economic models that encompass experimental and behavioral economics as well as cognitive and social psychology. Most recently, the latest computational tools delivered additional perspectives from evolutionary biology, computational anthropology, and computational mathematics. Empathy-based approaches are applied across all industry domains from healthcare to education and from technology to warfare.

The meaning of empathy in the 21st century has thus evolved to be multifaceted and diverse. Among its multiple definitions, modern-day empathy is adjacent to the psychological phenomenon known as "emotional intelligence." First introduced by social psychologists Peter Salovey and John D. Mayer in 1990,[7] it was later popularized by scientific journalist Daniel Goleman to signify an individual's "ability to recognize, manage, and influence personal emotions and the emotions of others."[8] Empathy has become recognized as a requisite leadership trait, especially in times of crises.

For example, New Zealand's head of state Jacinda Ardern became known as one of the world's most empathetic leaders during the pandemic crisis. In contrast to the traditional stoic models of leadership, Ardern's governing philosophy was explicitly based on kindness and empathy. In an interview with *The Guardian*, she presented her choice of leaning into empathy in the following way:

> … kindness, and not being afraid to be kind, or to focus on, or be
> really driven by empathy. I think one of the sad things that I've seen
> in political leadership is—because we've placed over time so much

emphasis on notions of assertiveness and strength—that we probably have assumed that it means you can't have those other qualities of kindness and empathy.[9]

The fact that New Zealand fared best of all countries in the pandemic is often attributed to Ardern's empathetic style of leadership and her decision to forego economic considerations in favor of public health.

Real-life applications of empathy are impacting many aspects of business today. Empathy influences design of products, services, emerging technologies, and for some could even define the future of humanity at large. Cultural observer and journalist Jeremy Rifkin elevated empathy to be the foundational human value in his 2010 book *The Empathic Civilization: The race to global consciousness in a world in crisis*.[10] In his book, Rifkin predicts that "empathic sensibility lies at the heart of the new management style" and that a "new empathic spirit" will transform "our businesses, our neighborhoods and even our biosphere."[11] As the service economy started to take hold, empathy became broadly recognized and accepted as an important business technique that allowed marketers and product designers to "shoe-shift," put themselves in the shoes of their customers and users in order to get into the mindset of the consumers.[12]

The empathetic approach to business offered product creators and service providers an ability to see beyond data, patterns, interviews, and surveys. Empathy as a design principle is low cost, intuitive, and uniquely human; it does not require an fMRI scanner to read a customer's mind. To be effective, it does require one to connect to one's own feelings and to learn an empathy technique.

Anti-Empathy Backlash

The meteoric rise of empathy as a powerful driver of the 21st-century zeitgeist has not gone unchallenged. The century-long prioritization of rationality and the legacy of subordinating humanity to the pursuit of profits has kept its fast hold over social and political institutions. Opponents to the promoters of empathy came from every corner of public life, including academia and corporate boardrooms. In industry and politics, empathetic choices were a rare exception rather than the norm.

Conservative critics claimed that the empathetic approach to solving problems was a grave threat to rational judgment, economic prosperity, and growth. When President Obama referred to the importance of empathy in governance, his detractors immediately associated it with the "wealthfare state" and with left-wing activism. All democratic government nominees in the Biden administration had to fend against accusations of being "socialist" for the mere sin of looking after the underserved.

In academia, a major push against unquestioning acceptance of empathy came from Paul Bloom, an influential Yale psychologist who launched a vigorous intellectual crusade against empathy as a credible approach. In his seminal tome titled *Against Empathy: The case for rational compassion*,[13] Bloom argued that empathy was fraught with biases, short-sightedness, and innumeracy. The downside of empathy, according to Bloom, was the innate human inability to step outside themselves and the immediate circumstances humans found themselves in. Empathy thus impeded effective decision making for a set of legitimate reasons:

- *Empathy is short-sighted.* It is anchored in the subjective reactions of an individual lacking perspective into the future. Emotional reaction today is always stronger than planning for the future with a well-timed perspective.

- *Compassion for the immediate "human size" problems.* Empathy for the suffering of one's own child could happen at the expense of statistically difficult to grasp numbers such as millions perishing in a genocide in another part of the world. The way it works in business is if a tweet from one disgruntled customer was prioritized over the opportunity to address a systemic market issue in the future.

- *The implicit bias.* Empathy is always stronger for the individuals who "look like us" over those who happen to be different.

• *Narcissism.* Empathy could be exploited to serve one's own immediate emotional needs in response to a situation in question rather than to prioritize objective and more effective measures and solutions.

Granted, some of Bloom's arguments may be valid but they are neither original nor new. Historically, the scales have always been tipped in favor of deliberate rationalization and dehumanization of decisions. Injecting empathy into that process has the potential to reveal human experiences that escape algorithmic logic and provide a missing link to an ambiguous solution. Prominent British psychologist Simon Baron-Cohen, who studied the healing qualities of empathy and the devastating effects of its lack in the context of autistic disorders, argued that empathy was "one of our most valuable natural resources. It has particular promise as an approach to conflict resolution, one that has advantages over viewing a problem through a chiefly military, economic or legal lens."[14] Baron-Cohen attributed the origins of evil to the lack of empathy.[15]

The debate between empathy enthusiasts and empathy detractors is ongoing. It highlights the importance of attending to both poles on the empathy spectrum—the emotional (affective) and the logical (cognitive). Neither side will hold up without giving credence to the other. Broadly applied in 21st-century organizations and social and industry domains, empathy may see some of its most spectacular successes and most instructive failures. The path to empathy becoming a superpower has just begun.

CASE STUDY
Empathy Deficit at Amazon

July 1, 2021 marked the date that Jeff Bezos, the world's richest man and the founder of Amazon, stepped down as the company's CEO. During his 27 years at the helm, Bezos built the world's most powerful internet juggernaut, ranked among the top five largest and most valuable companies in the world. Personally, he amassed a fortune larger than the GDP of 140 countries. Yet Bezos's leadership legacy was mixed. The tech oligarchs and investors both admire and envy his superhuman business acumen and his supreme customer obsession. At the same time the relentless pursuit of customer satisfaction has been achieved through unrelenting optimization and efficiency of employees' performance, stretching them to their limit. Bezos himself described his business philosophy as "always living in Day 1." In 2016, Bezos wrote in his annual letter to shareholders: "Day 2 is stasis, followed by irrelevance, followed by excruciating, painful decline, followed by death. And that is why it is always Day 1."[16]

Bezos's personal style of leadership is all about constant innovation, speed, and efficiency but empathy has never been one of his virtues. Amazon may look like the 21st-century version of the Biblical feet of clay or an unholy alliance between techno-utopia and techno-dystopia melded into one. In the words of one of Amazon's executives: "If you're not good, Jeff will chew you up and spit you out. And if you're good, he will jump on your back and ride you into the ground."[17]

Amazon would argue that the company simply sets high performance goals and expects the employees to be meeting them. But a closer look reveals that the ideal Amazon customer service model would involve no humans at all. Every year during his time as CEO, Bezos played the role of a customer service rep for a day with an experienced worker sitting next to him; he was quoted as saying "… because otherwise I would probably give really bad service. It's not that easy."[18]

It is too early to see if and how Amazon's culture will mutate post its founder's stepping away from the company's day-to-day operations. But on the day of Bezos's departure two new values were added to Amazon's leadership principles:

- "Strive to be Earth's best employer."
- "Success and scale bring broad responsibility."

The new added values ostensibly focus on employees and stakeholders and signal the first public recognition of the effort to close the deficit gap between the company's market success and its "soulless, dystopian workplace where no fun is had and no laughter heard."[19] Is Amazon looking to address the issue of "empathy deficit" in the core foundations of its culture? Will the pressures of ever-greater efficiency and scale be too overwhelming for the increments of humanity?

CASE STUDY

Can Empathy Save Technology from Itself at Microsoft?

In early 2021, the news about Bill and Melinda Gates' divorce brought out new facts about the former Microsoft CEO's personal indiscretions, calling forth new scrutiny of the company culture.[20] Satya Nadella, the current Microsoft CEO and Executive Chairman, was quick to respond in most unambiguous terms: "The Microsoft of 2021 is very different from the Microsoft of 2000 to me and to everyone at Microsoft."[21] Nadella, who rose through the ranks to take over company leadership in February 2014 after 22 years in the company, not only transformed the business but was laser focused on transforming the culture.[22]

"I feel that we have created an environment that allows us to really drive the everyday improvement in our diversity and inclusion culture, which I think is a super important thing and that's what I'm focused on," he added in the same interview.

Nadella's track record as a CEO is as remarkable and unique among top tech CEOs as his personal story. He is credited with reversing what became known as Microsoft's "lost decade," characterized by business stagnation and decline amidst a hyper-competitive internal culture. To him, restoring the business to its lost prime was also a story of a personal search for the "soul" of the company that he had spent over 20 years working for. In his book *Hit Refresh: The quest to rediscover Microsoft's soul and imagine a better future for everyone*,[23] Nadella shares his leadership philosophy and the origins of his worldview that he successfully translated into Microsoft's success story.

Nadella's unique quality that does not appear on the standard CEO list is his unquestioning embrace of empathy. Nadella turned empathy into the major source of innovation and customer success at Microsoft. Empathy became the differentiator that set Microsoft apart from its Seattle neighbor, Amazon. Nadella shares his personal sources of inspiration and success with unusual transparency and candor. Far from being the "soft skill" removed from the hard work of business, empathy is the foundation of the culture in today's Microsoft. In a letter to employees written on the first day of his new job as CEO, he revealed his personal story:

> I am 46. I've been married for 22 years and we have 3 kids. And like anyone else, a lot of what I do and how I think has been shaped by my family and my overall life experiences. Many who know me say I am also defined by my curiosity and thirst for learning. I buy more books than I can finish. I sign up for more online courses than I can complete. I fundamentally believe that if you are not learning new things, you stop doing great and useful things. So family, curiosity and hunger for knowledge all define me.[24]

Nadella does not make a secret of his personal drivers and the insights he gained from his own difficult journey as a father of a child with severe disabilities. In another letter to employees, he revealed the personal challenge that transformed his worldview and gave him a tremendous source of inspiration. His unique ability to translate technology into meaningful products comes through when he talks about having to come to terms and live with his son's disability:

> It has helped me better understand the journey of people with disabilities. It has shaped my personal passion for and philosophy of connecting new ideas to empathy for others. And it is why I am deeply committed to pushing the bounds on what love and compassion combined with human ingenuity and passion to have impact can accomplish with my colleagues at Microsoft.[25]

Nadella enjoys an "A+" rating among Microsoft employees that puts him in the top 5 percent of CEOs of comparable companies.[26]

Empathy by Design

When engineer and product designer David Kelley founded Stanford University's d-School (Design School) in 2005 he had already been in the product design business since 1978. Kelley merged the design company he founded (DKD) with what would become IDEO, the original global design thinking and innovation firm. "Changing the world through design" became the mission of IDEO's consulting and educational business. IDEO's way to achieve the mission was to develop its own "empathetic" design methodology and apply it to the creation of all products, to the solving of all issues, and to improving organizations of all types. The design thinking method is best used in thinking through "wicked" problems that do not lend themselves to linear or "waterfall-style" solutions. Despite its Ivy League pedigree, design thinking, according to Kelley, was a deeply democratic method anchored in the fundamentals of design and based on the uniquely human capacity to empathize:

> We don't believe in this notion of a bunch of smart people sitting around being clever. We believe in this notion that you hang out with the people who will benefit, and develop real empathy for them. Look for latent, nonobvious needs that they have. Then give it to the smart people to try to figure out innovation.[27]

The uniqueness of IDEO's and Stanford's d-School approach to empathetic design is that it is not only innovative but replicable and scalable. It balances the emotional and relational elements of empathy with a step-by-step framework. Empathetic listening is not precious in its methodology; it can easily be turned into a helpful guide and a call for action. It cracks the code on creativity, just like the title of Kelley's article that he co-authored with his brother, Tom Kelley, "Creative Confidence: A Path from Blank Page to Insight."[28] Cultural anthropologist Grant McCracken once said, "Anthropology is too important to be left to the anthropologists."[29] Kelley would second this view in the case of design. Just like one does not need to be an anthropologist to explore culture, one does not need to be a designer to learn how to design customer-centered solutions. The mission of the design thinking method is exactly that. It is being designed with everyone in mind and is made for all humans to use.

Since its founding, multiple schools of thought and methodologies have branched off the original design thinking model. For example, the Stanford d-School model has five steps: empathize, define, ideate, prototype, and test (a sixth step, assess, was added later). Interaction Design Foundation clusters nine steps into three groups: inspiration, ideation, implementation. NN Group combines six steps into three groups: understand, explore, materialize. IDEO has three stages: inspiration, ideation, implementation. Business Models Inc. use the double loop process which includes prepare, point of view, ideate, understand, prototype, validate, scale.

Regardless of the number of steps, the design thinking method is about empathy at heart. Empathy is the starting point of every step in the design process. To empathize is to create distance and novelty while generating the "beginner's mind" effect that all creators seek. Most organizations habitually overlook empathy, distracted by an unfortunate fixation on "best practices." Immediate customer needs have to come first before any company comparisons are invoked. It is the trigger for all subsequent steps—defining the problem, ideating the solution, prototyping and testing the product, and possibly repeating the sequence again and again. Without empathy, there is no design. It is that simple.

FIGURE 5.2   Empathy Map

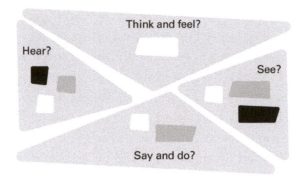

The Empathy Map illustrates best how such design methodology works. It is a brainstorming technique that allows observers to hear, see, and record what users "say," "do," "think," and "feel" about the topic at hand. An empathy map captures live conversation, comments, observations, and insights. Simple props such as whiteboards and color-coded Post-it notes help to visualize brainstorming results and visually document observable behavior. With the help of visualization, the Empathy Map helps to infer the emotional state of users and opens up new ways of looking at issues and developing creative solutions.

As technology continues to evolve, the natural question to ask is whether the greater ability to collect infinite amounts of data through algorithms cancels the need for the time-consuming and resource-intensive empathetic process. Could technology deliver the insights that would normally take a long time to get? Design thinking practitioners are attentive to the explosion of data technologies, but they remain undeterred. Augmenting empathetic stories with data collected through technology would make the outcome more powerful but could not replace the empathy step. The cumulative result generates "hybrid insights," and in the words of Tom and David Kelley, "Coupling insights based on empathy with analytic confidence within relevant target market may be the way to take the best of both approaches."[30] There is no question that access to data is going to continue to expand but the need to make sense of the available information from the empathy perspective and tell compelling stories is becoming even more urgent.

Let Empathy Not Numbers Drive Inclusion

There is no shortage of data made available today to track the state of organizational diversity and inclusion. Measurements and regulation are being introduced to benchmark diversity and inclusion practices and to set new baselines and assess commitments. Corporate boards are requesting their companies' Racial Equity Audits[31] and governments from the European Parliament to the US House of Representatives are demanding compliance with the new standards. In March 2021, for example, the US House of Representatives' Financial Services Committee and the Subcommittee on Diversity, Equity and Inclusion held virtual hearings titled "By the Numbers: How Diversity Data Can Measure Commitment to Diversity, Equity and Inclusion."[32] The focus on data is intended to develop a measurable set of criteria that would help foster diversity, equity, and inclusion in organizations across industry and public sectors. So far, the results have been mixed.

The design thinking community might offer an answer on how to move forward from data to action. Empathy, at times radical empathy, might be the missing link in the search for effective long-term solutions.

CASE STUDY
MIT AgeLab

MIT AgeLab is one such example of how the embrace of empathy as a decision-making tool and the integration of design thinking methods are being used to achieve AgeLab's mission of reimagining aging.

MIT AgeLab was created in 1999 in response to the ongoing demographic revolution.[33] Human lifespan in the West has increased on average by about 30 years since the 1900s, with life expectancy reaching into the 70s, the 80s, and beyond.

Joseph F. Coughlin, the founder and director of MIT AgeLab, writes in the introduction to his book *The Longevity Economy* that old age is a social construct that is "at odds with reality that constrains how we live after middle age—and stifles business thinking on how to best serve a group of consumers, workers, and innovators that is growing larger and wealthier with every passing day."[34]

Creating a more empathetic world for the aging population calls for a new generation of products and services. There is also a shared belief that these inclusive designs would not only accommodate the aging demographic but would improve overall quality of life for all. MIT AgeLab works with the whole ecosystem of businesses, governments, and NGOs, applying a customer-centered innovation approach to its product designs and services.

Using empathetic design, MIT AgeLab created their AGNES body suit. The "AGNES" acronym stands for "Age Gain Now Empathy System." AGNES is an empathy simulator that allows participants to jump from their 30-year-old body into the body of someone in their late 70s or early 80s and see the world from that age perspective. The simulator allows users from researchers to engineers and public officials to get on the inside of an aging person: yellow goggles make it difficult to see clearly, earplugs make hearing muffled, gloves reduce the sensation of touch and precision, a neck brace requires the rotation of the entire body, bands attached to the arms make it harder to reach high above the shoulders. The suit is used in conjunction with other data collection methods including interviews, focus groups, design thinking sessions—all for the purpose of getting as close to the first-hand experience of older adults as possible. The advantages of such an experience are hard to overestimate. AgeLab research specialist Samantha Brady explains how this empathy-based research project works: "When we have the designers wearing the suit do walk-throughs with local older adults, we can compare the experiences and see if there are smaller changes that can be made from a design perspective that improve accessibility."[35]

Originally developed by an occupational therapist and other age specialists at AgeLab, these simulator suits are in high demand. There are only four AGNES suits currently available and AgeLab is using them exclusively for research: "We've brought 'her' to do training at an assisted living facility and we've trained Harvard Medical School students who are interested in working with older adults—they understand the biology, but the empathy experience is really eye opening for them."[36]

One of the most important projects involving AGNES is the evaluation of public transportation systems around the US and in London from an accessibility perspective. Designers and architects wear the AGNES suits to evaluate the accessibility of what they are creating. Other innovations for the elderly are at play, including smart houses, robot carers, and glasses with built-in facial recognition. There is no equivalent to putting the designers themselves through the experience and using empathy as a guide in creating future products that are not only useful but also accessible.

Artificial Empathy (AE)

Empathy, as we have learned, is vital to building successful human relations. If properly understood, empathy could be converted into meaningful actions, designed into products and services, and made to benefit humans in multiple novel ways. It is in this context that computational modeling of empathy has emerged as one of the most promising avenues for modeling human behavior going forward. Advanced computational models reveal and help better understand the complex interlink between affective (emotional) and cognitive (rational) aspects of empathy. As virtual AI agents are equipped with artificial empathy (AE), they can better sense and process social and emotional signals and can more effectively respond to human emotions and reactions. Affective computing, speech and natural language recognition, voice recognition, and facial expression recognition are just a few among multiple innovations that attempt to simulate empathy via technology. The broader implications of these advancements for all aspects of society including business, education, the caregiving economy, law enforcement, and others are enormous but still not fully understood.

The real-life applications of these technologies have mixed results and are just now being scrutinized by researchers, technologies, and regulatory bodies. Take two applications of such technologies that have already been put to work in business:

- recognition of a person's internal state, including cognitive, emotional, and physical states;
- predictions into the person's response to various changing situations such as acting under stress, responding to positive stimuli etc.

Uses of affective technologies in call centers have been among the more successful applications. One such example is the MIT spin-off Cogito, the call center assistant that uses voice recognition to help call center reps assess the emotional state of customers calling in. It analyzes voice and tone patterns to prompt the appropriate response. Cogito has been successfully used to diagnose PTSD in veterans.[37]

By contrast, the use of video assessments in job interviews to identify job fit has so far had mixed results. HireVue, the pioneer in the field, boasts its technology's efficiency, cost savings, and scale.[38] Yet, the lack of human interaction in the recruitment process and the empathy gap are experienced negatively by the candidates. The results are mixed, to say the least. Even if the employers are happy with the return on their investment, the candidates report being ignored, poorly communicated to, and end up uncommitted to the potential employer. While the product may work, the relationship does not.

The caregiver economy presents the ultimate opportunity and a test for the new emotionally intelligent tools. Additionally, the ethical implications of using emotional technologies are consequential. The questions being asked are about the role of empathy in companion robots, as the introduction of artificial companions is already reality, not science fiction.

The Future of Empathy

Empathy is poised to play a supersized role in the economy of the future. The imbalance created through the disproportionate attention paid to what became known as "hard skills" at the expense of what are profoundly human "soft skills" is about to be corrected. In a plot twist, new research shows that the new empathetic robots can teach back those human skills to humans. Emotionally intelligent robots are being used to facilitate not only human–computer interactions but better collaboration among humans.[39] The best is still to come. It is possible to envision a future when emotionally intelligent machines will be teaching empathy back to humans and taking humanity back to its roots.

Endnotes

1 Northwestern (2019) Obama to graduates: cultivate empathy, "The world doesn't just revolve around you," https://www.northwestern.edu/newscenter/stories/2006/06/barack.html (archived at https://perma.cc/AL4W-BR7R)

2   Lanzoni, S (2019) The surprising history of empathy, *Psychology Today*, https://www.psychologytoday.com/ca/blog/empathy-emotion-and-experience/201911/the-surprising-history-empathy (archived at https://perma.cc/8YAU-HCDG)

3   Starr, GG (2013) *Feeling Beauty: The neuroscience of aesthetic experience*, Cambridge, MA: MIT Press

4   Evensky, J (2015) *Adam Smith's Wealth of Nations: A reader's guide*, New York: Cambridge University Press.

5   Ford, H and Crowther, S (1991) *My Life and Work*, Salem, NH: Ayer

6   Chen, J (2021) Homo Economicus, *Investopedia*, https://www.investopedia.com/terms/h/homoeconomicus.asp (archived at https://perma.cc/9A29-BCA6)

7   Salovey, P and Mayer, JD (1990) Emotional intelligence, *Imagination, Cognition and Personality*, **9** (3), pp 185–211

8   Goleman, D (2017) *What is Empathy?* Boston, MA: Harvard Business Publishing

9   Blackwell, G (2020) Jacinda Ardern: "Political leaders can be both empathetic and strong," *Guardian*, https://www.theguardian.com/world/2020/may/31/jacinda-ardern-political-leaders-can-be-both-empathetic-and-strong (archived at https://perma.cc/67SE-ZLKG)

10 Rifkin, J (2010) *The Empathic Civilization: The race to global consciousness in a world in crisis*, Cambridge: Polity

11 Ibid.

12 Sherman, JE (2021) Empathic intelligence: To put yourself in their shoes, unlace yours: How to become a better listener and empathizer, *Psychology Today*, https://www.psychologytoday.com/ca/blog/ambigamy/200905/empathic-intelligence-put-yourself-in-their-shoes-unlace-yours (archived at https://perma.cc/5LJM-Y6WL)

13 Bloom, P (2016) *Against Empathy: The case for rational compassion*, First edition, New York: Ecco, an imprint of HarperCollins Publishers

14 Baron-Cohen, S (2019) Only empathy can break the cycle of violence in Israel-Palestine conflict, *Guardian*, https://www.theguardian.com/commentisfree/2019/jan/22/empathy-cycle-violence-israel-palestine (archived at https://perma.cc/G8JP-NMSM)

15 Baron-Cohen, S (2011) *The Science of Evil: On empathy and the origins of cruelty*, New York: Basic Books

16 Bezos, J (2017) 2016 Letter to shareholders: Why it is always Day 1 at Amazon, https://www.aboutamazon.com/news/company-news/2016-letter-to-shareholders (archived at https://perma.cc/8MD3-D735)

17 Stone, B (2021) The Jeff Bezos paradox, *The New York Times*, https://www.nytimes.com/2021/07/03/opinion/jeff-bezos-space-amazon.html (archived at https://perma.cc/N3TN-JHG2)

18 Jopson, B (2012) The Bezos doctrine of ruthless pragmatism, *Financial Times*, https://www.ft.com/content/2398876a-c202-11e1-8e7c-00144feabdc0 (archived at https://perma.cc/EUD6-GNZ9)

19 Kantor, J and Streitfeld, D (2015) Inside Amazon: Wrestling big ideas in a bruising workplace, *New York Times*, https://www.nytimes.com/2015/08/16/technology/inside-amazon-wrestling-big-ideas-in-a-bruising-workplace.html (archived at https://perma.cc/3WDX-8CLM)

20 Flitter, E and Goldstein, M (2021) Long before divorce, Bill Gates had reputation for questionable behavior, *South Florida Sun Sentinel*, https://www.sun-sentinel.com/news/nationworld/ct-aud-nw-nyt-bill-gates-divorce-20210516-34h5kcrfanfzbgkurwu57sor2m-story.html (archived at https://perma.cc/W8G4-R2Y4)

21 Akhtar, A (2021) Satya Nadella addresses Bill Gates controversies: "The Microsoft of 2021 is very different from the Microsoft of 2000," *Business Insider*, https://www.businessinsider.in/tech/news/satya-nadella-addresses-bill-gates-controversies-the-microsoft-of-2021-is-very-different-from-the-microsoft-of-2000/articleshow/82838218.cms (archived at https://perma.cc/RAU4-PCHD)

22 Weinberger, M (2019) The rise of Satya Nadella, the CEO who totally turned Microsoft around in 5 years and made it more valuable than Apple, *Business Insider*, https://www.businessinsider.com/the-rise-of-microsoft-ceo-satya-nadella-2016-1 (archived at https://perma.cc/Q9KH-KG68)

23 Sadella, S et al (2017) *Hit Refresh: The quest to rediscover Microsoft's soul and imagine a better future for everyone*, First edition, New York: HarperBusiness

24 Nadella, S (2014) Satya Nadella email to employees on first day as CEO, Microsoft, https://news.microsoft.com/2014/02/04/satya-nadella-email-to-employees-on-first-day-as-ceo/ (archived at https://perma.cc/C4B7-6GDU)

25 Nadella, S (2017) The moment that forever changed our lives, LinkedIn Blog, https://www.linkedin.com/pulse/moment-forever-changed-our-lives-satya-nadella/ (archived at https://perma.cc/J3M5-SFHR)

26 Satya Nadella Microsoft CEO Rating (2020) Comparably, https://www.comparably.com/companies/microsoft/ceo-rating (archived at https://perma.cc/E3KN-NGWH)

27 Whiting, S (2007) David M. Kelley's journey from designing Apple's mouse to fostering creative thinking, *San Francisco Chronicle*, https://www.sfgate.com/magazine/article/David-M-Kelley-s-journey-from-designing-Apple-s-2588245.php (archived at https://perma.cc/7XXC-NVYB)

28 Kelley, D and Kelley, T (2013) Creative confidence: A path from blank page to insight, *Harvard Business Review*, https://store.hbr.org/product/creative-confidence-the-path-from-blank-page-to-insight/ROT217 (archived at https://perma.cc/7VNE-5VAN)

29 Kelley, D and Kelley, T (2013) Why designers need empathy, *Slate*, https://slate.com/human-interest/2013/11/empathize-with-your-end-user-creative-confidence-by-tom-and-david-kelley.html (archived at https://perma.cc/G2XN-K6ZY)

30 Kelley, D and Kelley, T (2013) *Creative Confidence: Unleashing the creative potential within us all*, Crown Business

31 Tavis, A (2021) Why racial equity audit matters, *LinkedIn*, https://www.linkedin.com/pulse/why-racial-equity-audits-matters-anna-a-tavis-ph-d/ (archived at https://perma.cc/V93J-GRC4)

32 Subcommittee on Diversity (2021) Virtual hearing – by the numbers: How diversity data can measure commitment to diversity, equity and inclusion, https://financialservices.house.gov/calendar/eventsingle.aspx?EventID=406121 (archived at https://perma.cc/9PJU-YYPN)

33 https://agelab.mit.edu/about-agelab (archived at https://perma.cc/5UU8-7M38)

34 Coughlin, JF (2017) *The Longevity Economy: Unlocking the world's fastest-growing, most misunderstood market*, Foreign Affairs

35 Coughlin, J (nd) Empathy suit helps us understand ageing, Atlas of the Future, https://atlasofthefuture.org/project/agnes-mit/ (archived at https://perma.cc/6XDR-B2SR)

36 Ibid.

37 Cogito (nd) Elevate human connections in real time with Cogito: Augment your workforce with the AI coaching system for the contact center, https://cogitocorp.com/ (archived at https://perma.cc/R528-XAQA)

38 https://www.hirevue.com/platform (archived at https://perma.cc/YYQ8-X9NL)

39 Kramer, J (2020) Empathy machine: Humans communicate better after robots show their vulnerable side, *Scientific American*, https://www.scientificamerican.com/article/empathy-machine-humans-communicate-better-after-robots-show-their-vulnerable-side/ (archived at https://perma.cc/NE4H-695W)

06

From Customers to Employees: Employees Are the New Customers

"They're Not Employees, They're People"

In 2002, Peter Drucker, the founder of management consulting, wrote an article in the *Harvard Business Review* provocatively titled: "They're not employees, they're people."[1] The view of employees as people first was central to Drucker's management philosophy. He laid out his case arguing that companies needed to be concerned with managing all workers, including contract and temporary ones, as an organization's most valuable assets. He wrote that all employees mattered, without exception.

Drucker's philosophy ran counter to the leading Human Resources Management practices of his time. "Talent" was all the rage in the wake of the publication of McKinsey's study "The war for talent"[2] (1997) and the subsequent book (2001) of the same title.[3] However, talent did not mean "all employees without exception." The definition of *talent* was popularized by management consultants who claimed that the same *Pareto* principle that governed key principles of corporate performance—20 percent of investments deliver 80 percent of business outcomes—applied to people management; this meant focusing on just 20 percent of the people. The focus in general management and in the Human Resources function was on managing *talent* or the "vital few." According to the Talent Management doctrine, organizations needed to identify, reward, and develop up to about 20 percent of their employees—the *talent*—who were expected to deliver 80 percent of the company's results. This 20 percent were selected for their in-demand skills that were hard to recruit. HR set up specialized Talent Management functions to shepherd high-potential "talent" through the entire "life cycle" from recruitment to development, rewards, and ultimately promotions. It was assumed that the remaining 80 percent were at best "meeting expectations" and were treated accordingly, as "personnel" would have been.

Drucker's management thinking represented a challenge not only to his contemporary Talent Management opponents but to his generation of Human Resources professionals. Organizations were in the midst of the Total Quality Movement (TQM) and Six Sigma transformation at the time; management was more focused on how to become "lean" and to reliably deliver products and services on time than on who made it happen. Customer trust and loyalty was thought to be earned through efficiency, expediency, and quality.

Drucker warned against underinvestment in the workforce. He would have cautioned organizations about outsourcing critical employee relations functions and cutting back on internal services. Yet the idea that it was critical to find out what was important to all employees—not just the 20 percent—seemed wasteful at the time. It took organizational management over two decades and the disruptions of the Great Recession and the pandemic to revisit Drucker's position. Today Drucker's view of the importance of people is becoming widely accepted and HR is working to incorporate it into mainstream practice.

McKinsey's post-pandemic report titled "Back to Human: Why HR Leaders Want to Focus on People Again" made the case for the importance of people. The European CHROs interviewed for the study felt strongly that people were at the heart of their business. The road to customer success came through attending to the employees and allowing them to "bring their whole self to work."[4] This represented a sea change from the idea that you could ignore employees and expect practices like TQM to win customer trust.

McKinsey was not alone in this view. Sir Richard Branson, Virgin CEO, insisted in an often-cited interview: "Clients do not come first. Employees come first. If you take care of your employees, they will take care of the clients."[5] Branson put that idea to work in all of his 400 businesses. Simon Sinek, motivational speaker and author, built on Branson's idea and made it popular: "Happy employees ensure happy customers. And happy customers ensure happy shareholders—in that order."[6]

In this chapter we argue that the transition from focusing on the 20 percent of high potentials to enterprise-wide employee relationship management, personalization, and employee experience did not happen as a result of the internal evolution of HR practices. It first came from outside of HR. The U-turn in people management happened because of advancements in workplace technologies, access to data, and, most importantly, the precedent of innovative practices in marketing and customer services. Marketing and customer services have always been the yin and yang of HR management. The connection between quality customer service and employee experience is tangible, present, and measurable.

As we will show in this chapter, the hospitality industry deserves full credit for first elevating the critical role of employee experience to the level of management philosophy and making it one of the most urgent business issues.

CASE STUDY

Employees Discovered: The Ritz-Carlton Experience

Steve Jobs once said, echoing Pablo Picasso: "Good artists copy; great artists steal."[7] In the early 2000s, Jobs was searching for a breakthrough concept for the first Apple Store. The idea of vertically integrating all touchpoints with the customer was compatible with Apple's emerging business model. One such business model that inspired him at the time was the experience of immersive hospitality at Ritz-Carlton Hotels.

The idea of reimagining the tech store by focusing on the immersive customer "experience" in the style of Ritz-Carlton was new and bold. Twenty years later, if you walk into any of the current 512 Apple Stores in any of the 22 countries, you are greeted by a friendly employee who will ask you for your name no matter how busy the store is. Today, the Apple store set-up resembles a hotel more than a traditional tech shop. The Genius Bar represents a repurposed concierge desk just like in a hotel. As for the customers who are waiting for service, there are plenty of entertaining and educational activities available in the store. Those include trying new Apple devices or taking classes that keep customers entertained and learning.[8] Trained on the Ritz-Carlton model, Apple employees are expected to anticipate customer problems rather than just "fix" existing ones. The model of focusing on employees who take care of the customers paid off for Apple shareholders as well. Apple Stores have five times as many sales per store as their closest competitor Best Buy, and the customers keep coming back, at a 90 percent-plus loyalty rate.

Ritz-Carlton's employee-centric hospitality culture ran against the mainstream practice of their day. The dominant "best practice" at the time was one of "efficiency" and of treating employees as a cost center and expense. The Ritz-Carlton chose to go against the "lean approach" to managing people while still focusing on quality of service. That is what Steve Jobs saw and successfully adopted for the Apple Stores.

Ritz-Carlton Hotels was the only hospitality company to receive the highest quality and performance award twice. Its two Malcolm Baldrige National Quality Awards in 1992 and 1999 set Ritz-Carlton apart from its peers. It was the culture and values that elevated its employees above all else and showed how focusing on employees first helped deliver the "Ritz-Carlton Mystique." The company's "Golden Rules" of service are posted on its website and are transparent and explicit to employees, customers, and the world. The "Golden Rules" include: the Motto—"Ladies and Gentlemen serving ladies and gentlemen"; the Credo—"the finest personal service for guests; the Three Steps of Service—warm and sincere greeting, anticipating guests' needs, and saying a fond farewell while always addressing them by their name; the Service Values that are all about employees' personal responsibility for superior service; and finally the Employee Promise.[9]

Now widely known, Ritz-Carlton's Employee Promise states that:

> At Ritz-Carlton, our Ladies and Gentlemen are the most important resource in our service commitment to our guests. By applying the principles of trust, honesty, respect, integrity, and commitment, we nurture and maximize talent to the benefit of each individual and the company.[10]

The stories of how Ritz-Carlton employees deliver their magic service to its many loyal customers are legendary. Behind the scenes, there is a deliberate culture woven into every process that goes into the "WOW stories" that staff members share at the "Daily Lineup" that starts every shift. The lesser-known side of the Ritz-Carlton hospitality success story is its extensive use of technology and data. There is an abundance of data being collected daily, from individual guests' personal preferences to general hotel maintenance data such as room cleanliness. The data is organized and communicated to the staff to make decisions about every hotel guest. As more technology and data are introduced, so is the opportunity for the "unscripted" staff behavior that delivers personalized guest service. Employee selection, onboarding, coaching, and training become ever more important.

When Ritz-Carlton founder and ex-CEO Horst Schulze was asked about his position on the role of technology and data in his industry, he prioritized employees' empowerment again.

> My advice for hotels would be identify the technologies that empower employees and truly make the life of the guest easier and more pleasant. Too often I see hotels (and companies in other industries) purchase technologies almost, it seems, for the sake of it—iPads on the reception desk that no one uses, lighting systems in hotel rooms that are too complex for more guests to fully understand, I could go on. General managers need to ask themselves whether the technology they are about to invest in improves the lives of the guest or empowers service staff to improve the life of the guest. If the answer is yes, then go ahead."

Two lessons from Ritz-Carlton's unique hospitality model continue to be relevant today. First is the focus on empowering employees and creating a culture that delivers exceptional customer outcomes. The second lesson is that the abundance of customer data and the most advanced technology—though invisible to customers—became effective tools to power Ritz-Carlton's highly personalized, customer-focused culture. Data and technology were the enablers, no more, no less. Steve Jobs should be credited for not only recognizing Ritz-Carlton's hospitality formula but for successfully "borrowing" and transforming it to fit the needs of selling technology, scaling it through the global Apple Store network.

Customer Experience Sets the Stage

At the start of the chapter, we wrote that employee experience did not happen as a result of an internal evolution of the HR practice; it was the result of adopting ideas developed in marketing and customer

FIGURE 6.1 From Customer Experience to Workforce Experience

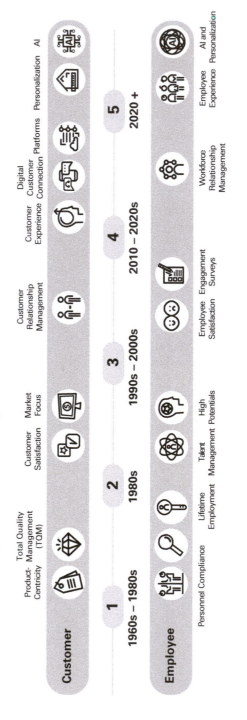

service. The historical parallels in the evolution from customer experience to employee experience are hard to miss. We see five distinct stages in the customer-centric journey that are reflected in the employee experience as well.

- Stage One (1960–1980s): Product-centricity and the Total Quality Management movement (TQM).

- Stage Two (1980s) Customer satisfaction focus and market vs product orientation.

- Stage Three (1990s–2000) Customer Relationship Management.

- Stage Four (2010–2020) Customer Experience, Digital Customer Connection, Platforms.

- Future: Total Personalization and AI.

On the employee side, the customer-centric stages are mirrored in the following employee-centric phases.

In **Stage One** (the Product), business organizations were engaged in process improvement in the wake of the TQM and Six Sigma movements. The focus was for the producers to reliably deliver products and services on time, with the least "waste." Product quality was the ultimate goal. Experts had the answers. The idea was it was critical to find out what customers wanted from a product. "Customer experience" seemed secondary if it was considered at all.

At **Stage Two** (Satisfaction), customer primacy was still a novel idea. The new approach's aim was to ultimately achieve customer satisfaction. Several new methodologies were developed in aid of improving customer satisfaction.

Noriaki Kano, Professor of TQM at Tokyo University of Science, is credited with introducing the most enduring model that connected customer satisfaction with the product development process.[12] Kano worked with the Toyota Motor Company and proposed a model that sorted out product features into five categories depending on anticipated customer needs. Those features included: threshold, performance, excitement, indifferent, and dissatisfier qualities.[13] In the product development process, features that satisfied customers most were prioritized while dissatisfiers were supposed to be avoided.

Another measurement instrument of customer satisfaction—SERVQUAL—was developed by a US marketing team to capture consumer expectations and perceptions of service quality.[14] The model focused on five criteria of service quality—quality (termed tangibles), reliability, responsiveness, assurance, and empathy. SERVQUAL introduced the first universal measurements of customer satisfaction.

At **Stage Three** (Customer Relationship Management (CRM)), many companies saw technology as a key to good customer relations. CRM systems, such as Salesforce, provided a technical capability to support an efficient process of managing information about customers.

At the same time, access to vast amounts of customer data marked the "golden age" of traditional market research. Customers finally "got noticed," and the discovery gave rise to a flurry of customer satisfaction surveys and focus groups.

The classic marketing mix of 4Ps—product, price, place, and promotion[15]—was expanded to 7Ps to include people, process, and physical evidence.[16] 7Cs—customer, cost, convenience, communication, consistency, content, and credibility—were then supplemented with 3Cs—company, customers, and competitors—the elements that signal a pivot towards people and market orientation.[17]

At **Stage Four** (Customer Experience), the new marketing focus on people, customers, and competitors came full circle. One of the most insightful observations by Peter Drucker describes what customer experience is in the following way:

> The customer rarely buys what the business thinks it sells him. One reason for this is, of course, that nobody pays for a "product." What is paid for is satisfaction. But nobody can make or supply satisfaction as such—at best, only the means to attaining them can be sold and delivered.[18]

The pivot from "selling" a product to catering to the customer "experience" made marketers expand away from the traditional product to new ways of gauging customer experience. Getting to customer experience involved building a broader network of cross-disciplinary alliances and "borrowing" data from adjacent disciplines including sales, supply chain, manufacturing, and not least, the company's employees.

As marketers were going through the transition to the customer-centered approach, they discovered that employees played an important role in supporting and promoting a company's brand. The notion of "people as products" was already being broadly discussed in marketing circles in the late 1980s–1990s. The concept that employees were not just producers but rather products themselves became the consensus in marketing.[19] The services industry—hospitality, tourism, financial services—was the industry that ran with the concept that employees were essential to the company or brand's success. In his *HBR* article "Selling the Brand Inside. You tell your customers what makes you great. Do your employees know?" Colin Mitchell, a veteran CMO, made an impassioned case for taking the brand to employees first. The effort of communicating the brand to employees should be no less than taking it to external customers.[20] The acknowledgment of the role of employees stayed on and continued to evolve with marketers, customer relations, and communications managers. The business cases of Apple, Ritz-Carlton and Best Buy illustrate the power of the employee-centric service model.

Employees Are the New Customers

There is no more precarious position for a business to be in than to lose the trust and commitment of its employees. There is a new realization that an organization's overall success is becoming increasingly dependent on the quality of the relationship between the organization and its employees.

The Covid-19 pandemic put that relationship in the spotlight; the real stress test for organizational cultures was the risk to employees' health and overall wellbeing. However, the overnight physical-to-digital transformation presented its own challenges and risks. At the same time it offered incredible opportunities for the future of work, the workplace, and the workforce, coming full circle back to Drucker's original insight about the importance of treating employees as people.

CASE STUDY
Best Buy

To understand what it means to treat employees as people, let's turn to a specific example in a well-known retail chain. When Hubert Joly was named the CEO of Best Buy Co in the summer of 2012, the company was in trouble. Stock hit a low of $11 per share, stores were closing, and Joly's appointment was met with investor skepticism as he was seen as unqualified. However, Joly had led a luxury hotel chain, Carlson Companies, before joining Best Buy Co, and just like Steve Jobs, he brought the best lessons from his hospitality experience to the technology retail business, going against the mainstream "profits first" management philosophy.

In the nine years of his stewardship, the company stock price went up tenfold to $115. Joly attributes his business success to the deliberate and purposeful steering of the company culture towards human-centric priorities. He openly rejects the legacy of shareholder capitalism and outlines key principles of the new human-centric culture in his book: *The Heart of Business: Leadership principles for the next era of capitalism*.[21] Joly summed up his overall approach in the following way: "The human-centric approach was part of the Best Buy turnaround from the beginning. It's not just a theory for good times."[22]

Instead of starting with cuts, Joly started with people and treated profit as an outcome. His goal was to "Create energy. Get going. Celebrate small wins. Talk about problems." Empowering employees at the point of sale to match any online price and make those decisions on their own was how that approach worked day after day on the shop floor. To deliver consistent outcomes, Joly argues, the most important step a company needs to make is to create the right inclusive environment for its employees. Raising the minimum wage is just the start; goodwill towards employees needs to go beyond salary and consider benefits, such as mental health and the ability to vote. Skills development, professional growth, and manager investment in each and every employee's growth were high on Joly's list. In summary, Joly's fundamental philosophy is to restore the social compact between employers and workers. He argues that businesses have made a consequential historical mistake by following Milton Friedman and his shareholder primacy agenda rather than Peter Drucker and his advocacy of the stakeholders.[23]

Towards the Worker-Centered Economy

The industrialized world had come full circle to accept Drucker's "employees are *people*" position by the time the Covid-19 pandemic waned. In the middle of the global shutdown, the pandemic brought the two forms of employment traditionally seen as binary—full-time and contractor, part-time and freelance—closer together. The pandemic forced employers to relax legacy cultures of control and allow for flexible and remote working for full-time employees. At the same time, it was recognized that all workers mattered, including the essential and front-line ones. The effect of the systematic changes surprised even the most skeptical observers. Productivity went up and employees' sense of belonging has grown. The Edelman Trust Barometer, one of the world's most recognized global authorities on employment brands, came out in 2021 with findings that measured the world's changing trust levels among major social institutions such as governments, NGOs, media, and business. The results of the survey showed that business was both the most competent and ethical, surpassing other global institutions.[24]

Partial shutdowns of major parts of the service economy strained relationships between gig workers and platforms, exposing the tensions and inequities that had already existed before. As the pandemic shutdowns precipitated a new wave of layoffs and furloughs, it further exposed the fragility of self-employment and the gig work model in the US, where medical benefits are attached to one's employment. The business model of "gig" was set up to meet business priorities first, to be adaptive to market volatility, and to have access to an army of unattached contractors, consultants, freelancers, drivers, and other types of temporary roles. The pandemic tipped the scales towards recognition that all types of workers deserved protections and benefits.

The US Labor Secretary, Marty Walsh, announced early in the Biden administration that the government considered gig workers to be employees and would expect to be reviewing national guidelines in favor of the workers. He stated, "We are looking at it but in a lot of cases gig workers should be classified as employees... in some cases they are treated respectfully and in some cases they are not, and I think it has to be consistent across the board."[25]

In September 2021, New York City became the first to introduce aggressive legislation to improve the conditions of food delivery workers working for app-based employers such as Uber Eats, Grubhub, and DoorDash. The new rules set minimum pay levels and other requirements to improve the working conditions of the army of these essential workers in New York.[26]

In the UK, the Supreme Court decided early in 2021 in favor of labor groups and ruled that the vast network of independent contractors from food workers to cleaners and Uber drivers were considered employees.[27] In France, Germany, Italy, and Spain similar legislations have been passed or are pending.

The worker-centric economy may be closer than we think. Peter Drucker was its guide, marketing offered the model and the direction, the pandemic accelerated progress, and technology will play a critical role for generations to come.

Endnotes

1 Drucker, PF (2002) They're not employees, they're people, *Harvard Business Review*, 80 (2), pp 70–128

2 Foulon, M and Handfield-Jones, H (1997) The war for talent, *McKinsey Quarterly*

3 Michaels, E, Handfield-Jones, H, and Axelrod, B (2001) *The War for Talent*, Boston, MA: Harvard Business Press

4 Khan, T et al (2021) "Back to human": Why HR leaders want to focus on people again, McKinsey&Co, https://www.mckinsey.com/business-functions/people-and-organizational-performance/our-insights/back-to-human-why-hr-leaders-want-to-focus-on-people-again (archived at https://perma.cc/2CNL-5V9Q)

5 Schurenberg, E (2020) Richard Branson: Why customers come second at Virgin. In an exclusive Inc. interview, Sir Richard explains who rates highest at Virgin. And it's not investors, either, *INC Magazine*, https://www.inc.com/eric-schurenberg/sir-richard-branson-put-your-staff-first-customers-second-and-shareholders-third.html (archived at https://perma.cc/32DT-PKR4)

6 Sinek, S (2009) *Start with Why*, East Rutherford, NJ: Penguin Publishing Group

7 PBS (1996) Television special "Triumph of the nerds: The rise of accidental empires," Transcript Part III, Steve Jobs speaking, pbs.org/nerds (archived at https://perma.cc/X2PB-9N6L)

8 Gallo, C (2012) How the Ritz-Carlton inspired the Apple Store, *Forbes*, https://www.forbes.com/sites/carminegallo/2012/04/10/how-the-ritz-carlton-inspired-the-apple-store-video/?sh=293475c3449c (archived at https://perma.cc/VQ6M-4Q3F)

9 https://www.ritzcarlton.com/en/about/gold-standards (archived at https://perma.cc/4PKY-H2L4)

10 Ibid.

11 Sorrells, M (2019) Q&A: Ritz-Carlton founder Horst Schulze on tech's role in luxury hotels, *Phocuswire*, https://www.phocuswire.com/q-and-a-ritz-carlton-founder-horst-schulze (archived at https://perma.cc/Y44Y-YQYJ)

12 Kanji, GK (1995) *Total Quality Management: Proceedings of the first world congress*, Dordrecht: Springer Netherlands

13 Kanomodel.Com (archived at https://perma.cc/2V9G-FLVZ)

14 Parasuraman, A (1988) Servqual: A multiple-item scale for measuring consumer perceptions of service quality, *Journal of Retailing*, **64** (1), pp 12–37

15 Hunt, SF and Goolsby, J (2011) The rise and fall of the functional approach to marketing: A paradigm displacement perspective (originally published in 1988), reprinted in *Review of Marketing Research: Special Issue – Marketing Legends, Vol. 1*, ed Naresh K. Malhotra, Bingley, UK: Emerald

16 Booms, B and Bitner, MJ (1981) Marketing Strategies and Organizational Structures for Service Firms, in James H Donnelly and William R George (eds) *Marketing of Services*, Chicago, IL: American Marketing Association, pp 47–51

17 Ōmae, K (1982) *The Mind of the Strategist: The art of Japanese business*, New York: McGraw-Hill

18 Drucker, P (2012) *Managing For Results*, Hoboken, NJ: Taylor & Francis

19 Hirschman, EC (1987) People as products: Analysis of a complex marketing exchange, *Journal of Marketing*, **51** (1), pp 98–108

20 Mitchell, C (2002) Selling the brand inside, *Harvard Business Review*, **80** (1), pp 99–126

21 Joly, H and Lambert, C (2021) *The Heart of Business: Leadership principles for the next era of capitalism*, Boston, MA: Harvard Business Review Press

22 Johnston, P (2021) Former Best Buy CEO Hubert Joly on leading through the company's turnaround, National Retail Federation, https://nrf.com/blog/former-best-buy-ceo-hubert-joly-leading-through-companys-turnaround (archived at https://perma.cc/YJ9E-4NW4)

23 Gelles, D (2021) Hubert Joly turned around Best Buy, now he's trying to fix capitalism, *International New York Times*, https://www.nytimes.com/

2021/07/15/business/hubert-joly-corner-office-best-buy.html (archived at https://perma.cc/F3PR-HPLN)

24 Edelman (2021) Trust Barometer Special Report: Trust, the new brand equity, https://www.edelman.com/trust/2021-brand-trust (archived at https://perma.cc/3V6L-DKRJ)

25 Bose, N (2021) Labor Secretary throws his support behind classifying gig workers as employees, Reuters, https://www.reuters.com/world/us/exclusive-us-labor-secretary-says-most-gig-workers-should-be-classified-2021-04-29/ (archived at https://perma.cc/P8JS-USKY)

26 Mays, JC (2021) New York passes sweeping bills to improve conditions for delivery workers, *New York Times*, https://www.nytimes.com/2021/09/23/nyregion/nyc-food-delivery-workers.html (archived at https://perma.cc/5VM7-H5AS)

27 Satariano, A (2021) Uber drivers are entitled to worker benefits, a British court rules, *New York Times*, https://www.nytimes.com/2021/02/19/business/uber-drivers-britain.html (archived at https://perma.cc/9VTH-SX3G)

PART THREE

Workplace

07

Where Work Happens

The Return of the Hybrid Workplace

"When disaster struck, work from home (WFH) saved the day. Work from anywhere (WFA) will win the decade," announced the founders of LiquidSpace.[1] Since its founding in 2010, LiquidSpace has emerged from the fringes of commercial office real estate to be at the heart of one of the greatest workplace transformations ever. Its mission is to bring maximum flexibility to employers of all sizes, workers, and the growing community of entrepreneurs. It offers workspace rentals *à la carte* from a few hours to a few months in multiple locations ranging from megacities to smaller towns. It now offers over 10,500 flexible office spaces across 2,700 localities. As the 2020–21 global healthcare crisis sped up the transition away from HQ centers towards distributed multilocation options, LiquidSpace saw a perfect opportunity to step up and offer a solution. This flexible, wired "work from anywhere" platform brands itself as a "matchmaker" not a broker. It positions itself as the maximum workplace flexibility provider for companies looking to accommodate their remote workers with exactly the right location options.

The pendulum of workplace locations historically swung in response to the changing economic times and developing technologies. The trajectory of the last two centuries was to bring workers closer together under one roof. Once pre-industrial artisan workshops were abandoned and work became organized and streamlined around the production lines in factories, centralization became impossible to escape. In the later 20th century, workers were nested in sprawling call centers, and for office workers, within open-plan office spaces—all gathered under one roof.

With the pandemic at their doorstep, the sprawling early 21st-century corporate campuses overnight transformed themselves into virtual cyber communities of remote workers. While the future of the workplace is unknown and we are still trying to figure out what comes next, it is worth revisiting the pre-industrial artisanal models and imagining their 21st-century return.

Before the Industrial Revolution (1760–1840), dispersed networks of craft-based workshops were housed in dedicated spaces often adjacent to the artisans' homes. Imagine a boot maker rolling out of bed in the morning, having some porridge, and then walking to his "workplace," which was just a room in the dwelling next door. Individual craftspeople worked independently and had control over their own work within the norms prescribed by their respective guilds. The boot makers may have shared suppliers of leather, the marketplaces, and the apprentices. With urbanization on the rise and the growing concentration of the population in a few urban locations, the private workshop system was transformed into the "putting out" or domestic system. The "putting out" system involved urban-based merchant-employers "contracting out" materials to rural producers who worked primarily in their homes. For efficiency purposes these independent workshops were eventually brought under one roof, thus giving rise to the historical factory and today's office.[2] With the "putting out" system the artisans' work looked similar to today's contracting, except that for the most part it was dependent on one client, and offered less control over what one did. Once the work became centrally controlled and the artisans had to leave their workshops, foundries, ateliers, and mills to report to the factory, the world of work changed forever.

The historical parallels between the artisanal economy and the post-pandemic world of work are hard to miss. With all the differences in purpose, technology, and execution, we are witnessing a historic turn towards a world of semi-autonomous employees working remotely but in sync with their employers representing the modern-day guilds. The historical analogy is not only "interesting" but also helpful in our thinking and planning for the next world of work yet to come.

Why Working From Home Is Not the Answer

The key issue at the heart of today's workplace debate is not about worker productivity. Neither is it about saving on real estate costs, or whether working from home is a better use of workers' time than the daily commute. It is not solely about which collaborative technologies to adopt either. The receipts from the pandemic are in and the results are instructive. There is no short answer to the question of where work needs to happen. It is complex. Today's work is first and foremost about tapping into the skills, resourcefulness, and resilience of world-class workers no matter their origins, gender, race, age, or ultimately their location. It is about creating a culture where these workers can be at their best.

Let's look at three contrasting cases of the "working from home" results: Sir Isaac Newton's scientific discoveries, Goldman Sachs' analysts' revolt, and Microsoft's lessons from tracking remote workers.

To begin with one of the best-known fables from the history of science, Isaac Newton's discovery of the law of gravitation has more parallels to today than previously imagined. As the story goes, Newton was at home on leave from Cambridge University sitting in his garden when the fabled apple fell on his head. The timing of the event is of note; it coincided with the outbreak of the 1665 bubonic plague when the university was closed. Would the young, unknown Newton have arrived at the scientific breakthroughs and his discoveries of the theories of gravity, calculus, and optics were he not "working from home" and enjoying the flexibility of having time to himself away from the confines of his elite college?

Fast-forward to the pandemic of 2020. A year into the lockdown, a group of Goldman Sachs junior analysts released a slide deck describing working around the clock, with a grueling 95-hour work week and five-hour sleep breaks at best. They rated their job satisfaction at 2 out of 10 and predicted leaving the firm in a few months if conditions did not change. The response to the publication of the deck in *The New York Times* was mixed.[3] While some blamed Wall Street employment practices, others pointed to the explicit compact of the six-figure salaries for the freshman class at Goldman. Some veteran financiers' commentary was most relevant to today. Starting their jobs in a virtual setting with the deal flow being at its highest, there was no chance of leaning into the unofficial support network while learning the "tricks of the trade." In the past, a new hire would be sitting right next to more experienced peers. When they ran into a problem a more seasoned analyst would show them the shortcuts. In a pandemic, a brand-new recruit would be alone in a studio apartment in New York faced with a daunting flow of work they barely understood. Management by email has also proven to be alienating, especially to new employees with no ability to push back or ask for help. The open question from the public standoff between Goldman management and the analysts was whether working from home made it more unbearable for the apartment-bound junior analyst.

Microsoft research tracked the company's remote workers from the start of the pandemic. It revealed the "unbearable inequity" of experiences among those working from home. It turns out that the isolation of the pandemic taxed the younger generation heavily, while the more senior, more established, more affluent, and better-connected cohorts embraced the autonomy and mostly "thrived."[4] Judging from the abundance of "working from home" reports, surveys, and informal data, it became clear that the key differentiator of employee experience for the most part was not the technology or daily convenience. What tipped the scale was the very human, often "soft" and "intangible" factors such as the quality and depth of the existing workplace and personal connections, the quality of employees' living situations, and workers' ability to maintain a work-life balance.

Isaac Newton benefited from the autonomy of working from home surrounded by family and nature. For Goldman Sachs junior analysts, working in isolation in their New York apartments became an occupational hazard. Microsoft's research confirmed that working from home could be a tale of two cities. In short, context matters, management matters, and company culture can make or break the success of any type of work arrangement.

The Future of Work Is Hybrid

There is an almost unanimous consensus in industry that there is no going back to the office as we left it in 2020. For many, working from home is not a long-term solution either. The workplace location pendulum will most likely settle in the middle, supporting flexible "hybrid" work arrangements. Hybrid work maximizes employees' productivity and work experience through flexible and personalized workplace arrangements. Most companies are in the process of deciding what would be the optimal workplace set-up for their business and for their people. There is no one size fits all. Every employer must reflect on their experience with remote work, their strategy going forward, weigh the pros and cons of the arrangements they will be willing to make, and finally, experiment.

GM's choice to call their post-pandemic return to work approach "work appropriately" is a good example of how an employer may choose wisely. GM's decision goes back to CEO Mary Barra's days as the company CHRO when she tossed out the 10-page HR manual prescribing the appropriate dress code and replaced it with "dress appropriately" guidance. That culture of trust is now extended to an employee's decision to choose how they want to work between the office and home. For GM, this move was not motivated by cost considerations. In fact, GM's management admitted to not having done all the math before making the announcement. GM's strategic focus today is on attracting an in-demand workforce. As GM is pivoting towards electrical vehicles, they are in competition for the technical talent that is not native to the Detroit area. The early report is in and the strategy is working. GM's highly skilled workers can now be found hundreds of miles away from HQ.[5]

Another place to look for the best examples of "return to work" decision-making processes is Microsoft. The company that leads innovation in the remote workplace suite of tools has been remarkably transparent about how its own workplace decisions are being made. Microsoft's approach was experimental and iterative from the start. Traditional linear timelines clearly did not work. "Though we don't know how far off a new normal is, we are adapting to a new way of working with an expanded understanding of flexibility," wrote Microsoft executive Kurt DelBene in a blog.[6] Microsoft innovated in response and created a new tool, the *Hybrid Workplace Dial*. It is easy to move up or down the dial depending on the situation in a specific global location and on how the pandemic is fluctuating. The dial has six stages of opening: closed, mandatory to work from home, work from home strongly encouraged, soft open, open with restrictions, and open. Kurt DelBene explained how they arrived at their philosophy and how they made the decision to meet Microsoft employees where they were while continuing to innovate, develop, and adopt new remote working technology to stay productive and connected.[7]

All decisions were data based and rigorously tested. Microsoft collected their own employee data, reviewed peer company research, and solicited expert insights related to the hybrid workplace. The

FIGURE 7.1   The Stages of the Hybrid Workplace

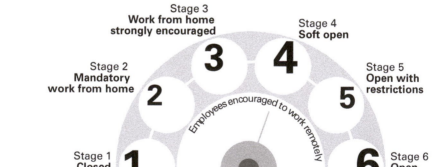

result was the release of Microsoft's 2021 Work Trend Index, appropriately titled "The Next Great Disruption is Hybrid Work—Are We Ready?"[8] Highlighted were seven trends that were prioritized for the hybrid work culture:

1 Flexible work was the company's way of the future.

2 Leaders needed to understand and acknowledge that employees' experiences were different.

3 The productivity numbers were misleading and masked an overworked workforce.

4 Gen Z was about to become the lost generation, missing out on education and genuine connections.

5 The diversity of the networks suffered, replaced by the broad and less committed Zoom conferences.

6 There was a need to return to authenticity.

7 Talent was everywhere in the distributed world.

These seven trends exposed hard truths about the pandemic and highlighted opportunities to act. The negatives had largely to do with inequities in the workplace that the pandemic exposed and exacerbated. The opportunities lay with the commitment to flexibility, true global reach, and the need to restore authenticity to employee experiences.

All in all, every company's decision to go hybrid requires learning from their own experiences with remote working and choosing the appropriate flexible operating model. These models will not be effective without deliberate investment in more inclusive workplace practices supported by user-friendly collaborative technologies.

Co-working Spaces Re-enter the Scene with a Vengeance

Alternatives to traditional workplaces sprang up in the shadows of the official office culture prior to the pandemic. The ubiquitous coffee shops serviced the entrepreneurial ecosystem with free public Wi-Fi, claiming the middle ground between office cubicles and kitchen tables. A familiar feature at a local Starbucks would be a recent college graduate cranking out a business plan, while texting a friend to arrange a meeting.

It was in these in-between spaces that the first alternatives to the office came into their own, competing with the coffee shops for their first tenants. The number of users of co-working spaces grew exponentially, doubling every year through the pandemic.[9] The number of people working in co-working spaces in the US is projected to go up to 1,076,000 in 2022 and will continue to grow.[10] Today's workers are ready to move away from crowded traditional offices but are fatigued from pandemic confinement at home. Workers are ready to experiment and are open to alternatives.

Taking Work to People Rather Than People to Work

CASE STUDY
WeWork Comes Back

When WeWork entered the co-working market in 2010, its very existence became synonymous with the rise of the shared economy. Its aesthetic was based on what neither workplaces nor home-based working could offer. It provided attractive collaborative spaces and the sense of a community of like-minded innovators. In its design approach, WeWork personalized each one of its 600-plus locations around the world, blending the mass-market approach with one-off and locally appropriate design. At the time of its failed first IPO in 2019, 40 percent of WeWork's portfolio of clients consisted of companies with over 500 employees, along with the likes of PepsiCo, IBM, PwC, and others. For those traveling on business or enrolled in online courses, WeWork offered spaces on demand in multiple locations.[11] The convenience of the national and global network of offices, the aura of sharing spaces with the most entrepreneurial global community, and the relaxed creative vibe of a comfortable living room successfully branded these co-working locations as true alternatives to the cubical culture of major corporations at the time.

The story of WeWork Co has had multiple labyrinthine plots and a few dead ends but the co-working brand it represented has sustained. With new leadership at the helm, the company is recalibrating for a promising return. The difference between today and when WeWork started is that the space it occupies is much more crowded with creative and promising alternatives.

Employers' decisions to relax "back to the office" rules opened the real possibility of multiple alternatives to the traditional workplace. The "work from anywhere" model promised to take work to people rather than people to work. It was pushing out of the urban centers into outlying suburban locations and further into rural areas. A new generation of real estate entrepreneurs responded to the emerging new market with creativity and speed. The opportunity to create a breakthrough business model and reinvent the workplace has become too irresistible to miss, and the number of innovative breakaway companies that sprang up right around the pandemic is promising.

Let us start with a spin-off from WeWork, Daybase. Founded by a pair of former WeWork executives, Joel Steinhaus and Doug Chambers, Daybase was launched in the commuter suburbs of New York as the pandemic started to wind down. The company's model was to turn abandoned retail spaces into furnished offices. It offered an affordable common charge of $50 and the option of private offices and meeting rooms at an affordable cost. *The Wall Street Journal* profiled the company to its readers.

"People want their homes back, and they want to see their colleagues again, but they don't want the long daily commute and monotonous routine that a full-time return to the old office entails," said Doug Chambers, Daybase COO. "This is where Daybase comes in."[12]

Another of the experimental new companies reinventing the workspace is Codi, the "hyperlocal" "walk to work" company that marries the concept of Airbnb with WeWork's co-working amenities.[13] Codi's services are offered in major cities where real estate is at a premium and homes are small. Codi affords private workspaces for single users or small groups in the neighborhood's homes with office support services minus the commute. It is as simple as entering one's zip code on the Codi website. One can find a few local sites for use as office space away from the office and in proximity to one's home. It appears to be a win, win, win. A win for companies that can provide a quality office environment for employees at a fraction of the cost of an office, a win for employees who can literally "walk to work," and a win for local property owners able to make additional income from their expensive urban real estate.

During the lockdowns, Codi pivoted to a business-to-business model, offering safe alternatives for companies concerned about their workers suffering from isolation and burnout. At an affordable monthly price, the "walk to work" solution might be particularly attractive in urban centers where homes are small and peak-hour commutes to the office are crowded.

The largest residential property owners, Equity Residential and AvalonBay Properties among them, are also looking into offering additional smaller private office spaces within their properties that tenants can rent as offices.

We conclude where the chapter started, with LiquidSpace—an end-to-end online marketplace that promises to deliver work from anywhere solutions. The LiquidSpace platform offers a choice of workspaces for individual employees and hubs and can accommodate teams of several hundred people. LiquidSpace workplaces do not require long-term contracts. They are available on demand, monthly, weekly, and by the hour if needed. CEO Mark Gilbreath posted on the company's website that it was set to expand across North America.[14]

The great pandemic of the 21st century brought about perhaps the second-largest workplace migration, on the scale of the Industrial Revolution and urbanization of the past. The move away from the corporate towers towards worker-centered locations is about to reverse the 200-year-old trend towards centralization of work. It is taking us back to the workplace's artisanal roots with all the benefits and opportunities that offers.

Endnotes

1 https://liquidspace.com/ (archived at https://perma.cc/9S35-VBXS)

2 Davis, H (2020) *Working Cities: Architecture, place and production*, Abingdon, Oxon; New York, NY: Routledge, Taylor & Francis Group

3 Karaian, J and Ross Sorkin, A (2021) "I'm in a really dark place": Complaints at Goldman Sachs set off a workplace debate, *New York Times*, https://www. nytimes.com/2021/03/19/business/goldman-sachs-analysts-workplace-complaint.html (archived at https://perma.cc/PL75-STA3)

4 Singer-Velush, N, Sherman, K, and Anderson, E (2020) Microsoft analyzed data on its newly remote workforce, *Harvard Business Review*, https://hbr. org/2020/07/microsoft-analyzed-data-on-its-newly-remote-workforce (archived at https://perma.cc/CJZ5-3C7C)

5 Lareau, JL (2021) GM reveals its post-COVID-19 plans, *Detroit Free Press*, https://www.freep.com/story/money/cars/general-motors/2021/04/20/gm-work-appropriately-remote/7288363002/ (archived at https://perma.cc/2FP9-USQT)

6 DelBene, K (2021) The philosophy and practice of our hybrid workplace, Microsoft Blog, https://blogs.microsoft.com/blog/2021/03/22/the-philosophy-and-practice-of-our-hybrid-workplace/ (archived at https://perma.cc/E9US-LLBF)

7 Ibid.

8 Microsoft WorkLab (2021) The next great disruption is hybrid work—are we ready? https://www.microsoft.com/en-us/worklab/work-trend-index/hybrid-work (archived at https://perma.cc/5JRK-RVHU)

9 Statista (2021) Number of people working in coworking spaces in the United States from 2015 to 2022 (in 1,000s) https://www.statista.com/statistics/797564/number-of-people-working-in-coworking-spaces-us/ (archived at https://perma.cc/UU79-CBXC)

10 Statista (2017) Number of people working in coworking spaces in the United States from 2015 to 2022, https://www.statista.com/statistics/797564/number-of-people-working-in-coworking-spaces-us (archived at https://perma.cc/FGH9-PUM8)

11 Zaleski, O (2018) WeWork is turning its offices into study halls, *Bloomberg News*, https://www.bloomberg.com/news/articles/2018-01-22/wework-is-turning-its-offices-into-study-halls (archived at https://perma.cc/FGH9-PUM8)

12 Putzier, K (2021) Suburban homes and retail are the budding new office hotspot, *Wall Street Journal*, https://www.wsj.com/articles/suburban-homes-and-retail-are-the-budding-new-office-hotspot-11620129603 (archived at https://perma.cc/3BWJ-9T9J)

13 https://www.codi.com/ (archived at https://perma.cc/8VLG-C7BU)

14 Newswire (2020) LiquidSpace launches the largest curated network of enterprise-grade flexible office spaces for enterprise clients, *PR Newswire*, https://www.prnewswire.com/news-releases/liquidspace-launches-the-largest-curated-network-of-enterprise-grade-flexible-office-spaces-for-enterprise-clients-301187786.html (archived at https://perma.cc/DJH7-U7N9)

08

Work at Scale: Organizations as Platforms

The Platforms Have Arrived

The spring of 2021 started with a market disruption caused by a platform. The wild ride of the GameStop stock left professional investors and regulators alike bewildered by the sudden havoc caused by a clique of amateur traders. The group that called themselves WallStreetBets organized on a subreddit to discuss what stocks to trade on the brokerage platform Robinhood. In a matter of days, WallStreetBets caused unprecedented stock volatility and disarray in the regulated investment markets.[1] To the outsiders, the incident was seen as a standoff between intrepid, self-organizing day traders and professional asset managers. The media portrayed the event as an act of "democratization" of the trading process, a digitized version of the "Occupy Wall Street" movement, with the day traders winning the battle even if they lost the war.

The advance of platforms such as Robinhood that are capable of exploiting vulnerabilities in established organizations has put additional pressure on traditional businesses to keep up or risk getting disrupted or left behind. As the platforms continue to penetrate the market, they take down the scaffolding of the established organizational structures and practices. Disruption has always been a way of doing business; what's new is the speed, frequency, and scale at which these changes occur today. The lesson learned by "the adults in the room" is that platforms set their own rules. Yes, they make things possible that might have been unthinkable before, but at the same time, they create a range of new issues for which the playbook has not yet been written.

A look at platforms' historical antecedents and their impact helps better understand their intent. Pre-internet platforms enabled economic and social activities for millennia. Green markets brought farmers and city residents together. Indian matchmakers found the right matches for their wealthy client families. The invention of Gutenberg's printing press in Renaissance Europe connected authors with their distant audiences and helped spread ideas, which eventually led to the Protestant Reformation. Twenty-first-century digital platforms have unprecedented reach. While many towns still have farmers' markets, consumers can also choose to get fresh produce delivered directly to their homes through Fresh Direct. Match.com provides an alternative to traditional matchmaking, and while subscriptions to major national media continue, more than eight in ten Americans get their news from digital platforms.[2]

Akin to the historical impact of the printing press vs handwritten scrolls, digital platforms by far outperform their analog predecessors but they also bring along a set of unexpected consequences. Technology skills are needed but they are not the only ones in play. Organizations need to be quickly reskilled to prepare for the digital age of the platforms at multiple levels. The Robinhood scenario should serve as a cautionary tale. Just like institutional investors in the GameStop saga, traditional HR may find themselves left behind and holding the bag.

Talent Platforms Break Through the Firewall

The key difference of the platforms is that they have multiple purposes. It's not the iPhone that matters, but the underlying digital platform that provides access to multiple tools.

While Apple's success has been often attributed to the iPhone's distinct design and functionality, what really distinguished Apple from its competitors was the radical positioning of its devices as a platform. The iPhone, for example, entered the market not only as a provider of mobile telephony but also as a provider of access to a broad range of services including music and cameras available through the iCloud and its App Store. The platform strategy creates a new service model. Rather than selling a single product, they also provide a means of interacting with a variety of other products and services. Platforms enable a shift from leveraging resources to increasing the "network effect" for users and service providers on their platform. There are many such disruptive platforms that provide users with a wide variety of services in one setting. Amazon, Airbnb, Alibaba, Uber, and DoorDash lead the way among thousands of other standout platforms across all industry domains. They punctured the siloed industry verticals and began to redraw market boundaries in new innovative ways. HR has traditionally been one of the most siloed, internally focused functions claiming exemption from market rules. In this chapter, we explore how the rapid growth of platforms in people management has provided an impetus for the People function to reinvent itself.[3]

People operations started to transition to platforms in the 2000s, as early as the platforms themselves. Internal platforms were first introduced in companies that were in the business of creating platforms. To deliver the product they sold to others, these companies needed to redesign their own organizational structures first. Internal operations, leadership styles, and even cultures had to be consistent with the way platforms operated for their customers. Reskilling and transformation of management processes started to take place. All others were taking note.

The first, most commonly adopted platforms were in recruitment. The first ATSs (Applicant Tracking Systems) were built for applicants who were actively seeking jobs and applying for work at the organizations of their choice. An ATS serves as a central hub for organizing job postings, processing resumes, scheduling interviews, and tracking applicants as they move through the recruitment process, and manages onboarding once they are hired. Today, there are over 300 ATSs and most companies are using them.[4] The limitation faced by the first ATS was that it was built around job vacancies and automated the transactional side of the hiring process.

The job-matching process became the next automation opportunity and priority for organizations. The technology and rationale for matching talent to jobs were already well developed and in place through the evolving gig marketplace infrastructure. The gig economy has grown largely because of the growth of a great variety of talent platforms, the largest among them being Upwork, TopTal and GitHub. These external talent platforms elevated contract hiring to the science and art of matching freelancers of different specialties to a broad variety of projects globally. For example, help with a new company logo and brand positioning for entrepreneurs could not be easier to get with Fiverr. By putting your job out for a bid, ideas and offers keep coming in and the entrepreneur then decides on the best for their business. The logical next step was to transfer existing matching technologies to meet internal talent mobility needs within organizations.

Contrary to earlier predictions that competitive gig marketplaces would lead to the eventual dissolution of internal company structures in favor of flexible contract work, the opposite has happened. Companies responded by bringing variety and flexibility of projects and job offerings to their internal talent pools. Today, powerful internal talent marketplaces are helping companies to become much better competitors for their own talent. Parallel with the technical advances, the platforms accelerated transitions towards a more inclusive, employee-centric philosophy of talent.

Take the example of the high-performing companies of the industrial era. General Electric, IBM, Unilever, Schneider Electric, Standard Chartered, and Procter & Gamble became known for their centrally planned and expertly managed talent management operations. They had two primary goals: 1) to identify and develop high-potential upwardly mobile employees, and 2) to ensure adequate succession management and continuity of management culture.

These classic talent management approaches were built on the understanding of talent management as a series of career ladders built out of the finite set of career options. The upwardly mobile, carefully selected A-players were developed on a narrow set of selection criteria and structured competency models. That approach screened out 80–90 percent of the employee population from the possibility of ever moving upward to any position of leadership responsibility. The purpose served was one of bringing carefully chosen high-potential employees up the management ladder in a relatively stable hierarchy to fill senior roles and perpetuate companies' cultures. By the start of the 21st century, the culture created through the highly selective talent system had outlived its usefulness and led to organizational stagnation and non-competitiveness against the external talent markets.

The new talent marketplace positioning is designed to include all employees, broaden everyone's career choices, and significantly increase internal career mobility. The intention is not only to match workers to tasks for which they are the best fit but also to support targeted skills development by customizing learning offerings across the entire organization.

Key Talent Marketplace Players

There is no shortage of external providers of talent marketplace technologies today, and each vendor has its particular benefits. Leading the pack is Gloat, the market leader in internal mobility today. Gloat owes its rise to starting in recruitment. Gloat's talent approach is to "democratize career development, unlock skills, and future proof the workforce."[5] Gloat's platform InnerMobility technically and from the user experience perspective is perhaps one of the most successful in the market. Gloat's clients are some of the well-recognized Talent leaders of the past, including Seagate, Schneider Electric, Unilever, and others.

Hitch Works,[6] another popular vendor, grew out of a larger enterprise, HERE Technologies,[7] which is a leading provider of digital location mapping using in-car navigation systems across multiple applications and industries. Here Workplace may be of relevance in the "work from anywhere" environment, bundling talent mobility services and workplace location strategies. Among other Talent platforms that are claiming their share of the market are Fuel50, 365Talents, Eightfold.ai, Pymetrics,[8] and others.

On the tech enterprise side, the leading technology companies have been aggressively building their own Talent solutions. IBM, Microsoft, and SAP have designed their internal platforms with use by their customers in mind. Workday, a leader in HRIS (Human Resource Information Systems), is working toward getting its own talent marketplace across the line and to its customers.

Connectivity across a variety of internal systems provides unprecedented access to enterprise and employee data. The aggregated data must be used ethically and intentionally to enable the next big step towards integration and management of the entire employee experience in one place. Platforms create a waterfall effect of changes across the entirety of people management processes and programs, and enable an employee-centered redesign of the entire company culture.

CASE STUDY
Microsoft Enters Employee Experience (Ex) Relay

Companies today are in a race to win the competition for Employee Experience (EX) solutions. An estimated $300 billion is spent annually on a variety of internal employee initiatives including recruitment, learning and development, pay, time off, safety, training, wellbeing, and various supporting technologies. The required degree of integration of processes and tools at the enterprise level would have been unthinkable without the functionalities offered through digital platforms.

The creation and launch of Microsoft Viva,[9] the first-of-its-kind Employee Experience and Workflow Management platform, illustrates best the strategic shift towards such total integration of people management. Microsoft Viva provides a single point of entry, a gateway that opens access to all available employee services in one place. Communications, knowledge, learning, resources, and insights powered by Microsoft 365 are accessed primarily through Microsoft Teams. Viva was developed in the context of Microsoft's own experience managing its global workforce that effectively became the platform both their employees and their customers could use. The message from CEO Satya Nadella, delivered at the launch of Microsoft Viva, confirmed the company's commitment towards a fully integrated employee experience: "As the world recovers, there is no going back. Flexibility in when, where and how we work will be key."[10] Head of Microsoft 365, Jared Spataro, defined the goal of the Viva platform this way: "We need to stop thinking about work as a place, and start thinking about how to maintain culture, connect employees, and harness human ingenuity in a hybrid world."[11]

The first four Viva EX platform modules include Viva Connections, Viva Insights, Viva Learning, and Viva Topics—with more modules promised in the future. Viva Connections involves video-enabled collaboration and communication tools. Viva Insights aggregates individual and company productivity reports and tips; it involves workplace analytics and pulls data from third-party platforms such as Workday, Zoom, and SAP. Viva Learning is an enterprise learning platform that serves up curated training content to employees in Teams. Viva Topics uses AI to mine enterprise data and create "Topic Pages" with information about that topic, and identifies company experts on that topic.

Employee experience powered by Viva realigns the HR agenda further towards investing in the culture of personalization, equal access, and internal mobility all in one place. All employee services are being linked together with a powerful analytics engine capable of supercharging its personalized delivery of individual employee experience. For Microsoft, there is no difference between the quality of service and ease of use they offer their clients and their customers. Customer and Employee Experience become a merged strategic goal enabled through enterprise-wide platforms.

How Platforms Are Changing People Practices

Mike Cannon-Brookes, the co-CEO and co-founder of Atlassian, kicked off his company's annual conference, Team 21, with a three-way conversation among his fellow technology CEOs, Stewart Butterfield of Slack and Eric Yuan of Zoom. The three companies have been remarkably successful in building collaboration tools on which most organizations get their work done today. Atlassian pioneered agile project management tools, Slack has all but replaced intracompany email, and Zoom innovated the video conferencing space. These companies' successes could be attributed not only to the products and services they offer but equally to the organizations they built. Here is how these platform companies achieve their goals within their own cultures.

An organization as a platform is neither hierarchical like a traditional business nor fully organic and uncoordinated like an ecosystem. It has a unique design that links employees, suppliers, and clients together into a dynamic network of relationships united by an overarching purpose and governed by a combination of shared core principles and complementary practices. What makes organizations as platforms distinct from their traditional forbearers are their three staples:

1 Platform leadership.

2 Platform-enabled internal operations.

3 The unique sources of motivation/incentives/rewards for employees.

Why Industrial Leadership No Longer Works

We start by highlighting the contrast between traditional industrial-age leadership and the three company CEOs who kicked off Atlassian's annual company event. Jack Welch, GE's legendary CEO (1981–2001), introduced management practices that became the gold standard for business organizations through the end of the 20th century. The espoused purpose of leadership was to exercise maximum control over company assets. Power cascaded down from the top and information flowed through delegation and subordination within management ranks. Job descriptions and employment contracts codified relationships to management authority and defined the limits of the specific roles. The management function that traditionally looked after "personnel" became known as Human Resources Management (HRM).[12] HRM practices were designed with the goal of extracting maximum productivity from employees, and "winners" were those companies that could best systematize and "lean out" their internal processes while maximizing outputs in the form of units per hour.

CASE STUDY

Leadership Lessons From the Atlassian Summit

The three tech founders speaking at the Atlassian summit each shared an episode from their Covid-19 work lives. The stories included awkward Zoom appearances and details of personal lives. The idea was to come across most "unplugged" and human in front of the conference attendees and employees who were tuning in. Authenticity was the gauge by which those leadership stories were judged at a meeting that took place in the middle of the pandemic.

Connecting to the traditions of servant leadership, the platform leaders are the ones that show foresight, relentless drive, and humility all at the same time.[13] It is not accidental that the most successful early 21st-century digital economy leaders assimilated many of servant leadership's key principles into the way they led their organizations. As the saying goes, "the first servant leader in any successful organization is its founder." Eric Yuan of Zoom, Stewart Butterfield of Slack, and the two founders of Atlassian built their organizations following in the steps of the agile platform leaders.

To be a platform leader means first and foremost to play on your company's team. When it comes to platforms, there are no longer traditional managers but coaches and facilitators. Platform leaders do not overuse their power of "no," they replace it with "tell me more...." They listen, adjust and facilitate the team's work. The most important quality of the platform leader is that of commitment to learning; they learn from other CEOs, from their families, and from their employees. They learn from mistakes fast. They embrace the words of John Wooden, a legendary American basketball coach: "Failure is not fatal, but failure to change might be."[14] And yet, leaders must make decisions and move fast, on the platform or not. The following four principles have been pulled from the vast repertoire of leadership strategies by the platform leaders themselves:

Principle #1. "Disagree and Commit," a core "and" leadership principle that invites the discussion, debate, and dissent but once the arguments have been considered, it expects everyone to commit in the end. First introduced into the leadership canon by Scott McNealy, CEO of Sun Microsystems, it was later adopted and made famous by Jeff Bezos. In his 2016 Letter to the Shareholders, Bezos described how this principle applied equally to leaders and teams in his organization. He shared a story of how he disagreed with his Amazon Studios team but committed to supporting their decision anyway. "... given that this team has already brought home 11 Emmys, 6 Golden Globes, and 3 Oscars, I'm just glad they let me in the room at all!"[15]

"Disagree and Commit" accelerates decision making for platform leaders and allows them to successfully navigate inclusion and focus on execution at the same time. Sun Microsystems, Amazon, GitLab, Qatar Airways, Venture L, Zalando, and other companies have embraced this leadership principle.

Principle #2. "Tell me more...." The platform leader is always ready to listen and invite an explanation in order to learn and be willing to be persuaded. This principle is more about the leadership posture of listening, paying attention, and expecting to learn. A syndicated Public Radio show named "Tell me More" was built on the principle of going behind the scenes and getting to the bottom of complex issues.[16]

Principle #3. "Argue as if you are right and listen as if you are wrong." This leadership principle was first formulated by Michigan psychologist Karl Weick and later popularized by Adam Grant of Wharton business school.[17] It captures the leadership posture of persuasiveness and willingness to be persuaded. A leader who succeeds in managing the platform organization can do both: lead by persuading and listen to learn and be persuaded.

Principle #4. The 80–20 percent authenticity principle. The standard textbook advice to leaders is to project optimism, confidence, and resoluteness. That is what leaders do 80 percent of the time. What sets them apart is the 20 percent of the time when they are who they really are and have their guard down. The ability of leaders to show that 20 percent of themselves makes them most powerful.

CASE STUDY

How Atlassian Does Things

While traditional organizations tend to rely almost exclusively on the low-powered incentive of paying employees recurring wages in exchange for their labor, the platform organization requires higher-powered commitments from all employees. Atlassian's culture is an experiment in its own right; it is an extension of the company's broad portfolio of collaboration tools. "Work Open" is the foundational philosophy of how Atlassian operates. It is fundamentally a "learning by doing and from each other" culture, untethered from employees' status, tenure, and rank. Work outcomes are being captured, analyzed, and generously shared across the internal platform and within the ecosystem of customers, contractors, and all those who are willing to listen.

Atlassian's Annual Summit is a public square where all the stakeholders come together to share and to learn.

According to the Great Place to Work rankings, Atlassian's employees gave their company a 93 percent approval rating compared with an average of 59 percent for US companies in 2021.[18] *Fortune* magazine recognized Atlassian as #8 on the list of the Best Technology Companies to Work For. Atlassian's excellent market performance is often attributed to the deliberate attention leaders pay to their culture. The company's "Work Open" philosophy has delivered to employees who give their company the highest ratings on honest business practices, pride at working for the company, and getting the supportive environment to succeed.

The "Work Open" culture has been built on three levers that drive its success. Supporting the levers are working principles that promote the desired behaviors at work. These tenets are validated through surveys of the employees and customers.[19]

Lever One: Understanding one another
Ensuring that people got to know each other "as people, not skill sets" and
    building trust was the overriding determinant of team performance.

Lever Two: Access to information
"No more closed-door meetings, everyone can join" is the company's operating
    model. The leaders of the company believe that every big idea is always a
    sum total of many smaller ideas.

Lever Three: Receptiveness to candid feedback
To adapt to the culture of "Radical Candor," teams use regular "retrospectives"
    beyond project management. To improve the future, teams commit to
    learning from the past.

Success at Atlassian is defined not just by the technology they sell and the skill sets they hire for. Atlassian's commitment to being an adaptive, networked, and collaborative culture is genuine and it is working. It stands out as the exemplar for companies to study if operating as a platform is their goal. One may argue that it is easier for a company that makes collaborative agility tools to be collaborative and agile. Truth be known, platforms are transforming all industries, whether financial services, education, healthcare or hospitality. All companies are technology companies today, and all companies need to be ready.

Organizational Considerations for Implementing Platforms

As with every technology adoption to date, transitioning to platforms has consequences. Choosing a platform is more than a technical decision. Platforms bring with them new ways of working that present big challenges to traditional management. Flat structures, transparency, active informal networks, and the central role of teams are vital to getting the work done on a platform. Such transformation creates tensions within the existing work structures and requires a deliberate approach to organization redesign. The following three steps are foundational to a successful transition to a platform.

Orchestration of Work

Hierarchies are replaced with a complex orchestration of work. New work design involves building into the platform specific requirements that align with the values and levels of risk tolerance in the organization. These five foundational standards and protocols support the new work style:

1 What needs to get done: work requirements, specifications of the deliverables.

2 Who will do the work: number of people needed, profiles and skill sets to do the work, structure of the team.

3 Who are the stakeholders, their expectations and level of involvement?

4 How will the result be evaluated: quality requirements, evaluation criteria, who will do the evaluation?

5 How will the value be established: intellectual property ownership, rewards, recognition, reputation building?

Permeability of Organizational Boundaries

By design, platforms bring flexibility in accessing talent pools and orchestrating work in a more agile way. Platforms also break down traditional organizational boundaries—be that between teams, internal functions or even with the external labor market. Work flows unrestricted between units engaged in projects and information about the quality of the team, work environment, conflicts, progress, and so on is freely shared. This permeability of boundaries might result in leakage of intellectual property or data, in exposure of internal conflicts to the external world, and potentially in talent leaving the original team because of making connections with other teams or being "poached" by an external organization.

Transparency and Its Risks

Transparency enabled by the platforms can expose both the positives and the negatives of working cultures. This exposure requires a more deliberate shaping and management of reputation across all stakeholders: individuals, teams, units/functions, leaders, and organizations as a whole. As with anything where there is something to lose or gain, it is important to ensure that transparency doesn't lead to reputational losses or manipulation by some mal-intentioned players.

The workplace is the next frontier for the advancement of the new generation of powerful digital platforms. Such technologies are already reshaping workers' experience at large. A note of caution is called for when considering a transition to platforms. The business cultures at Atlassian and Microsoft could serve as a case study of just how to set an organization up for success, how to leverage organizational strengths, and how to control for the downsides.

Endnotes

1 Tufekci, Z (2021) It's all rigged, *The Atlantic*, https://www.theatlantic.com/technology/archive/2021/02/gamestop-mess-shows-internet-rigged-too/618040/ (archived at https://perma.cc/HX47-U727)

2 Shearer, E (2021) More than eight-in-ten Americans get news from digital devices, *Pew Research Center*, https://www.pewresearch.org/fact-tank/2021/01/12/more-than-eight-in-ten-americans-get-news-from-digital-devices/ (archived at https://perma.cc/3LNX-24HY)

3   Van Alstyne, MW, Parker, GG, and Choudary, SP (2016) Pipelines, platforms, and the new rules of strategy: Scale now trumps differentiation, *Harvard Business Review*, https://hbr.org/2016/04/pipelines-platforms-and-the-new-rules-of-strategy (archived at https://perma.cc/86ZK-9MZX)

4   Costa, D (2018) Everything you need to know about applicant tracking systems, *Skeeled*, https://www.skeeled.com/blog/ats-everything-you-need-to-know-about-applicant-tracking-systems (archived at https://perma.cc/ZD52-TGLY)

5   https://www.gloat.com/ (archived at https://perma.cc/5FG8-58TS)

6   https://hitch.works/ (archived at https://perma.cc/HA58-2A3H)

7   https://www.here.com/platform/workspace (archived at https://perma.cc/NG2H-8TN6)

8   https://www.pymetrics.ai/ (archived at https://perma.cc/JS4V-RTXE)

9   https://www.microsoft.com/en-us/microsoft-viva (archived at https://perma.cc/V8V8-27XB)

10 Lardinois, F (2021) Microsoft launches Viva, its new take on the old intranet, *TechCrunch*, https://techcrunch.com/2021/02/04/microsoft-launches-viva-its-new-take-on-the-old-intranet/ (archived at https://perma.cc/M9VR-7DQB)

11 https://news.microsoft.com/2021/02/04/microsoft-unveils-new-employee-experience-platform-microsoft-viva-to-help-people-thrive-at-work/. (archived at https://perma.cc/8TR9-GYUN)

12 Marciano, VM (1995) The origins and development of human resource management, *Academy of Management*, 8 (1), pp 223–27

13 Sendjaya, S and Sarros, JC (2002) Servant leadership: Its origin, development, and application in organizations, *Journal of Leadership Studies*, 9 (2), pp 57–64

14 Wooden, J (1997) *Wooden: A Lifetime of observations and reflections on and off the court*, 1st edition, McGraw-Hill

15 Bezos, J (2017) 2016 Letter to shareholders: Why it is always Day 1 at Amazon, Amazon Website, https://www.aboutamazon.com/news/company-news/2016-letter-to-shareholders (archived at https://perma.cc/75F7-BR54)

16 WNYC (nd) About 'Tell Me More', https://www.wnyc.org/shows/tell-me-more/about/ (archived at https://perma.cc/8YTV-AMKT)

17 Weick, K (nd) Leadership when events don't play by the rules, iMpact Web Portal, https://www.bus.umich.edu/FacultyResearch/Research/TryingTimes/Rules.htm (archived at https://perma.cc/2S77-DHR4)

18 https://www.greatplacetowork.com/certified-company/1100234 (archived at https://perma.cc/CG9B-REY2)

19 Atlassian (nd) We believe all teams can do amazing things when they work Open, https://www.atlassian.com/practices/open# (archived at https://perma.cc/FH3M-237M)

PART FOUR

Worth

09

Why Work? The Rise of Employee Experience

The Turnover Tsunami

In the summer of 2021, major Wall Street investment banks announced increases in the salaries of their junior-level associates.[1] Goldman Sachs, Citi, Morgan Stanley, and JPMorgan Chase responded to media reports of their employees' grueling 90-hour work weeks, unrealistic deadlines, and total burnout while working from home. David Solomon, Goldman Sachs' Chief Executive, sent a voice note to all bank employees pledging that help was on the way. More associates were to be hired, work had to be more evenly distributed, and the firm pledged to uphold the "Saturday rule." Goldman's Saturday rule was established in 2013 and required employees to stop working at 9 pm Friday night until 9 am on Sunday in order to guarantee at least one full day of rest each week.[2] It was clear to the Wall Street stalwarts that financial incentives alone would not buy employee loyalty and stave off workers' growing disengagement.

At the same time, 36,500 front-line workers at McDonald's-owned restaurants across the United States received a 10 percent raise as the company was looking to hire 10,000 additional workers. The company is particularly proud of its benefits packages for hourly employees, which include paid time off, educational benefits through the Archways to Opportunity program, and an employee assistance program for employees and families. "Our first value is taking care of our people, and today we are rewarding our hardworking employees in McDonald's-owned restaurants for serving our communities" was the statement from Joe Erlinger, President of McDonald's USA.[3]

From the investment banks to the fast-food chains, companies' internal employee listening radars were registering high levels of fatigue, burnout, and job restlessness. Early on, SHRM (the Society for Human Resource Management) surveys picked up on the warning signs of the "turnover tsunami," aka the "great resignation," the phenomenon when significant cohorts of workers are considering heading for the exit.[4]

For those paying attention, the reasons for the post-Covid surge in talent mobility could have been predicted. The pandemic further "unmasked" the "great decoupling." Starting in the late 1980s, the vital link connecting work with prosperity and ultimately with happiness was broken.[5] Pay and median family income did not keep up with the relentless advancements in technology. The "War for Talent" yielded winners and losers while general employee engagement levels were plummeting despite significant productivity gains.

The post-Covid generation was reclaiming YOLO, the decades-old acronym that stands for "you only live once."[6] The majority of workers spurned their employers' "back to the office" policies and chose new jobs that allowed them to work more flexibly or work from anywhere. Others looked to turn the page to the next chapter of their careers, became entrepreneurs, chose to pursue their hobbies or special passions, relocated to a place of their choice, or took time off altogether. The trickledown of departures that started in the pandemic with those who could most afford it turned into a waterfall of daily transition announcements on LinkedIn. A few employers were beginning to get in front of the trend and were putting containment measures in place to stave off the impending worker deficit. The traditional response was to return to the basics and pay workers more as a short-term containment measure. More generous benefits were also considered, including flexible work arrangements that were also becoming requisite perks. These are all familiar strings in the employers' bow, the classic hygiene factors that should be considered at the start.[7] The bigger unresolved questions that both employers and employees must wrestle with are deeply human, acutely relevant, and also urgent: why we work and what kind of work is worth showing up for. It is about the new truths about work that the pandemic revealed and about the new set of accommodations and strategies that workers and employers have to settle on to keep moving forward.

The great exodus of employees after the pandemic was a sign that the days of the transactional employment contract were ending. Patience was running thin and the new era of purposeful employment was arriving fast.

Defining Work

FIGURE 9.1   Work: Push vs Pull

The workplace does not exactly run by the laws of physics, but it borrows its core principles and terminology from science and many of the core scientific principles apply to the workplace.

In physics, *work (W)* is defined as "the energy transferred to or from an object via the application of *force (F)* along a *displacement (s)*."[8] Work by itself has no direction. Work transfers energy from one place to another, or one form to another. Without applied force and energy, there is no work. With the evolution of technology, the "labor" or "force" is delivered through intelligent machines while the human workers contribute direction, meaning, innovation, and ultimately deliver outcomes.

To be meaningful and fulfilling, work requires intentional, human organization to achieve desired outcomes. There is no work without a worker. Workers give work energy and direction. The workers come together to work on teams, in organizations, and create work cultures. In return, as Stephen Hawking pointed out, "work gives you meaning and purpose, and life is empty without it."[9]

The story of a NASA custodian's encounter with Robert F. Kennedy is a fitting illustration of how the force of human intention changes the meaning of work. As legend has it, in 1962, President Robert Kennedy was on his first visit to NASA when he encountered a custodian carrying a broom down the hall. When asked what he was doing at NASA, the custodian replied, "I'm helping to put a man on the moon."[10] This employee's excitement to connect his daily work with the direction and purpose of his organization is what every employee and every employer should be aiming to achieve. It is what most organizations today are aspiring to reach.

The hard work of rethinking the purpose of employment and redesigning the workplace to align with that purpose had already been underway before the pandemic, and it has accelerated ever since. Newly discovered "experience of employees" is the best way to connect work purpose with employees' search for meaning in life. Commitment to center people strategy on Employee Experience (EX) offered employers a way to tap into the new sources of organization energy and direction. It also ties up with the organization's pursuit of innovative ways to access work's most powerful force, ie employees' commitment, loyalty, creativity, and drive.

Employee Experience: What Took So Long?

From Silicon Valley to Silicon Alley, today's companies are embracing EX with a vengeance, making it the leading people strategy to date. Yet, to organizational outsiders, EX technology and methods are not new; they look just like an organizational application of the user-centric design principles. By the time the principles of behavioral design finally found their way into organizational management thinking, they had already been around for at least two transformative decades. Donald A. Norman, a computational psychologist, founder of the user-experience approach (UX) and human-centered design evangelist, wrote a decade earlier in his book *Living with Complexity*, "We must design for the way people behave, not for how we would wish them to behave."[11]

Since the Experience Economy arrived in the late 1990s, behavioral-based design principles have transformed economics, product, and technology development, and turned marketing and customer service on their heads. To quote Donald Norman again: "It is not enough that we build products that function, that are understandable and usable, we also need to build products that bring joy and excitement, pleasure and fun, and, yes, beauty to people's lives."[12] Businesses began to prioritize the experience data along with and in addition to operational scorecards. Transparency, feedback, journey mapping, personas, consistency, affordance—these are the terms that capture the fleeting "experiences" that inform key elements of any design.

The first experience-focused cohort of companies such as Starbucks (1971) and Apple (1976) captured the imagination of the new generation of customers to become the world's most valuable brands. Starbucks' iconic Siren logo was also deliberately made asymmetrical to capture some of that imperfect human beauty that everyone could relate to. Apple was called "the original Human" for masterfully capturing the emotional side of technology long before it became commodified. The fact that the first Macintosh computer was designed to have a personality and say "hello" was a huge hit.

As these transformations were taking place in the external market, organizational and people practices behind the companies' firewall were continuing the traditions of the industrial age. Charged with looking after people management, HR was engaged in a campaign of renaming itself "Business Partners." Fundamentally, the HR function continued to maintain its largely administrative role charged with looking after the workforce as a cost center. The Learning and Development departments were faced with staff reductions and ongoing campaigns to justify their existence by proving the ROI of their worth. In the second decade of the 21st century, it was all about to change, with the businesses' "discovery" of Employee Experience. The origin story of EX as a leading people management practice is worth revisiting. It is a story of outsiders to the HR departments who were inspired by a new set of ideals and took a designer's approach to the businesses they set out to create.

CASE STUDY

Airbnb Changed People Management Forever

In late 2020, Airbnb (launched in 2008) conducted the largest IPO of the pandemic year with an improbable valuation of $47 billion. The meteoric market success of the maverick hospitality startup is legendary in its own right. Airbnb's second and often underplayed contribution to the disruptive business model is its deliberate company culture. The founders Brian Chesky and Joe Gebbia, a duo of design school graduates, wanted the company's mission of #belonganywhere to be embedded in all aspects of Airbnb's work culture. Elevating EX as the company's primary focus meant that people management had to be reimagined, redesigned, and measured against a new set of values—the experience of its employees. To achieve those goals, Airbnb had to abandon the centuries-old "scientific management" principles; it got rid of the functional name Human Resources and replaced "People Operations" with EX once and for all. In 2016, Airbnb was ranked #1 on the prestigious Best Places to Work list and EX became the next best way of managing people as the disruptive trend took off.

If you look at the Airbnb logo long enough, you will see in the letter A people, places, love, and a heart.

As Airbnb describe their journey, the turn to EX is the story of returning to the values of a community, of investing in relationships and doubling down on a shared sense of belonging. Belonging used to be the value communities were built on. When people lived in villages, everyone knew each other, and everyone knew where each other's homes were. With the Industrial Revolution and urbanization came alienation, loss of trust, and people felt disconnected from each other. Airbnb believes that they are in the business of recovering and investing in communities and restoring the lost sense of belonging in their customers and hosts as well as in their employees. Airbnb want to be known for restoring the value system where rewards are not financial but relational and fundamentally human:

> That's because the rewards you get from Airbnb aren't just financial—they're personal—for hosts and guests alike. At a time when new technologies have made it easier to keep each other at a distance, you're using them to bring

people together. And you're tapping into the universal human yearning to belong—the desire to feel welcomed, respected, and appreciated for who you are, no matter where you might be. Belonging is the idea that defines Airbnb.[13]

In the words of Mark Levin, Airbnb's first Employee Experience officer, to create the culture of "belong anywhere" he had to design memorable work experiences across all interactions with the employees including recruitment, development, work environment, volunteer experiences available to the employees, even the food they share at work. Being the first in the EX business, the company continued to experiment and iterate. On Glassdoor, 90 percent of Airbnb's employees recommended working for the company 90 percent of the time, making it the top employer several years in a row.

The true stress test of the Airbnb business and its value system came in the first two months of the pandemic when all travel came to a halt. To stop the bleeding the company had to lay off 25 percent of its global workforce, to pivot and innovate from its business model. CEO Brian Chesky was in the spotlight. The steps he took set the bar high for those companies committing to follow EX and the "belong anywhere" culture.

At the time the employee layoffs were announced, Chesky wrote an open letter to the employees communicating his empathy and commitment to do the best the company could do in the situation they were in. "To those leaving Airbnb, I am truly sorry. Please know this is not your fault."[14] Chesky went on to explain the benefits that the company was extending to all leaving the company including year-long health insurance benefits—life-saving during the pandemic—and setting up an external website to help employees find new jobs.

From the lowest point during the pandemic to the U-turn in the business and an off-the-charts IPO, Airbnb stayed the course on its commitment to putting its stakeholders' experience first. The company sees the experience of belonging as giving its business the energy, drive, and resilience it needs to remain the innovator and pioneer in the hospitality business it is committed to continuing to reinvent.

Employee Experience Is Not About the Tools

Employee Experience is often defined as an intentionally designed employment journey: from candidate experience and recruitment to employee onboarding, performance and feedback, learning and development, career progression, succession, rewards, recognition, benefits and finally, the exit. The employment journey is monitored and technologically supported through its multiple stages. The stated intention is to increase employee retention, engagement, and productivity. The key design idea is to mirror the established customer journey mapping process into the workforce. The sheer volume of collected employee data and complex technology tools that support the implementation of the EX process makes this approach heavily dependent on advanced analytics support and workplace technology infrastructure. It is also a question of scale and reach and the availability of highly skilled analytics and technology professionals to support EX initiatives in distributed organizations.

The costs of running a competent and adequately supported EX function represent perhaps one of the most significant financial and human capital investments companies can make into workforce support and development. According to Josh Bersin, the leading workplace technology analyst, the total global spend on EX technologies and processes to date may be close to $200 billion.[15] The question that naturally comes up is why today? What is the real value of EX investment? How is the successful EX function being measured and what can go wrong?

Work tech analysts and organizational consultants may successfully try to convince Chief HR Officers that the EX trend is about technology and process implementation. From the evolution of technology and data analysis perspective, EX tools sit on top of the organizational maturity pyramid. But starting on the EX path with technology alone can divert attention and resources from the larger cultural project and lock companies into expensive technology programs with no tangible outcomes. There is a growing awareness among the technology community of the limitations of their own thinking when it comes to the impact and leverage that their tools have on humans:

> I can safely say that we in tech don't understand the emotional aspect
> of our work, just as we don't understand the moral imperative of what

we do. It is not that all players are bad; it is just not part of the thinking process the way, say, "minimum viable product" or "growth hacking" are.[16]

Where most organizations stand now, there is an unquestioning deference to technology and data experts within people management departments. When it comes to setting up a successful EX function the project cannot be left to the consultants and technology vendors alone. The adoption of EX technologies needs to be based on the considerations of company culture, its purpose, and the desired impact on the employees. Done right it is about the culture change first and technology and process second.

Here are a few important questions to ask before selecting EX technology:

- What assumptions about employees is this technology built upon?
- What impact will it have on the current culture?
- Whom will this approach benefit most?
- What new skills does this technology require?
- What jobs and tasks will this technology displace?
- How will this technology change other aspects of people management?
- How will this technology affect the way employees relate to each other and collaborate?
- How will this technology affect how employees, managers, and leaders communicate?
- What new practices will this technology cultivate?
- What current practices will this technology displace?
- How does this technology reallocate management's/employees' time?
- What unintended consequences might this technology entail?
- Who will take full responsibility for the consequences of this technology?

When Airbnb launched EX, the company's leaders were singularly focused on creating a shared sense of belonging and community among employees. They were looking to recapture the lost sense of community in modern life. They wanted to seek the deeper meaning of work. The technology to support their mission was developed later, after the culture of EX took off. Companies embarking on the EX journey today have the advantage of learning from many others ahead of them. Yet, they cannot outsource the hard work of thinking through the meaning of the EX approach to their work and their culture. They need to know exactly what it will require to succeed in this project.

The Search for the Meaning of Work

Among many lessons the post-pandemic turnover taught the world was that most workers today still experience a "deficit of meaning" at work. Changing jobs in search of a better job fit could have been one of the reasons why so many headed for the exit once the pandemic receded. It seems that companies that seek to achieve the heights of engagement, loyalty, and commitment have to help their employees to connect with their true purpose at work. One should avoid the trap of assuming that technology and process could do the hard work of building a purposeful business and culture. It is also not the case that marketing and customer service could offer an authentic and lasting model. Researchers have confirmed in multiple studies that a positive link exists between people working and their sense of purpose.[17]

The destructive impact of consumerism in Western societies is a factor. Efforts by marketers, advertisers, and social media to replace the hard search for the meaning of life and work with seemingly easily accessible products led to the overall population's disengagement from work. Consumerism is at the heart of neoclassical economics; it encourages conspicuous consumption of goods and services as life's singular goal. In the consumerist society, people consume not to satisfy their basic needs but to meet all of their extrinsic goals.[18] Consumerism as an ideology has proven the existential harm it causes to individuals and communities alike. Critiques of consumerism as an economic and personal position in life are multiple; consumer-centered economics are blamed for the externalities leading to environmental and social damages globally.

From the workplace values perspective, consumerism is criticized for being a leading cause of a loss of satisfaction with work. Consumerism orientation in workers is associated with extreme status anxiety that may lead to stress and depression. Further psychological research shows that individuals who live their lives to achieve consumerist goals are prone to greater levels of dissatisfaction with their relationships at home and at work.

Researchers who study the meaning of work identify three categories of workers today: those who hold jobs, those who strive for a career, and the third group that pursues a calling. Each of these groups is motivated by a different set of incentives, and each experiences their workplace differently:

Extrinsic motivation. The majority of the working population, research shows, are job holders whose main source of motivation is extrinsic. Increases in pay and benefits are deemed to be the leading motivators for this group. The needs of these employees are easier to anticipate, track, and address. Regular performance reviews, engagement surveys, and the existing tech tools can perfectly identify issues and bring them to the manager's attention. The current EX platforms are designed to meet the needs of this group. Find out where the disconnect occurs on the employment journey and address needs in a timely way.

Career motivation. The second big employee category is those most invested in building a career. They are ambitious, upwardly mobile, and committed to learning and updating their skills. They may accept a compromise on extrinsic rewards for the benefit of learning, advancement, and professional exposure. Their journeys may not always be linear and their rewards are not always climbing up, but in the long run, great careers are being built, new businesses started. Technologies are catching up to meet the motivations of this career-focused group. AI, for example, is particularly well suited to meet this ambitious group's needs. When applied to learning and development, AI prompts and nudges employees to learn new skills, recommends a new project to take on, and helps build out networks and relationships. Granted that this technology is made available to all, it will take personal motivation to turn it into a skill and a career.

The third group are motivated by their *life calling*. These individuals are the most committed ones. They reach for the highest level of values on the values pyramid. These employees cannot be developed, they have to be recruited and brought on board. Like heat-seeking missiles, they find the work that aligns with who they are. The power of intrinsic motivation is so strong, almost sacrosanct, that management needs to look after these people to make sure that their needs are fairly addressed and their accomplishments are fairly rewarded.

In reality, there is always a hybrid type; employees whose motivations are complex and multiple, need autonomy and flexibility to adjust and realign their motives and their jobs.

We come full circle in the discussion of the rise of Employee Experience. To stave off departures and turnover, all aspects of EX need to be activated. Technology may diagnose and surface the issues but it comes down to having a worker-centric culture that helps with the bigger context and serves organizations a longer run. Airbnb got it right. They broke away from traditions of building organizations, changed the language they spoke about their culture, and most importantly, they prioritized the deeply personal goal of getting everyone to "belong." Airbnb built the culture before they brought the tools. It worked exceptionally well for the company that within one decade has gone from a bold idea to an experiment and on to market success. The most remarkable achievement is that they brought their workers along on the journey.

Endnotes

1 We discuss the case of Goldman Sachs analysts' PowerPoint presentation published in *The New York Times* in Chapter 7

2 Marshall, ED (2021) Goldman CEO to junior bankers: we are sending you more resources, *Reuters*, https://www.reuters.com/business/sustainable-business/goldman-ceo-junior-bankers-we-are-sending-you-more-resources-2021-03-22/ (archived at https://perma.cc/A3DQ-QYWG)

3 McDonald's (2021) McDonald's USA to raise wages at company-owned restaurants across the country, https://corporate.mcdonalds.com/corpmcd/en-us/our-stories/article/.mcopco-wage-raise.html (archived at https://perma.cc/ECS7-UWP3)

4 Mauer, R (2021) Turnover 'tsunami' expected once pandemic ends, *Recruiting News Network*, https://www.recruitingnewsnetwork.com/posts/turnover-tsunami-expected-once-pandemic-ends (archived at https://perma.cc/L8P5-X8EX)

5 Brynjolfsson, E and McAfee, A (2013) The great decoupling, *New Perspectives Quarterly*, 30 (1), pp 61–63

6 Roose, K (2021) Welcome to the YOLO economy, *New York Times*, https://www.nytimes.com/2021/04/21/technology/welcome-to-the-yolo-economy.html (archived at https://perma.cc/J45G-NG6X)

7 Meyers, A (2021) The pandemic has forced people to rethink what they want from a job, but pay, benefits still top the list, *Morning Consult*, https://morningconsult.com/2021/08/02/workplace-incentives-to-join-leave-polling/ (archived at https://perma.cc/RBT8-LL7D). The polling offers some insights into the motives of today's job hoppers. The largest group of those polled (31%) would opt for the higher salary and 29% for generous benefits and PTO. Flexible schedules (15%) and remote working (11%) also come as important categories of incentives. Though significant, flexibility is more likely to be targeted to specific demographic groups, especially women. The third group of emerging items is worthy of note, and reflects today's issues: 6% of respondents would join a company that does not make any political donations; 3% would join companies that require vaccinations and observe strict health protocols; and 2% would go with an employer that does not enforce masks and vaccines

8 Work (physics) (nd) *Wikipedia*, https://en.wikipedia.org/wiki/Work_(physics) (archived at https://perma.cc/Q6ST-EDTN)

9 ABC World News with Diane Sawyer (2010) Conversation with Stephen Hawking

10 Nemo, J (2014) What a NASA janitor can teach us about living a bigger life, *Biz Journals* (blog), https://www.bizjournals.com/bizjournals/how-to/growth-strategies/2014/12/what-a-nasa-janitor-can-teach-us.html (archived at https://perma.cc/KM99-XTMG)

11 Norman, DA (2011) *Living With Complexity*, Cambridge, MA: MIT Press

12 Ibid.

13 Airbnb (nd) belong anywhere, https://blog.atairbnb.com/belong-anywhere/ (archived at https://perma.cc/6FRW-EDL9)

14 Chesky, B (2020) A message from co-founder and CEO Brian Chesky, https://news.airbnb.com/a-message-from-co-founder-and-ceo-brian-chesky/ (archived at https://perma.cc/5977-2S7G)

15 Bersin, J (2021) Employee experience, https://joshbersin.com/ex-definitive-guide-2021/ (archived at https://perma.cc/D7FQ-E3PE)

16 Malik, OM (2021) Technology and the moral dimension, https://om.co/2014/11/26/technology-and-the-moral-dimension/ (archived at https://perma.cc/42FM-MXMN)

17 Baldoni, J (2012) *Lead With Purpose: Giving your organization a reason to believe in itself*, New York: Amacom

18 Hayes, A (2021) Consumerism, *Investopedia*, https://www.investopedia.com/terms/c/consumerism.asp (archived at https://perma.cc/Z2BQ-6EB5)

10

Work Reputation as Experience

❦

Four Historical Stages of Reputation

Reputation is work's social oxygen. Work does not happen in a vacuum but in the social context of a group, a team, an organization, and society at large. Reputation is work's traded social currency. Just like any currency, it changes with the times and in the context of different social and cultural realities. Reputation historically evolved as work's long social shadow from honor to brand and from a persona to an avatar. In this chapter we examine the evolution of reputation as a social and organizational asset. We review the effect of its evolution on the workplace and its connection to rewards. We discuss the opportunities offered by smart technologies in the building of reputations, and reflect on the significance of reputational downsides. We review four stages in the development of reputation and work:

1 Reputation as honor (Pre-Industrial).

2 Reputation as an asset (Industrialization and early Internet).

3 Reputation as a currency (Platforms, Avatars, AI).

4 Reputation as an experience (Metaverse).

Because reputation as a social institution reaches deeply into the cultural fabric of society at large, each historical stage remains present in the subsequent reputational conventions surpassing it. At each of the four stages, a new order of social incentives is created to seek and

FIGURE 10.1   Evolution of Reputation

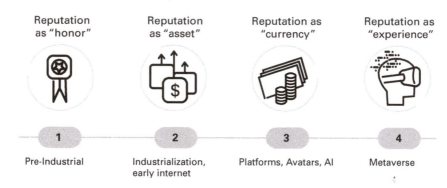

Reputation as "honor"	Reputation as "asset"	Reputation as "currency"	Reputation as "experience"
1	**2**	**3**	**4**
Pre-Industrial	Industrialization, early internet	Platforms, Avatars, AI	Metaverse

maintain certain reputations. Reputations are rewarded in multiple different ways. As much as we need to pay attention to the building of reputations and understand their rewards, we need to pay attention to reputational losses, which often shed the most light on the specifics of each historical moment in reputation building.

Reputation and its Discontents

"On the internet no one knows you are a dog." This famous 1993 *New Yorker* cartoon by the artist Peter Steiner marked the coming of the new age in how reputations were shaped, evaluated, maintained, lost, recovered, and ultimately rewarded. It is fair to say that the '90s was the watershed time when the powers of the internet were being discovered by advertisers, companies, and consumers alike. Even though it would take another decade for social networks to come online and become a social force, the very existence of the internet made it abundantly clear that the connecting lines between one's image and one's actual behavior, performance, accomplishments, and expertise were becoming more and more tenuous.

FIGURE 10.2   Everyone is a Dog on the Internet

With technology platforms replacing "word of mouth" as the medium in which reputations live and flourish today, the new era of reputation management has transformed what reputation used to be into a standalone social asset. Technology added significant new opportunities and set up dangerous traps for developing reputations. Today's challenges facing "reputation" in organizations were best described by the actor Matt Damon playing Tom Ripley, a fictional character representing the original con man. Ripley's line, "It's better to be a fake somebody than a real nobody," captured the disconnect and perverse incentives built into the institution of reputation today.[1] One of the growing challenges today is that present-day reputations are being transformed into brands that command significant financial and social rewards. Individuals, teams, companies, and society at large are faced with significant stakes and consequences where their reputations are concerned. The "fake it 'til you make it" phenomenon, memorialized as early as 1968 in Simon and Garfunkel's single "Faking It," has developed into a present-day movement commanding its own trends in pseudoscience, philosophy, and politics. It has been amplified with the proliferation of "fake news," online "bots," and further with synthetic voice and video, including deep fakes. A sprawling service industry has emerged and is thriving, focused on manufacturing, repairing, and augmenting reputations and public identities. A disproportionate share of marketing attention and financial investment has been given to the technologies that extend the reaches of reputation in the media and beyond. We now must equally commit to putting some serious brakes on what technology is able to do with reputation building and perform authenticity and ethics audits before its connection to reality is completely torn down.

Historically, the concept of someone's "reputation" has been defined as "the opinion that people in general have about someone or something, or how much respect or admiration someone or something receives based on past behavior or character."[2] Societal order was built on the continuity of shared reputations and wielded significant power of social control over citizens. Any individual or organization today has to prioritize their commitment to authentic, "nuclear" values and missions along with creating an image of themselves that they project to markets, communities, and their own employees/workers. Companies striving to scale and amplify reputational rewards should be equally concerned with investing in and preserving authentic "nuclear" reputation over the external brand. Maintaining a balance between committing to a reputation and pursuing its rewards is becoming more challenging. It is getting easier than ever to cheat in favor of incentives and skip on building the "nuclear" reputation itself. A healthy reflection on how we got to this point offers important lessons for the future.

Reputation as Honor

A cursory detour into the history of Western civilization shows that "reputation" has been a central theme in life, literature, and societal mores for millennia. Up until the Industrial Revolution, reputation was often referred to in the form of "honor," "fame," and "integrity." Honor (reputation) was traditionally defined by the nature of the bond between a person and society, and was derived from a personal power one acquired as a consequence of moral and ethical excellence and personal uprightness.[3] Honor could be traced back to the most ancient social institutions and stood for integrity, service, and continuity of one's reputation recognized and rewarded by the community. Despite all the changes that technologies and social habits have introduced to reputation since then, "honor" persists in its original form in certain professions even today. It is represented in the military, police officers, and firefighters who give up their lives in the service of everyone's safety.

When it comes to the origins of "reputation," all roads lead to Greece. Take *The Iliad*, an epic poem about the war between the Greeks and the City of Troy. It was written down circa the 8th century BC from multiple narrative accounts and is attributed to the Greek poet, Homer. Together with *The Odyssey*, its sequel, it is considered to be the first recorded masterpiece of Western literature. Pursuits of honor, pride, and glorious reputation represent central themes in both *The Iliad* and *The Odyssey*. The Iliad starts with a conversation among warriors about military honor and glory, asserting that Troy's surrender was "a thing... whose glory shall perish never." Military honor in ancient Greece was afforded through the recognition and respect of others and was the most sought-after signifier of status in the eyes of the ancient Hellenes. Loss of honor was equivalent to being ostracized in the eyes of peers and banished from society. Restoring lost honor was the only way to prove oneself worthy of being a member of a community.

The discussions of honor are central throughout the Bible. Defined as "honesty, fairness, or integrity in one's beliefs or actions," honor is afforded not only to people of authority but to all people who deserve to be treated with dignity and respect. "Honor everyone. Love the brotherhood. Fear God. Honor the emperor."[4]

For William Shakespeare, the theme of "honor" takes center stage in all of the plays and throughout his work. There is a famous line in *Richard II* that captures the importance of the "honor" theme in this historical tragedy: "Mine honor is my life, both grow in one. Take honor from me, and my life is done"[5] (1595). Wars were fought and lost defending one's honor and in the service of it. "Life every man holds dear; but the dear man holds honor far more precious dear than life," Shakespeare wrote again in *Troilus and Cressida*, a play dedicated to the Trojan war.[6]

The Framers of the US Constitution signed into the Declaration of Independence a line about upholding an "honor": "We mutually pledge to each other our Lives, our Fortunes and our sacred Honor."[7] The culture of honor was emphatically followed in the American South. The extremes of upholding honor were manifested in the duels that took place during the early 20th century; by participating in duels, men defended their honor, often at the expense of their lives.

There are at least two ways in which the "honor" tradition continues to live and to be relevant in today's organizations. It is the cornerstone of company "culture" as it relies on the shared norms of collective behavior, not on compliance and employment laws. Just like the "honor code," strong cultural norms are more powerful enforcers of behaviors than explicit rules, compliance requirements, and written directives. On a personal level, it is the observance of the "honor" system and integrity that drive desired workplace behaviors and habits rather than top-down management. Personal "honor" remains the foundation of every reputation; it matters on a team, in an organization, and in society at large.

Reputation as an Asset

"It is not from the benevolence of the butcher, the brewer, or the baker that we expect our dinner, but from their regard to their own interest."[8] This famous comment by Adam Smith in *The Wealth of Nations* marked the transition to labor. From that time on, reputation began to be viewed in economic terms. What Smith's observation reflected was the societal transformation from artisanal end-to-end production to the division of labor. Industrialization broke down craftsmanship into tasks and assigned discrete skills to the execution of those tasks. The early machines could not operate without human assistance and humans became extensions of the machines. Worker productivity rose through specialization and was priced against the market depending on how skilled the workers needed to be to execute the particular tasks.[9]

Human capital took center stage, first with the transition from agrarian societies to early industrialized ones in the 18th–19th centuries, and later with modernization in the early 20th century. Artisans were replaced with laborers; labor was seen as distinct from craftsmanship; work was broken down into tasks; tasks required possession of certain skills associated with those tasks. The complex interplay between unskilled, mid-skilled, and highly skilled occupations and their linkage with developing technology and tools has continued in the much-expanded job market today. Whereas demand for low-skilled and middle-skilled occupations has ebbed and flowed, the steadily growing need for highly specialized professions that started in the mid-19th century has continued to today.

The demand for professional, technical, and managerial qualifications never declined. Education became a proxy for the complexity of skills required in those jobs. Higher levels of schooling became associated with access to mid- and higher-level employment that guaranteed sustainable economic success. Wages and reputations were distributed according to the market and social value of those skills.

The very first recorded promotion of a professional background goes back to Renaissance Italy and is attributed to Leonardo DaVinci. In 1482, at 30 years old, DaVinci had an account of his skills and accomplishments written down while seeking the patronage and sponsorship of the Duke of Milan. He did get hired and was commissioned to paint *The Last Supper* for his employer and patron, Ludovico Sforza.

The fact that several centuries had to elapse before the *résumé* (French for summary) or *curriculum vitae* (CV, the life journey) came into their own to become a required record of one's professional background signals that professional reputation was primarily a product of one's position in society while employment was found through family relationships and close-knit connections. Jobs were for life. Attending certain universities guaranteed access to premier employment opportunities that bestowed social status. It was not until the early 20th century when the job market became more diversified and distributed that there was a need for a resume. An independent record of one's professional background became essential as social mobility increased. In the 1930s–1950s resumes became common. One's age, height and weight, marital status, even family origins along with a photo of oneself were required items, and career experts warned against inflating one's accomplishments too much for fear of appearing conceited.

Reputation as Currency

Back to the *New Yorker* cartoon of the dog in the 1990s, the internet engine and the anonymity of digital media widened the gap between a person and their reputation. As jobs became plentiful, job mobility increased and most skills grew to be more sophisticated and diversified, "resumes" became ubiquitous, and reputations took on a life of their own. Creating professional reputations through resume writing and interview preparation grew to be a multi-billion-dollar market. Resumes turned into a product to sell rather than an accurate record of an individual's skills and experiences.[10] As more recruiters began to use automated services to screen incoming applications, standardization of resume writing became a feature. With automation came standardized, formulaic templates that made such services more accessible and affordable. When it came to traditional reputation building, personal references and recommendations continued to serve a critical role. Online transparency became the path to social validation and—as with everything internet—it turned out that referrals and recommendations could also be hacked.

The launch of LinkedIn (2002) marked the new digital era in professional reputation building. There was no question of the advantages of an online professional presence over traditional handwritten resumes. Digital profiles allowed the information to stay current, updated with latest jobs, projects, skills development, and most importantly, more recent recommendations. That made one's professional networks transparent. What became apparent though is that trust and accuracy of the information provided could be in question.

How can an online reputation be validated, double-checked, and cross-referenced against reality? Although LinkedIn has come up as the most trusted social media platform,[11] there is still a gap between one's online presence and the reality of a person behind their online profile. The competition for followers and likes on LinkedIn is no less real and fierce than on the battlefields of Troy, although unlike the Trojan war, key battles are now being fought in the comfort of the digital domain. Today's online popularity contests have replaced war heroes and honor duels; a different skill set is involved in winning digital reputational battles.

One's professional reputation today runs on two distinct and at times overlapping tracks. On the one hand, it is the internally focused "self" that is based on real-life experiences, education, work, and hobbies. On the other, it is the online persona created, validated, and cheered on by the audience it seeks. In fact, the meaning of a reputation today is associated primarily with the external image and perception of performance rather than the performance itself. Present-day "reputation" is used interchangeably with branding, image building, and online identity. It is becoming further removed from the authentic person themselves. The era of the reputational economy has arrived. From individuals to organizations and from governments to countries and their institutions, reputations have proliferated into all aspects of life and work to become a highly sought-after social "currency."

Reputational rewards are often ranked higher than financial rewards. Reputations are set up to proactively anticipate an audience's needs and influence public perceptions as well as seize opportunities to cater to those expectations. Digital media made digital reputations accessible to all and they are now being proactively cultivated and shaped by individuals and organizations alike.

In 2012, the *Oxford Handbook of Corporate Reputation* became the first definitive compendium on the questions of corporate reputation. After two decades of disruptive innovation and experimentation, key questions of what business reputations really were finally got their answers.[12] The questions asked of an organization's reputation were the same as those of individuals, but the answers were different:

- What do "good" or "bad" reputations really mean today?
- What is the value of a reputation?
- How could that value be measured and managed?
- How could particular reputations be pursued or avoided?
- How does an organization's reputation align with those of individual employees?

Any company's reputation management today creates new opportunities and a new set of challenges from a workplace perspective. The digital speed with which reputations travel makes companies' firewalls much more permeable. The reputations of a company and its employees are more intertwined, and every company today needs to pay attention to its employees, not only its external stakeholders, its customers, investors, and suppliers. Companies are uniquely dependent on what their employees do and how they think.

The platform Glassdoor (2007) built its business as the site that conducts internal company reviews, receives salaries information directly from employees of large to medium companies, and openly shares them for the public to see. Glassdoor's genius was in creating a virtual public square for employees and their employers to openly negotiate their companies' reputations based on crowdsourced data. The bad and good reviews on Glassdoor matter equally and so does a company's response. As noted on Glassdoor's site, almost eight in ten (76 percent) of Glassdoor users admit that their perception of a company improves after seeing how an employer responds and acts on a review:

> Whether or not that review is critical—maybe even more so if it is
> negative—job seekers want to know how a company responds to
> adversity because it reveals the true character of your company culture.
> How a company handles obstacles and stumbling blocks will define
> their reputation for future employees. And being silent doesn't mean
> you're not in the conversation—it just means you're not leading it.[13]

As organizations' reputations become more fluid and interdependent, attention needs to be given to closing multiple reputational gaps: between external reality and internal perceptions, between a company's values and the employee experience, and between actual performance and reputation management. One thing is certain—the value of reputational currency is on the rise. As new technologies are coming online, the next generation of "reputation management" in the workplace will have new challenges to face and new solutions to offer. The reputational stakes are getting higher and the social goalposts are constantly moving. What has become abundantly clear is that the parallel set of governing structures, protections, rights, norms, and social obligations that has ruled real-world interactions does not exist in the digital world. Everything from surveillance to "nudging" and to reputation manipulation—all outside of any governing constraints—leads to an urgency to design reputational systems that would change the entire ecosystem and its governance in anticipation of the next technological shift.

Reputation as Experience

In late July 2021, Mark Zuckerberg, Facebook's CEO, announced on the earnings call the launch of public testing for Horizon Workrooms, a free app for Facebook's Oculus Quest 2, the virtual reality headset.[14] The device lets users participate in virtual meetings as avatars.

Facebook announced on its website that its vision for the future of work was to add a third solution to the debate about the hybrid workplace: the Metaverse. For a few years prior, Facebook had been experimenting with Horizon Workrooms for the company's internal meetings, letting teams meet in the three-dimensional world. Zuckerberg himself wrote in a company blog that in the future, people would be using the Metaverse primarily to work together.

> Workrooms is our flagship collaboration experience that lets people come together to work in the same virtual room, regardless of physical distance. It works across both virtual reality and the web and is

designed to improve your team's ability to collaborate, communicate, and connect remotely, through the power of VR—whether that's getting together to brainstorm or whiteboard an idea, work on a document, hear updates from your team, hang out and socialize, or simply have better conversations that flow more naturally.[15]

Simply put, the Metaverse is being promoted as the successor environment to mobile internet technology. Instead of looking at the flat screen from outside, such as with Zoom meetings or smart phone screens, one could be inside that medium, interacting with colleagues, traveling, shopping, or generally going about one's virtual business. It is the three-dimensional world in which virtual reality (VR), augmented reality (AR), and extended reality (XR) merge with physical reality. *The Wall Street Journal* described the Metaverse as "an extensive online world transcending individual tech platforms, where people exist in immersive, shared virtual spaces. Through avatars, people would be able to try on items available in stores or attend concerts with friends, just as they would offline."[16]

Facebook is not the only one prospecting in the Wild West of today's Metaverse. Microsoft's CEO Satya Nadella, just a few days after Zuckerberg's call, made a revealing admission about his company's commitments: "As the digital and physical worlds converge, we are leading in a new layer of the infrastructure stack, the enterprise Metaverse."[17] Other players, investors, creators, and entrepreneurs have been laying claim to different parts of the Metaverse real estate. Cryptocurrencies are claiming to be beginning to seriously compete with the dollar-backed global financial system. Decentraland, a virtual blockchain-backed world launched in 2017, uses its own currency, MANA. The Decentraland community fluctuates between a few hundred people to a few thousand at its peak. Ownership of virtual land in Decentraland is bought and sold in the form of non-fungible tokens (NFTs). A non-profit Decentraland foundation governs the virtual land that is more of a virtual infrastructure than a real place.[18] Gaming companies such as Epic Games have been in the virtual world and avatar business the longest. NFTs are overtaking the creator economy, promising opportunities it never had before. In short, the Metaverse is more than the familiar virtual world, it is a new domain of interconnected business where interactions and transactions are taking place.

Facebook's Horizon Workrooms asserts the first real claim to the mixed reality workplace, creating new rules of engagement in the new world of work where one can recreate one's physical office everywhere one goes, participate in virtual meetings, and collaborate with others beaming in or in person. Here is how Mark Zuckerberg describes a Horizon Workrooms meeting:

> A lot of the meetings that we have today, you're looking at a grid of faces on a screen. That's not how we process things either. We're used to being in a room with people and having a sense of space where if you're sitting to my right, then that means I'm also sitting to your left, so we have some shared sense of space in common… In the future, instead of just doing this over a phone call, you'll be able to sit as a hologram on my couch, or I'll be able to sit as a hologram on your couch, and it'll actually feel like we're in the same place, even if we're in different states or hundreds of miles apart.[19]

What does the Metaverse have to offer to the ever-evolving institution of Reputation? Just like before, this technology represents a double-edged sword of opportunity and threat. Today's reputations are largely dependent on knowing the real person and on others' ability to predict the person's/organization's actions and rely on this predictability in future decisions. Online reputations are still largely moored in reality via technology; they are a sum total of multiple and verifiable data points about a person or an organization. Imagine a future where individuals and companies spend more time in virtual worlds where little or no data aggregation is available and could be easily traded. All data will be owned by sovereign individuals themselves or controlled by sovereign entities in the Metaverse. Personal data will be anonymous, unstructured, and decentralized by a degree much greater than anything existing today. This begs the question of our ability to access authentic facts, data, and humans. Will the Metaverse amplify the very real challenges that emerged with the introduction of the internet in the 1990s? On the bright side, what new opportunities will it create for building and maintaining reputations? How should we prepare for the coming benefits and unanticipated costs and harms the Metaverse may inadvertently create?

Next to no oversight exists in the Metaverse today. There are no agreed-upon norms and standards and its denizens are predominantly male. Cathy Hackl, the futurist, author, and one of the very few female participants, noted on the challenges of Metaverse: "I don't want to turn to the Metaverse to escape reality. I don't want to have that dystopian view of it. In some ways the Metaverse is an extension of humanity and creativity, where we're heading next."[20] Hackl reminds us that "escaping reality" is a very real possibility in the Metaverse if the technology is left to the geeks alone. Without the vigilance of guardians in the service of humanity, the dystopian world we have been reading about in science fiction may be closer than we think.

Reputation has been intrinsically associated with work through the ages. Reputation, as did work, evolved from the highly personal system that valued "honor" higher than life, to being a personal asset and a social currency in the industrial and information ages. Today, both work and reputation are faced with the real possibility of being further and further disassociated from each other, from the humans responsible for them, and from real life. The question of how to keep humanity human, reality real, and life meaningful has never been more consequential. In this book, we tried to raise these questions, but the answers still have to be collectively discovered.

Endnotes

1 Minghella, A (1999) *The Talented Mr. Ripley* (Movie)
2 *Cambridge Dictionary of the US Language*: Reputation
3 Johnson, S (1983) *A Dictionary of the English Language*, London: Times Books
4 *The Holy Bible*, New International Version, NIV (1973) 1 Peter 2:17
5 Shakespeare, W (2015) *Richard II*, Minneapolis, MN: First Avenue Editions, A division of Lerner Publishing Group (1.1.182-185)
6 Mētsē, E (2019) *Troilus and Cressida: A critical reader*, London: The Arden Shakespeare

7 Library of Congress Law Library, Issuing Body (1987) *The American Constitution: Its global heritage*, Washington, DC: Law Library, Library of Congress

8 Smith, A, Skinner, AS, and Drexel University, FO (1982) *The Wealth of Nations, Books I-III*, Penguin Books

9 Katz, LF and Margo, RA (2013) Technical change and the relative demand for skilled labor: The United States in historical perspective, *National Bureau of Economic Research*, https://www.nber.org/papers/w18752 (archived at https://perma.cc/7K3H-7HY5)

10 IBISWorld (2019) Resume writing and editing services in the US industry trends (2015–2020), https://www.ibisworld.com/united-states/market-research-reports/document-preparation-services-industry/ (archived at https://perma.cc/NLN8-B9QW)

11 Business Insider (2020) US Trust Study of Social Media, https://www.businessinsider.com/us-digital-trust-study-from-insider-intelligence-2020-9 (archived at https://perma.cc/785L-ZEU9)

12 Barnett, ML et al (2012) *The Oxford Handbook of Corporate Reputation*, 1st edition, Oxford: Oxford University Press

13 Glassdoor (nd) What is employer branding? https://www.glassdoor.com/employers/what-is-employer-branding/ (archived at https://perma.cc/Z344-NMPV)

14 Stein, S (2021) Mark Zuckerberg on Facebook's VR future, *C/NET*, https://www.cnet.com/features/mark-zuckerberg-on-facebook-vr-future-new-sensors-on-quest-pro-fitness-and-a-metaverse-for-work/ (archived at https://perma.cc/2PQV-AY86)

15 Facebook (2021) Introducing Horizon Workrooms remote collaboration reimagined, https://about.fb.com/news/2021/08/introducing-horizon-workrooms-remote-collaboration-reimagined/ (archived at https://perma.cc/4KXH-QEK6)

16 Bobrowsky, M (2021) Roblox, Facebook see the Metaverse as key to the Internet's next phase, *Wall Street Journal*, https://www.wsj.com/articles/roblox-facebook-see-the-metaverse-as-key-to-the-internets-next-phase-11629286200 (archived at https://perma.cc/KB86-VBUB)

17 Nadella, S (2021) Q2 earnings call 2021, https://www.microsoft.com/en-us/Investor/events/FY-2021/earnings-fy-2021-q2.aspx (archived at https://perma.cc/UB6X-VHA7)

18 Decentraland.org (archived at https://perma.cc/F2NP-3C5W)

19 Stein, S (2021) Mark Zuckerberg on Facebook's VR future, *C/NET*, https://
www.cnet.com/features/mark-zuckerberg-on-facebook-vr-future-new-sensors-
on-quest-pro-fitness-and-a-metaverse-for-work/ (archived at https://perma.cc/
VR5P-EHPC)

20 Hackl, C (nd) The Future Insiders Podcast with Cathy Hackl, https://
futureinsiders.com/ (archived at https://perma.cc/EQR8-CLMB)

Conclusion

Instead of writing a summary of what was already explained in the book, we want to end our journey together with a manifesto, the Humans at Work Manifesto.

What Is a Manifesto?

A manifesto is a public declaration by an issuer (one or a collective of individuals) that articulates their position, ideas, and opinions. It is written in the name of a group with a common purpose, ideology, or point of view. It is typically authored by nonconformists and at the core articulates moral guidelines and principles to lead the way into the future. They usually start a movement.

As with most of the concepts described in this book, there is a long history of manifestos. There are manifestos that govern societies, such as the UN's Universal Declaration of Human Rights,[1] or define political governance, such as the Labour Party Manifesto.[2] They also shape professional fields such as design, with the "First Things First 2000, A Design Manifesto,"[3] or software development, with the "Agile Manifesto."[4] Some manifestos are highly controversial and polarizing, such as the "Industrial Society and Its Future"[5] (Unabomber Manifesto) or the Cypherpunk's Manifesto,[6] focused on cyber-privacy.

Why a Manifesto?

We believe there is an urgency to act. Now is the time to make big decisions about the workplace. In a standoff between tech and humans, tech is beginning to prevail. We need new ground rules for how we engage with WorkTech to ensure that humans are not displaced in pursuit of automation. We need to reimagine the workplace and create an inclusive environment for everyone to flourish. Humans need to shape their destiny and lead the work of the future.

Humans at Work Manifesto

FIGURE 11.1   Humans at Work Manifesto

1 **People** over Human Capital.

2 **Work** over Jobs.

3 **Workplace** over Office.

4 **Stakeholder Value** over Shareholder Value.

5 **Worker Journeys** over HR Processes.

6 **Worker Experience** over Worker Efficiency.

7 **Human-centric WorkTech** over Smart Tech.

8 **Impact** over Productivity.

9 **Iterations** over Transformations.

10 **Inclusive** over Standardized.

11 **Simplicity** over Complicatedness.

12 **Networks** over Hierarchies.

13 **Trust** over Control.

1 People over human capital

People are not human resources anymore. *People* at work are unique in their needs, aspirations, life stages, and expectations. Start with people, not resources, nor labor, nor assets, nor means of production, nor capital, and not the unicorns that will match all the requirements a manager would ask for.

2 Work over jobs

Work is not the job description. Distill the essence of what needs to be done and find *who* can do it. It is a matter of work orchestration vs "unicorn" hunting.

3 Workplace over office

Workplace is not the office. Rethink and integrate physical, remote, hybrid workspaces to enable people to do *the work*.

4 Stakeholder value over shareholder value

Stakeholders are more than shareholders. Create value for all stakeholders, especially for workers and their communities.

5 Worker journeys over HR processes

Worker journeys are holistic employment relationships, not a collection of standardized contracts. Map and understand where *worker* journeys start and where they lead. Invest in relationships throughout.

6 Worker experience over worker efficiency

Worker experience extends beyond the ease of working and productivity targets. Efficiency is the outcome of good work design, not its destination.

7 Human-centric WorkTech over Smart Tech

WorkTech comes with responsibility. Smart Tech is agnostic to long-term outcomes. Technology needs to serve the improvement of the human condition, not replace humans at work. Do no harm!

8 Impact over productivity

Success is about impact. It is not about productivity, growth, or efficiency alone. It is about metrics and empathy taken together.

9 Iterations over transformations

Work experience is made human through good design and small steps. It rarely needs large transformations to flourish. Start by listening, be agile, and design work with humans in mind.

10 Inclusive over standardized
Include all, do not standardize for all. Make the work experience personalized for individual needs, work styles, life stages. Make it as personal as possible and as standard as necessary.

11 Simplicity over complicatedness
Simplify the work context for focus, do not complicate for effort. Complicatedness erodes value and dehumanizes the work environment. Keep it simple!

12 Networks over hierarchies
Most work happens in teams, groups, communities, and across networks. Strive for accountability by way of reputation and trust. Invest in informal connections, not structural hierarchies.

13 Trust over control
Trust always trumps control. Give people space to work and trust them to do it well. Let people flourish!

We hope this manifesto will help you create workplaces that work for all.

Endnotes

1 Universal Declaration of Human Rights. 1948. United Nations

2 Labour Manifesto 2017

3 https://www.readingdesign.org/first-things-first (archived at https://perma.cc/4ZC8-DUJW)

4 Manifesto for Agile Software Development (2001) Agilemanifesto.com (archived at https://perma.cc/ME6N-VK24)

5 Kaczynski, T (1995) *Industrial Society and its Future, The Washington Post*

6 https://www.activism.net/cypherpunk/manifesto.html (archived at https://perma.cc/V4WU-X23W)

APPENDIX 1: (4+3) WS FRAMEWORK

The (4+3) Ws Formula

To simplify the concepts discussed in the book we created a (4+3) Ws Framework.

FIGURE A.1   (4+3) Ws Framework

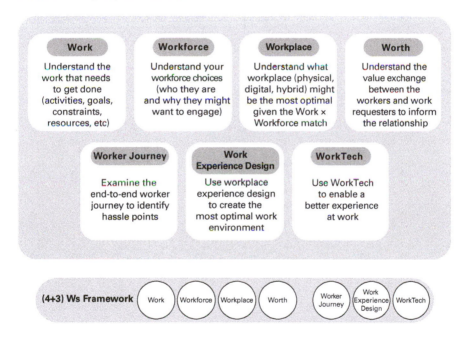

The intent is to provide a series of constructs of the work environment. There are four core elements—Work, Workforce, Workplace, and Worth—and three enabling elements—Worker Journey, Work Experience Design, and WorkTech. The goal of the frameworks is to assist in thinking through the transformation of each of these key elements. There is no right or wrong place to start and depending on the organizational complexity and level of impact, the journey can start at any point in the framework. The rest of the appendix provides further details about each of the constructs, the enabling elements, and how they can be applied in the organizational context.

APPENDIX 2: WORK

Work Construct

Definition: "Work" is not the effort needed to perform the work ("labor"), nor the capabilities and skills (talent), nor the position in which one is employed ("job"). We define "work" as the exertion of mental or physical effort to create goods, assets, or services of benefit to those who are interested in acquiring these outputs and exchanged for similar goods, assets, or services of tangible and intangible value perceived as fair to those who do the work. For example, most project manager roles will include a standard list of activities such as building project plans, managing project schedules, overseeing deliverables production, running project meetings, tracking risks and issues to resolution, or allocating resources. Of course, the specifics and complexity of each of these work units are contextual, and will vary between companies, projects, and the problem to be solved.

On Work Deconstruction

Imbalances in the labor market were historically cyclical in nature; however, over the past decade the "skills shortage"[1] has become a persistent issue, with organizations struggling to find qualified talent.[2] This imbalance is compounded by the mass exodus from the labor market[3] of women who prioritized childcare responsibilities and baby boomers with health conditions or who gave up on job searches and decided to pursue early retirement. The challenge to some degree is a shortage of workers with specific skills but there is a larger fundamental issue that needs to be investigated here.

Organizations hire based on job descriptions. The requirements of those job specifications might have been written a while back. When the incumbent leaves and the job needs to be filled, the manager or HR department inserts a few new skills or *fresh* requirements to update it with the latest technology or capabilities nomenclature. Many times, these job descriptions will require someone who could be described as a "unicorn," since they incorporate a mix of skills and experiences that will be nearly impossible to find in a single individual. First, the "unicorn" might not be interested to do a job they've already done and have already checked all the boxes on the requirements. Second, they might be unaffordable to the organization. And last, the job description rarely depicts the reality of the job, daily activities, and interactions. So much emphasis is put on the job description to filter out qualified talent only because they might be missing a very specific skill that was not critical to performance in the first place.

When examining work, consider the following dimensions and characteristics of the work activity/work unit and understand the trade-offs that might be possible when changing the nature of work activities within and across dimensions. For example, should the work be real-time, or can it be scheduled? Should it be manual, or can it be augmented by technology? Is it still necessary or can it be eliminated altogether? All these examinations and new choices could provide different options organizations can use to identify workers who can perform the job or create a workplace environment where it can be done.

The following are some of the work dimensions to consider evaluating:

- *Temporal dimension* describes the timing characteristics of the work unit (time zone-specific, shift work, hourly work, seasonal work, etc).

- *Technology enablement dimension* describes the degree of technological enablement in support of executing the work unit (fully automated, mechanized by certain equipment, hybrid, augmented by technology, etc).

- *Teaming dimension* describes the degree of collaboration required to perform the work unit (can be done by an individual, might be done via crowd work, requires collaboration, could be done through a "swarm," etc).

FIGURE A.2   Work

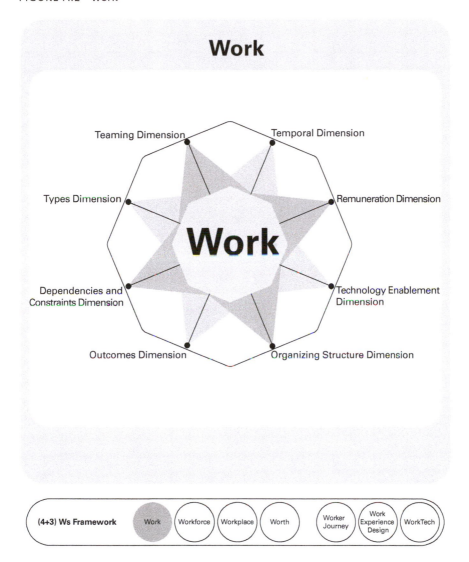

- *Organizing structure dimension* describes the kinds of formal or informal structures required to organize the work (project, gig, job, contract, artisanal, etc).

- *Types dimension* describes the categories and types of work (routine, specialized, standardized, intellectual, artistic, physical, etc).

- *Dependencies and constraints dimension* describes specific requirements for being able to perform the work (location-dependent, requires fluency in a certain language, needs to be performed in a certain sequence, requires judgment and discretion, requires specific skills, needs supervision, etc).

- *Outcomes dimension* describes the characteristics of intended outcomes (tangibility, efficiency, impact, effectiveness, quality, remunerability, etc).

- *Remuneration dimension* describes the remuneration practices relevant to the work unit (salaried work, overtime pay, in-kind remuneration, reputational value exchange, pay per unit, etc).

How Can This Framework Help?

Talent shortages could be partially alleviated by moving away from a rote use of job descriptions towards a more nuanced way to identify and select talent. Specifically, there are opportunities to be found by examining the *work* that needs to get done—not what is listed in the job description, but the essence of what needs to get done and the most optimal workers mix needed to do it. We describe workforce types in Appendix 3.

Endnotes

1 Cappelli, P (2014) Skill gaps, skill shortages and skill mismatches: Evidence for the US, NBER Working Paper 20382

2 Hilsenrath, J and Chaney Cambon, S (2021) Job openings are at record highs. Why aren't unemployed Americans filling them? *Wall Street Journal*, https://www.wsj.com/articles/job-openings-are-at-record-highs-why-arent-unemployed-americans-filling-them-11625823021 (archived at https://perma.cc/4K9F-TPTG)

3 Guilford, G and Chaney Cambon, S (2020) Covid shrinks the labor market, pushing out women and Baby Boomers, *Wall Street Journal*, https://www.wsj.com/articles/covid-shrinks-the-labor-market-pushing-out-women-and-baby-boomers-11607022074 (archived at https://perma.cc/9J74-JCDP)

APPENDIX 3: WORKFORCE

Workforce Construct

Definition: Workforce in the context of this book is expanded beyond the terms "employees" or "non-traditional workers" (such as contractors or temp workers) and describes the two key roles played by the workforce. We might also refer to the workforce as *work entities* that participate in the execution of work. These work entities could be individuals, teams, networks, organizations and institutions, digital labor, or any mix of these entities that are either requesting or performing the work. The following are the two roles performed by the work entities:

- *Work requesters* are those who need the work done. These can range from large entities such as organizations and institutions, to smaller units such as teams and individuals. These are entities that have specific problems to be solved, or unmet needs for goods, assets, or services. They also possess assets (such as money, access to markets, reputation etc) they can use to compensate or exchange elements of value with the work doer.

- *Work doers* are the entities involved in getting the work done. Their scope is not limited to the general *employees*-only categories but is significantly broader and includes all types of workers, groups or entities participating in executing the work. These can include the base workforce currently working for the organization, contractors and vendors, and other non-traditional workforce types such as freelancers, internal and external talent communities,[1] third-party talent clouds, and freelancer communities. It can also include affiliations and institutions that are represented by members of the political and regulatory environment influencing the regulatory landscape of the work environment, other employers, service partners such as benefits providers, equipment rental, travel, learning, tax services, relocation services, risk, security, insurance, and so on.

On Meta Identity (MI)

Each of the entities involved in the work and value exchange has a *digital identity* that we will interchangeably refer to as *social identity* or *digital personas*. The digital persona is the online footprint created by the workers to represent who or what they are. Typical information that would be captured on the digital identity includes identification information (name, picture, contact info etc), interests (hobbies or supported causes), capabilities (skills, experience), work history (work or projects portfolio, feedback on projects, tags or likes, status updates), credentials (certifications, degrees), strengths (awards, reputation), feedback (recommendations, work-related feedback), and network (social network, groups and teams, people in common, common interests).

There are many social media platforms where an individual or entity would have a distinct digital identity specific to that platform. These include networks with specific target use, such as LinkedIn for business networking, Instagram for sharing images or marketing own content, YouTube for videos, or Angie's List for home maintenance services. The social identity on these platforms may include digital identity details (link to website, title or social handles), reputation or level of influence (size of network, number of likes on posts, number of stars, GitHub resume), groups or networks the individual belongs to, communities they are affiliated with, and information about specific access rights and authentication levels that allow them to consume information and interact with the platform's features and with the other members of the network.

While very targeted (by design), the lack of portability of information across these networks is a limitation. Over time the notion of a *single* digital identity might emerge and will represent the convergence of different social identities that are currently on separate social media platforms. Such a unified and consolidated identity of identities—that we would like to refer to as *meta-identity (MI)*—could represent the "digital passport" of an individual.

As an easy illustrative example of how MI could be applied in the context of work, a worker has a social identity that has certain characteristics and experiences that they choose to disclose to the hiring entity. This identity becomes enriched with new skills and experiences acquired during the employment relationship. When the individual moves to the next entity for work purposes they can "check in" to the new destination with the updated profile. Contrast this with the need to apply anew to every organization, and a career that represents a collection of independent segments of the employment record that last only for the duration of the employment relationship with that particular employer. The primary evidence of that specific employment segment is usually an updated line on the resume and scant information in the employment verification records.

Technologies such as blockchain are starting to allow the storage of such data in a secure way, offering control over what gets disclosed to whom and for what reason, and enabling workers to "own it." Adoption of such technologies is starting to shift the power balance away from social media platforms that currently get our data in exchange for free tools or services, and then build lucrative businesses that monetize that aggregate collection of data about us.

The MI includes the information the work requesters and work doers share, disclose, and more importantly *choose* to publish on their website, social media channels, and networks, as well as the external market perception of the work requester or work doer—in other words, their reputation.

On Strength or Reputation

The MI typically would have a quantified or implied general reputation as represented on social and professional channels and communities. Reputation is much more difficult for work entities to control and shape the narrative around. Such a narrative is influenced by many factors such as the actions taken (or not) by work entities, by how they shape relationships with their customers or stakeholders, the quality of their offerings, their stand on certain social issues, by their impact on the community, environment, financial returns and so on. Reputation can be user generated (think of

FIGURE A.3   Workforce

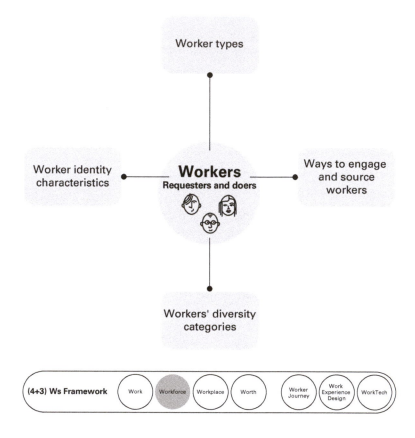

"five stars" ratings) or inferred (aggregate sentiment based on the analysis of sentiment-bearing keywords on social media posts, or aggregate feedback, or ranking on GitHub).

How Can This Framework Help?

When it comes to re-evaluating workforce composition choices, an organization can start with considering new combinations of the elements defined below. Of course, this will require resolving tensions and tradeoffs of the current management structures and norms. At the same time this approach widens the choices of workers and brings much-needed flexibility by tapping into talent pools not traditionally used, or engaging them in new ways:

- Consider the full spectrum of *worker types* (the kinds of worker categories and ways of clustering to provide a specific way of performing the work) that could potentially be tapped into that might have the skills, abilities, interests, and other characteristics appropriate to perform the work unit/activities that are sought by work requesters. For example, individual workers, contingent workers, teams, frontline workers, networks, managed service providers, crowds, swarms, shared services organizations, partnerships, alliances, digital labor, and so on.

- Re-evaluate the *engagement and sourcing types* (ways of engaging workers based on specific needs, time, cost value exchange, and other negotiating factors between the work requesters and work doers) to engage the workers based on the optimal match of intents of both requesters and doers. For example, hire an individual, contract or hire on a temporary basis, develop skills over time, retain key talent using milestone- or performance-driven rewards, transition out non-performing individuals, hire former workers, automate the work, hire entire teams, exchange talent (temporarily or permanently) with other organizations or institutions, engage with one single source/organization/entity that offers several solutions, or mix and match the options above.

- Determine the *diversity types* (the traits, characteristics, and circumstances that might create different needs and wants of the workers) or rather the unique needs of the individual—circumstances, abilities, and life stages that might require different work conditions and accommodations. For example, gender identity, sexual orientation, racial or ethnic identification, age, life stage, physical or cognitive impairments, caregiver status, marital or partnership status, veteran status, community affiliation such as refugee, immigrant, first generation, formerly incarcerated, neurodiverse, older worker, language ability, and performance.

- Consider the *meta-identity characteristics* (professional and personal experience, capabilities, and relationships that in aggregate will form the footprint of work entities that represents who or what they are). It is important to have different degrees of access to such information so that is up to the individual to decide what is to be kept private, what can be shared with whom, and what might be part of the general data commons that is publicly available. Examples of the information included in the MI include identifiable information, capabilities, credentials, work history, feedback received, network size and quality, interests, brand, reputation, career aspirations, personal and impact motivators, and authenticity, which is the confirmation that the digital you is the same as the real you.

Endnote

1 Starner, T (2018) The remarkable power of talent communities, *HR Executive*, https://hrexecutive.com/the-remarkable-power-of-talent-communities/ (archived at https://perma.cc/N359-U7QM)

APPENDIX 4: WORKPLACE

Workplace Construct

Definition: Workplace is the environment where the work gets done. This includes the use of and combination of the following elements:

- *Workspace* spans the physical and digital work environments.
- *WorkTech* (defined in Appendix 8) provides the enabling technologies in support of getting the work done.
- *Work Context* encompasses the management system, rules, and norms that guide organizational culture and operations.

Workspace is the combination of physical and digital environments where the work entities such as *work requesters* (those who have something to be done) and *work doers* (those who have the abilities, aspiration, and capacity to do the work) are connected and provides a platform in support of getting the work done for those involved in work activities. Workspace is distinct from the labor market,[1] which primarily orchestrates the supply and demand of jobs. In that case the elements involved are jobs (not work), employees or workers (vs work doers), and employers (vs work requesters).

The workspace is the physical environment that is designed and equipped to enable all work activities. It is also designed to enhance and optimize worker productivity as well as create serendipitous encounters and interactions. This is not limited to just physical office spaces but also might include the use of co-working spaces, working at coffee shops, at the client site, at home or other remote spaces where the worker with the necessary equipment (laptops or other devices) is able to perform the work. It might also include a mix of physical and digital experiences delivered using virtual or immersive reality, telepresence, and other technological solutions described in Appendix 8, WorkTech, that augment the work experience.

FIGURE A.4   Workplace

WorkTech is a tech cluster that aims to enable the execution of work by improving the workplace experience for all workers. This cluster includes devices, systems, and the application of social science to improve or expand human ability as well as enable interactions in the workplace. WorkTech is to be distinguished from HR Tech, which is primarily focused on the improvement of Human Resource processes and activities.

WorkTech is focused on the human side of work, on the individual worker, and combines hardware, software, and wetware[2] to create the optimal environment for that individual to accomplish their goals while maximizing the positive experience. Given the complexity of this concept we provide a more detailed definition of the WorkTech components in Appendix 8.

Work Context is the collection of organizational constructs (such as leadership behaviors, processes, rewards, etc) that influences how the current workforce (in its totality) performs, behaves, and creates value. This includes a variety of constructs we describe below, many of which fall into the hands of HR to design and reinforce. The content that follows was inspired by the Smart Simplicity approach from BCG,[3] Behavior design models,[4] and complexity theory.[5]

Work context components include:

- *Purpose:* statements representing aspirational goals and expression of why the organization exists, who it serves, how it creates value, and the moral guidelines that drive its ability to accomplish those goals. It might include one or more of the following: purpose statement, vision, mission, strategy, values, stakeholders.

- *Power:* representing the formal organizational structure and hierarchy that describes how organizational entities and individuals relate to each other, and how the organizational decision-making power is distributed, aligned, and reinforced along the decision-making structure. It also includes the formal leadership of the organization (senior leadership, CEO, board of directors, board of advisors). Their behaviors, vision, office politics, decisions they make, who they value, promote, and sponsor are all indicators and provide cues about what the organization stands for and will influence or role-model for others who are aspiring to progress up the career ladder.

- *Payoff:* the compensation structures and systems of motivators (both intrinsic and extrinsic) that reward the following of the protocols and reinforce the expected behaviors and performance. This includes wages, benefits, development programs, career pathing.

- *Practices:* the cultural norms, customs, routines, and specific behaviors exhibited by people in day-to-day activities. These are not the theoretical constructs or espoused values, principles, and strategies, but rather the use of the beliefs, methods, and norms to make decisions and create a specific sense of "organizational culture."

- *Principles and Protocols* includes a variety of components that describe what, how, who, and where things get done. It can involve job descriptions, roles and responsibilities, team constructs, capabilities framework, policies, procedures, process descriptions, and so on—all with the intent to articulate how the purpose is accomplished through the established power structure in place.

- *Platforms and Places* includes systems, tools, infrastructure, workspace, and how these elements are designed to interact with each other to create an optimal environment to accomplish the work.

- *People:* the workers who bring and align their skills, capabilities, talent, reputation, energy, and interests to support the organization to accomplish its purpose. It can include single individuals as well as teams, business units, and other ways of organizing people into work-producing units.

- *Performance:* the effort people make and behavior they exhibit in response to the interplay of all the components described above. It is the natural reaction to the context in which people operate. Observational and analytical measures can be used to evaluate the effort and impact people make.

How Can this Framework Help?

In the early stages of an organization's formation many of the workplace elements are limited in their nature and impact (if they are even established at all). As organizations mature and evolve, new layers and complexities are added and many of them are not assessed for their usefulness going forward. Every time an organization takes on an internal transformation, there is opportunity to examine the components of the workplace—from workspace choices to technologies used and the organizational context—and determine what needs to be adapted, added, and more importantly, eliminated. The more complicated the workplace is, the less time and energy is spent on creating value for stakeholders, and more time is spent on compliance with these elements and tracking that compliance (aka following the processes vs accomplishing the intended result). Many of the decisions as well as checks and balances in place will outlive their usefulness and only become a source of irritation, perpetuate a sense of distrust, and ultimately create disengagement among workers. Thus organizations could greatly benefit from simplifying the workplace while enhancing the experience of everyone involved.

Endnotes

1 https://corporatefinanceinstitute.com/resourcs/knowledge/economics/labor-market/ (archived at https://perma.cc/7H9M-QZ57)

2 https://www.merriam-webster.com/dictionary/wetware (archived at https://perma.cc/JSJ7-59ED)

3 Backx, J et al (2017) Mastering complexity through simplification: Four steps to creating competitive advantage, BCG

4 Fogg, BJ (nd) What is behavior design? Behavior Design Newsletter, https://behaviordesign.stanford.edu/ (archived at https://perma.cc/LA9G-37ZC)

5 Uhl-Bien, M and Marion, R (eds) (2008) *Complexity Leadership Part 1: Conceptual foundations* (Leadership Horizons) Charlotte, NC: IAP (Information Age Publishing)

APPENDIX 5: WORTH

Worth/Value Exchange Construct

Definition: Worth in the context of this book is defined as the reciprocal transfer or exchange of value between work requester and work doer. It can include direct trade and execution that transcends traditional organizational constructs. It typically includes payments and incentives such as monetary compensation, common currency/cash, equity, services, benefits-in-kind, instruments to reduce risks (legal services, insurance coverage), and access to workplace services. It can also include many non-monetary rewards such as recognition, reputational boost, new skills, sought-after experience, great network of colleagues, and "psychic income."

At the individual level, the experience is quite variable and what matters is influenced by the learning and demand curve of the job. There is no way to create a consistent employment experience for everyone; such attempts might lead to centralized mediocrity. Instead, organizations need a system that understands and accommodates variability.

Figure A.5 represents the complexity of the employment value proposition. The elements of value described can guide the development of processes and experiences that address deeply held needs, needs the workers might not yet be able to articulate. These elements were inspired[1] by Bain's B2B Elements of Value.[SM,2]

Guidelines on How to Work with the Employment Values Pyramid

It is important to gather the key stakeholders and ensure it is an inclusive group representing different organizational levels and networks. This group can review each of the values and sort them

Worth / Value Exchange

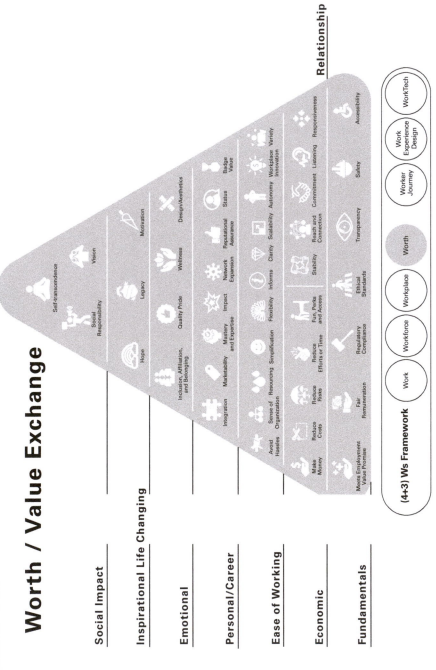

Social Impact

Inspirational Life Changing

Emotional

Personal/Career

Ease of Working

Economic

Fundamentals

Relationship

into the following categories based on the perception of the importance of each value:

- need to have (company should provide);
- nice to have (company's discretion to provide);
- not critical (not expected for the company to prioritize).

From the category "need to have," decide which of the values your organization wants to be known for (it should not be more than 10 values in total). These values can then be used to inform decisions about the work environment and workplace practices. This will ensure transparency in communicating those values and supporting employment value proposition to the candidates that are aligned with them.

Importantly, when choosing these values, organizations must identify what might be the relevant measures of success. How would one quantify the impact on the organization? For example, an organization that is committed to creating an accessible work environment will also commit to hiring and retaining individuals with physically and cognitively diverse abilities.

Employment Values

The following are the categories grouping different employment values:

Fundamentals

- Meeting the employment brand promise: an experience that conforms to the worker's understanding of the employment contract/relationship.
- Fair remuneration: the provision of fair, acceptable remuneration for the services rendered from the workers.
- Regulatory compliance: compliance with regulations.

- Ethical standards: performance of activities in an ethical manner.
- Transparency: visibility of decisions impacting the workers and workplace.
- Safety: a safe and inclusive work environment.
- Accessibility: experiences and environments that enable workers with diverse abilities to be equally effective.

Economic

- Make money: support for workers in improving their financial wellbeing.
- Reduce costs: cost reduction for the workers.
- Reduce risk: protection of workers against loss or unnecessary risk.
- Reduce effort or time: goal accomplishment with less effort.
- Fun, perks, and access: an environment where it is enjoyable to go to work or otherwise rewarding to be an engaged worker. Access to information, goods, services or other valuable items.

Ease of Working

- Avoid hassles: hassle avoidance or reduction.
- Resourcing: provision of the necessary resources to do one's job.
- Flexibility: work flexibility that maximizes individual performance.
- Informs: provision of reliable and trusted information.
- Clarity: clear expectations.
- Sense of organization: support in helping workers become more organized and efficient.
- Variety: a variety of experiences to build skills and expertise.
- Simplification: reduction of complexity, keeping things simple.
- Scalability: easy and quick expansion in response to increases in workforce demand, processes, or tasks.

- Autonomy: trust in the workers' ability to manage their work and themselves.
- Workplace innovation: innovative experiences for the workforce.

Relationships

- Listening: a culture of input-seeking from workers at different stages in their work experience.
- Responsiveness: prompt and professional responses to workers' needs.
- Commitment: commitment to the workers' own success.
- Stability: stability for the foreseeable future.
- Reach and connection: promotion of connections between workers internally and externally.

Emotional

- Wellness: a culture in which people worry less and feel more secure, improving their physical or mental state.
- Pride in quality: creation of high-quality goods or services.
- Design/aesthetics: aesthetically pleasing goods or services that are appealing in taste, smell, hearing, and other senses.
- Inclusion, affiliation, and belonging: a culture of supporting people in becoming part of a group or identifying with people they admire.

Personal/Career

- Integration: assistance in integrating work and life experiences for workers across different activities as they go through their daily experience.
- Mastery and expertise: supporting workers' growth and personal development.

- Network expansion: aiding colleagues' professional network expansion.
- Marketability: a culture of making users and colleagues more marketable in their field.
- Reputational assurance: a company reputation that does not jeopardize and may enhance the worker's own reputation.
- Badge value: the representation of achieved status or aspirations.
- Direct impact on outcomes: a worker's ability to contribute to a project that has a visible impact that provides a sense of personal accomplishment or improvement.

Inspirational/Life Changing

- Hope: the inspiration of workers' hopes for the future of their organization.
- Motivation: a culture that spurs people on to achieve their goals.
- Legacy: investment for future generations or leaving a mark on the world.

Social Impact

- Self-transcendence: support for other people or society more broadly.
- Vision: a philosophy of helping the workforce anticipate the direction of markets and influence the organizational strategy.
- Social responsibility: the promotion of a culture of social responsibility.

How Can This Framework Help?

Organizations will benefit from finding ways to meaningfully prioritize a few values and deliver on them to unlock the potential of the organizational promise.

The priority and importance attributed to the different value elements above will differ by the individual (some people come to work just to get a paycheck and perhaps we shouldn't insist on making them "be engaged") and by geographical location (some of the elements, especially economic ones, are provided by the country rather than as a company benefit—think universal health coverage). It will also be unrealistic for an organization to set goals to deliver on all the values above.

It is important, however, to identify a few and be explicit about the choices and reasons behind them, and more importantly, build those into all the messaging, internal and external communications, decision making, management practices, talent development, etc.

Endnotes

1 Similar to what we earlier described as the influence of marketing and customer relationship management on workplace practices, Bain's product design model inspired our own value pyramid. It has a similar intent, but a different set of elements customized for the workplace environment

2 Bain&Co (2018) Explore the B2B elements of value, https://www.bain.com/insights/explore-the-b2b-elements-of-value-interactive/ (archived at https://perma.cc/L3HN-CJ4N)

Worker Journey Construct

Definition: A worker or employment journey includes all stages of the relationship between the worker and the organization. This includes discovering the organization, deciding to join it (as an employee, contractor, intern, etc), being hired and on-boarded, performing and getting rewarded for it, pursuing development, progressing through different roles, experiencing career and life events, to eventually leaving the organization. It might also include returning as a rehire.

When entertaining efforts to transform the experience, it is important to first look at the experience from the worker's perspective (and not from a perspective of HR processes, or systems used, or business unit represented).

Focus on the "In-Between" Moments

The approach, taken by many organizations when attempting to improve the employee's engagement or retention, is to look at the "moments that matter." These would typically include career events (hiring, promotion, becoming a manager, going on an international assignment) or life events (changing marital status, having a baby, relocating). While these events are indeed important to transform, the worker experience happens in the day-to-day routines and actually *in between* those big moments.

It is important to look at the worker experience by observing the big and small details, barriers and hassles, and identify what can be eliminated, minimized, or transformed. Small issues and irritants accumulate over time, like papercuts, and can compound to an ultimate decision to disengage or even resign.

Worker Experience Is Not HR's Responsibility Alone

Another misconception is that workforce engagement and experience is the responsibility of HR. While HR has some impact through the processes and programs it deploys, workers spend very little time dealing with those processes. For example, participation in occasional training and development opportunities, running through performance management cycles, enrolling in benefits, updating personal information—all of those are periodic, cyclical, and usually limited in the level of effort the workers put into them. The actual experience happens when the worker is building deliverables, or collaborates with their peers on a project, or attends team gatherings and status updates, or interacts with the supervisor, or uses the tools and resources enabling their work.

Good Experience Is Contagious

Many organizations have invested heavily in managing their customer experience through improvements in their processes, communications, personalization, analytics, technology, and so on. A similar kind of upgrade is necessary for the worker. If the worker has no idea what a great experience is and looks like, how can they deliver it to the customers? A workplace that is enabling the workers to do their best work and is not a source of irritation and frustration can create the space for innovation, great collaboration, and an environment where people love to go and be part of. This then translates into benefits for the customer and other stakeholders.

Figure A.6 provides examples of subsets of the journey experiences as the relationship between the worker and the organization evolves. Below are the descriptions of each of the stages.

FIGURE A.6   Worker Journey

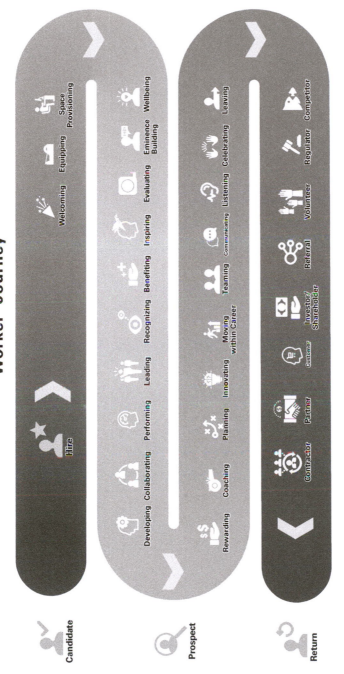

Worker Journey

Candidate

Developing · Collaborating · Performing · Leading · Recognizing · Benefiting · Inspiring · Evaluating · Eminence Building · Wellbeing

Welcoming · Equipping · Space Provisioning

Hire

Prospect

Rewarding · Coaching · Planning · Innovating · Moving within Career · Teaming · Communicating · Listening · Celebrating · Leaving

Return

Contractor · Partner · Customer · Investor/Shareholder · Referral · Volunteer · Regulator · Competitor

(4+3) Ws Framework

Work · Workforce · Workplace · Worth · Worker Journey · Work Experience Design · WorkTech

Prospect engagement

This includes discovering the brand via different internal and external sources of information such as social media channels, the company's career website, Glassdoor, LinkedIn, local or community-based events, community volunteering, or employee referrals. It also includes employment-focused advertising, clear employment brand and value proposition statements, diverse and inclusive sourcing channels, and distribution channels for job postings, etc.

Candidate experience

This includes the experience of a candidate who is applying for the job (one, multiple) and going through informational interviews, contacting other employees, and going through the screening and assessment, interviewing processes, as well as background verification, offer, acceptance, rejection, and all the associated communications throughout the process. The experience of those who didn't get the offer matters just as much since they will more likely than not share the negative aspects on social media and therefore further influence opinion about the organization.

Hiring and welcoming

This includes the post-offer communications and engagement, including manager's welcome, clarity of instructions about the next steps, and updating all the systems and records necessary for the worker to formally start work activities.

Onboarding, equipping, and space provision

This includes pre-boarding, onboarding, provision of access to work tools and equipment, performing team/organizational integration, initial development, and communications. It also includes provision of the equipment and space necessary to perform the work.

Benefiting

This includes understanding all the health and wellness offerings and choices for the worker, with the emphasis on personalization and flexibility of choice. It also includes wellness options, enrollment experience, ensuring that the benefits are tailored and customizable to different life stages (not just for parents, or for students), and all the related communications.

Supporting wellbeing

This includes the care and empathy the worker receives in support of their physical and mental wellbeing. This might include stipends for fitness programs and equipment discounts. It can also include meeting-free days, 4-day work weeks, team retreats without devices, or time off for mental wellbeing.

Collaborating

This includes the tools and settings that enable teams and groups to collaborate effectively. It can be design studios or spaces that support creative work. It can also be digital brainstorming tools. Increasingly different productivity, project management, and messaging tools are supporting this collaboration. Care and attention are to be given to distributed teams since their collaboration requires a more deliberate design and orchestration.

Coaching

This includes the formal and informal coaching a worker receives during their work experience. It can include peer coaching or a buddy system during the onboarding process or during career transitions, or life coaching when deciding to return to work after a career break or going through a divorce, or financial planning or career outplacement and so on.

Inspiring

This involves the efforts to engage and inspire the worker about the organizational mission, the team and work environment, the work outcomes, the impact on different communities and the environment, engagement with different stakeholders, the stand on social issues, etc. The goal is to build an emotional reaction that aligns the organizational and individual values.

Building eminence

This includes the activities and support the worker receives to build their reputation and eminence in the field of their work. This might include the ability to write papers, publish research, speak at conferences, collaborate with think-tanks, run externally facing projects, obtain education and development, or contribute to industry thought leadership.

Planning

This includes the ability for the workers to plan their work activities and have control over their workload and work environment.

Innovating

This involves the freedom and enablement of workers to come up with different ideas to help them perform their work better/more easily, or to help the organization come up with better or newer offerings. It requires a certain culture that not only invests in innovation but also tolerates mistakes and failures.

Communicating

This includes transparent, honest, personalized, and clear communications for the workers to understand the organizational context, priorities, processes, and updates.

Listening

This involves active and passive listening programs to understand the workers' sentiment. It can be as large as a company-wide listening program or it can be a small, targeted focus group, or a feedback loop along different parts of the employment journey— all with the intent to capture insights about the worker experience and make interventions to improve it based on those insights.

Celebrating

This involves the recognition of different professional and personal milestones and is not limited to big and significant ones. It might include small accomplishments and successes that allow teammates or the work group to have visibility and a shared experience of acknowledgment.

Teaming

This includes building a sense of belonging to a team or a group of individuals the worker is collaborating with. It might include things such as team onboarding, team cohesion building and bonding, networking, and conflict resolution.

Performing and evaluating

This includes the ability, enablement, and all the necessary means and clarity to perform the assigned work. It also includes goal setting, evaluation, feedback, performance interventions, and ways to address under-performance.

Rewarding and recognizing

This includes monetary and non-monetary rewards and recognitions including base pay, bonuses, equity awards, scholarships, products and services discounts, fairness and transparency of compensation decisions, ease of accessing information, ability to make exceptions, and autonomy of a manager to make decisions. It also includes recognition instruments such as spot awards, peer-to-peer recognition, badges or points to gamify the experience, recognition lists, and events to celebrate an individual's contributions.

Moving (within career)

This includes transfer to another role, including to another group or department, location, promotion, demotion, or a lateral move. It also includes key career milestones such as becoming a manager or an executive, a change in employment status or contractual relationship such as changing from a regular employee to a contingent worker, or from full-time to part-time, or to an outsourced provider, or to acquired/merger. It includes career pathing, career pivoting within the company, career coaching, and new role onboarding.

Developing

This includes all sorts of informal and formal development such as classroom-based learning, peer networks, on-the-job learning, external training and development, conferences, stretch roles or assignments, mentoring others, being a mentee, volunteering, shadowing (internally/externally), receiving feedback, doing work, skills and capabilities assessments, obtaining educational assistance, participating in apprenticeships programs, and obtaining different credentials (certifications, licenses, badges, points, etc).

Leading

This includes taking responsibility for leading a team or a project on a both formal and informal basis, becoming a first- or second-line manager, and in general showing leadership in whatever role or capacity the individual has the opportunity to do so.

Life events

This includes different life events such as having a new child, adopting a child, changing marital status, moving to another location, bereavement, leave of absence, taking a sabbatical, etc.

Leaving

This includes departure or exit from the organization due to layoffs or reduction in force, voluntary resignation, retirement, involuntary termination, offboarding, outplacement, and career transition processes. It also includes the alumni engagement processes the organization has established.

Returning

This includes the process of rehiring or the return of the worker to the organization in another employment arrangement such as leaving as an employee and returning as a contractor. It also includes returnship experiences where the worker has the chance to learn and transition into the organization after a period of absence from the workforce.

It is important to keep in mind that even after the worker leaves the organization, they continue to have a relationship in some capacity.

They might become a contractor, a partner or supplier. They might continue to purchase products or services (hence being a customer). They might continue to hold shares or equity in the company (hence being a shareholder). They might refer their friends or family to come to work at the organization or to purchase products or services. They might continue to participate in different volunteering and community programs. They might decide to be an investor or a regulator and influence the organizational direction or landscape in different ways. Lastly, they could become a competitor and target the market share.

How Can This Framework Help?

Transforming the worker journey can happen at three different levels:

- *Within a particular stage of the journey* where the goal is to improve a specific step, activity, experience. For example, workplace collaboration might involve improving the tools enabling the collaboration of distributed workers, teaming practices to ensure team collaboration, management skills to encourage it, or motivators and rewards that promote collaboration across business units. It is relatively easier to start by redesigning the experience at a particular worker journey stage since it limits the scope and impact and allows learning and iterations while the design mindset is taking hold inside the organization.

- *At transition points* where the goal is to ensure smooth transition between different stages and there is no stark difference in the experience from one stage to the next. For example, the candidate can have a wonderful hiring experience only to get to Day 1 of their employment and realize how poor their experience going forward will be. Many have had a lonely orientation experience in a sparsely furnished, windowless room reading slides on a computer screen about the organization, then signing a stack of papers that HR has ushered in, only to then be assigned to work on their first project and being informed that their company laptop will arrive in one week and their first meeting with their manager is scheduled around the same time. Another classic example is a still-practiced protocol of ushering in an unsuspecting long-tenured employee to tell them that they are being let go, and then having security escort them out of the building with a promise to mail their belongings.

- *For a lasting impact* with the goal to build a positive experience and lasting memories. It is tempting to design an *experience* and focus on the mechanics of it; however it is important to also focus on the *memory of that experience*[1] and the narrative the worker will build in their mind about that experience. A "great" experience can easily be conflated with "easy" and there are a lot of opportunities to simplify and reduce hassles for workers. An aspirational direction for a "great" experience is to create lasting memories of impact and purpose. For example, bringing a new sustainable product to the market, or transforming the procurement process so that suppliers are paid a living wage, on time, and have stability of contracts, or adopting practices where workers are trusted, empowered, paid equitably, and treated with dignity—all might be challenging efforts riddled with resistance, pushback, and political gamesmanship. However, the satisfaction, sense of pride, and purpose gained by being involved in such efforts will last a lifetime.

Endnote

1 Riis, J and Kahneman, D (2005) Living, and thinking about it: Two perspectives on life, in *The Science of Well-Being*, Oxford: Oxford University Press

APPENDIX 7: WORK EXPERIENCE DESIGN

Work Experience Design (WXD) Construct

Definition: Work Experience Design is the transformation of the work experience by using human-centered design principles and might include changes in how the work is structured, how the workflow is sequenced, how the team functions, how the individual is enabled to do the work and grow—all with the intent to deliver on the expected employment values (such as economic expectations, personal and career growth, relational, emotional, impact, etc) and enable the individual to get their work done to maximize their own and the organization's success.

Experience design starts with a mindset shift from "do it to them" to "do it with them." It comes so naturally to HR to create a new program or a new process and establish a cadence of building and deploying it. The idea behind WXD is to instead ask workers what *they* would change, what would be most impactful, and how would the ideal program look? The feedback will reveal both the minor irritants and the major barriers that prevent employees from bringing their full potential to work. Their participation in the design process may involve running focus groups, roundtables, WXD surveys, implementing a continuous listening solution, and/or forming employee advisory boards that help identify, design, and test solutions.

> Human-centered design starts from a place of not knowing what the solution to a given design challenge might be. Only by listening, thinking, building, and refining our way to an answer do we get something that will work for the people we're trying to serve.[1]

This process requires designers to build empathy with the end users (in this case employees/workers). Empathy is the capacity to walk a mile in other people's shoes, to understand their lives and experiences from the moment they wake up, get to the office (potentially with a long commute and a lot of traffic on the way), followed by getting to their desk, then attempting to log in to their workspace (along with a few expired passwords and cryptic error messages), then spending most of the day on conference calls with no time for lunch or breaks, and at the end of the day, after getting home and putting the kids to bed, logging back on to get the actual work done.

Human-centered design is about solving problems from a real person's perspective and requires immersion in another's world to "see new creative possibilities and leave behind any preconceived ideas and outmoded ways of thinking."[2]

Human-centered design brings solutions to problems at the inter-section of the following dimensions:

- *Desirability:* the solution addresses a specific problem, solves an unmet need, and provides something that the target audience will find of value.

- *Viability:* the solution is financially viable and affordable to the organization (ie generates income, saves money or time or errors, allows business or talent growth, maintains service level, etc).

- *Sustainability:* the solution is built in a way that is sustainable and does not create negative societal or environmental impact.

- *Feasibility:* the solution is possible to build (there is existing infrastructure, resources, technology that enable its creation and operation).

There are multiple schools, methods, and frameworks for the design process. For the purposes of Work Experience Design we will use the following four key phases that are intended to be iterative and ongoing (vs linear and static):

FIGURE A.7   Work Experience Design

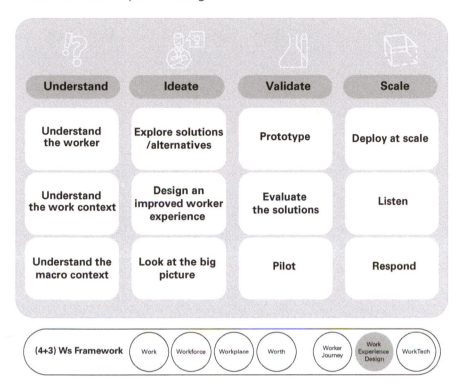

Step 1: Understand

Understand the worker: identify and build *personas* (canonical descriptions or archetypes of roles that include hopes, needs, fears, pain points, aspirations etc and that help rationalize multiple variations in the design process) and map the "moments that matter" and everything in between on their *experience journey/ employment life cycle.*

Understand the work context: articulate the problem to be addressed, goals and objectives of different stakeholders, work context elements and management system, constraints, and so on to gain clarity on the workplace system that influences the worker experience and the tensions that might have to be addressed in the redesign.

Understand the macro context: assess and understand the impact on the organization of external signals (demographic, economic, technological shifts), internal signals (financial, HR, workforce and customer indicators), and change triggers (business events such as mergers, acquisitions, and so on, natural disasters, laws and regulatory changes etc) to inform the external factors to be accounted for in the redesign.

Step 2: Ideate

Explore solutions/alternatives: identify new configurations within the elements or mix/match the elements that are part of the *(4+3) Ws framework*, such as exploring different workforce choices, work design, workplace choices, value exchange, and WorkTech enablement, and consider how these can be mixed to optimize for the goals of the redesign.

Design an improved worker experience: use inclusive design and human-centric design methods to transform the experience. Ensure accessibility to accommodate individuals with different physical, sensory, or cognitive impairments. Design the experience from the worker's point of view as opposed to the HR process or technology view.

Look at the big picture: evaluate the value of the solution from the end-to-end worker journey perspective. Redefine success measures and tie to desired outcomes.

Step 3: Validate

Prototype: build a low-fi or hi-fi prototype for solutions to be able to share it with others and evaluate its usability.

Evaluate the solutions: validate the prototype with the target personas, refine and improve.

Pilot: deploy the solution to a small subset of users, refine and iterate.

Step 4: Scale

Deploy at scale: implement the solution and allow for iterations and modifications.

Listen: establish workplace listening mechanisms to track success of deployed solutions and identify new areas to improve.

Respond: establish organizational structure and mechanisms to adequately address emerging needs.

How Can This Framework Help?

There is no right or wrong place to start. The most important thing is to start at all. To create a great workplace experience (WEX), it is important to start by critically evaluating the "pro and con" arguments internally and agree on the right organizational fit given the unique purpose and culture.

Acknowledge WEX. Organizations first need to commit to a culture of workplace experience and understand the ramifications of such a commitment. There is an inherent tension between investing in WEX and delivering on short-term shareholder value, so gaining the required support across many functions, and more importantly at the leadership level, will be critical to the adoption of WEX practices. The leaders might say they care about the employees, but if their decisions and actions prioritize financial outcomes above anything else, the WEX-related initiatives will have little chance of achieving lasting impact. Avoid making WEX transformation yet another HR initiative. As with any transformation, it is important to assess how ready the organization is for such change. There needs to be a compelling call to action and a story that will keep the organization inspired to continue the journey.

Ask. The easiest way is to ask the workers. What does your day look like? What gets in the way of you being productive and accomplishing your goals? What are the small irritants that, if solved, would remove the barriers between you and doing your best work? What would an ideal workplace look like for you? And really listen, without judgment. You might hear big "pie in the sky" results but more likely you will have a whole collection of small improvements that cost nothing or require little effort to make a change. Once you have a list, prioritize it. Better yet, involve employees in prioritizing it. Annual or quarterly employee engagement surveys are a good start, but the goal is to move to an ongoing feedback loop and "continuous listening." It is also important to ensure you have adequate technological support to collect data and an appropriate support model to respond efficiently to the employees' needs.

Act. Start small and go from there. Address the main irritants first. Use design thinking principles to act. Create a better understanding of the individual (persona) whose problems you are addressing and really get to the bottom of what they are thinking, doing, feeling, and saying. There are plenty of tools and resources you can use to organize this work. What motivates your worker? What are they coming to work for? You can repurpose existing constructs of assessing the elements of value from the consumer world. For example: Do your employees want a simple workplace environment where things *just work*? Are they looking for a community to belong to? Do they want to grow and build skills? Understanding the motivating factors will greatly help your solutioning process.

Understand their journey by observing a "day in the life" from the moment they wake up till they check out for the day (if they do). What does that experience look like? How are they interacting with your organization (refer to the components of the journeys framework)? With whom are they interacting? What are they doing and what stops them from doing it better, easier, and with more impact? How can you use technology, communication, simplification, the human touch, and other tools you have at your disposal to make a meaningful change in that journey?

Assemble teams. The best way to ensure that things get done is to assign accountability for the results. Some organizations create task forces with diverse representation and use them to not only solve specific problems but also to develop up-and-coming leaders with hands-on experiences (versus classroom-based leadership development programs). Some create dedicated organizations where the leader has the responsibility to integrate across all the participating silos. At some organizations, the employees form agile groups to solve specific problems.

Adopt a digital mindset. It is important to make digitization a cultural transformation, not merely a technological one. It will enable the organization to promote transparency, create more flexibility, provide alternative work arrangements, and bring Agile principles to day-to-day working. Adapting to change and getting used to "changing all the time" can become the next source of competitive advantage.

Advertise. Communicate. Communicate. Communicate. Throughout the entire process. There is no better way to show due respect to the process than to be very transparent and open about the changes you are making, why you are making them, and how you are making them. People need to know that you care and are listening. That alone will create a positive impact on the experience.

Assess. Measure your progress. It is important to think early in the process about the way you will define success and how you will track progress. These success measurements will help align stakeholders, open doors for additional funding or a widened scope of transformation, and, more importantly, show you where to focus next.

There are plenty of analytical tools and capabilities in modern organizations to enable you to aggregate data across the full life cycle and understand the relationship between improvements to the workplace experience and organizational outcomes (be it financial results, brand image, client satisfaction, or anything else that matters to your business).

Changing workplace experience can be perceived as a significant undertaking or effort that requires a lot of investment. That might be the case but frequently it is not so. Walking a day in workers' shoes might be very enlightening. Asking them directly will point to the main irritants that most likely will require simple changes to make an improvement. It can be as simple as broadband Wi-Fi onsite, or the ability to decide when to work from home, or time off not only for new parents but also for those who must care for their elderly parents.

None of us wants to work within systems where everyone is judged and compared against an unattainable and ever-moving goalpost, where decisions about pay, promotions, and successions are made by a select few behind closed doors, where the limited transparency of big organizational decisions is intended to keep the "troops" in the dark and under control. We all have the same basic needs: We want to be paid attention to. We want to be respected and listened to. We want to be doing something meaningful, satisfying, and to have a sense that *we* matter.

Endnotes

1 IDEO.ORG (2015) The field guide to human-centered design, https://www.ideo. org/perspective/the-field-guide-to-human-centered-design (archived at https:// perma.cc/4ZDP-GQJT)

2 Ibid.

APPENDIX 8: WORKTECH

WorkTech Construct

Definition: Technology Clusters

When it comes to defining *technology clusters*, the typical mental model would represent a mix of entities focused on advances in a specific field (think AI, quantum, etc), innovators and startups, venture capital funding, schools and universities, and a dynamic ecosystem of companies that employ many to deliver adjacent services. Typically, such ecosystems have a geographical footprint and ties with local research and educational institutions that ensure knowledge exchange.[1] Examples of such clusters are Silicon Valley with proximity to Stanford University, NASA's Ames Research Center, IBM's Almaden Research Lab, and a whole host of big tech companies such as Apple, Google, Netflix, Adobe, and even smaller ones aspiring to change the world.

Other kinds of tech clusters to have emerged are new domains where innovative technology is used to transform traditional sectors. For example, FinTech is aiming to provide greater or better access to financial services using smartphones, apps, and new protocols to deliver banking, investment, or borrowing services. HealthTech is devices, knowledge, medicines, vaccines, and procedures to address health problems and improve quality of life.[2]

Definition: WorkTech

WorkTech is a tech cluster that is focused on improving the workplace experience for all workers. This cluster includes devices, systems, and the application of social science to improve or expand human ability as well as enhance interactions in the workplace. WorkTech is to be distinguished from HR Tech, which is primarily focused on the improvement of Human Resource processes and activities. It is also broader than enterprise technology since we define the workplace to be broader than the physical office space or enterprise software, and it includes the integrated space—physical, digital, and social—where the work gets done.

FIGURE A.8   WorkTech

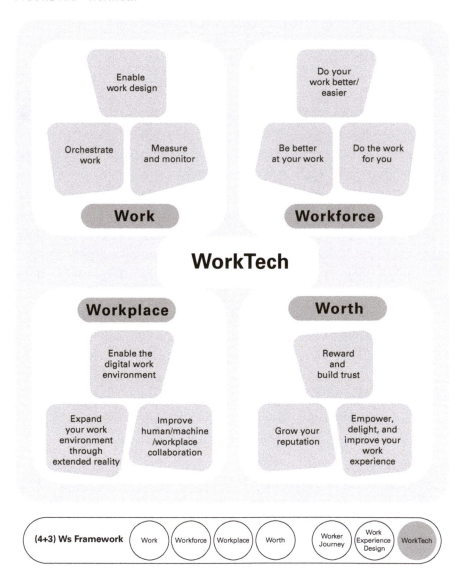

To reinforce the distinction: many technologies are used to improve processes, systems, activities, outcomes—all inanimate elements. WorkTech is focused on the human side of work, on the individual worker, and combines the hardware, software, and wetware[3] to create the optimal environment for that individual to accomplish their goals while maximizing the positive experience. When humans have that optimal environment, organizational success becomes a natural outcome[4] of this reconfigured and optimized human-cyber-physical system.

There are multiple models on the market describing the WorkTech cluster. In keeping up with the need for human-centricity, this framework approaches the definition with a focus on specific benefits, outcomes or goals that humans can attain using technologies. Specifically, we group technologies around the following four workplace experience goals.

Goal 1: Organize Work

The technology supporting this goal enables the orchestration of activities involved in getting work done in the following ways:

- *Enable work design.* Work design is the effort required in defining and designing the activities involved in completing a project and the description of intended results or outcomes. Work design helps frame what actionable requests can be done by the work doers, involving activities such as: defining the scope of work; considering the structure of the team or skills, and capabilities mix required to do the work; the way the work production will be managed; the fulfillment process to deliver the outcomes, and other details framing the request. This information can include the goals to accomplish and intended outputs, constraints, the resources available or necessary, the market mechanisms available to do the work, the quality expectations and control measures.
- *Orchestrate work.* These technologies support the triage of work across all the entities involved in performing the work. This

includes work-to-worker matching, which requires the use of sophisticated algorithms that consider the specifications of the work requirements and the qualities of the work doer, and finds the most optimal match that is driven by constraints articulated in the work design (pricing limits, timeline of the project and availability of the work requester, quality expectations, location where the work needs to get done and proximity of work request, and many other attributes). It also includes the contractual terms and processes that help formalize the work match so the work can begin. Such contractual details might include identity verification (is the person indeed who they claim to be?), terms of intellectual property transfer, any necessary liability coverage and insurance that both parties need to have to enter the agreement, evidence of compliant, safe, and secure processes, or compliance with certain labor laws and regulations, terms of data handling and privacy implications. Technologies included in this category are platforms, marketplaces, smart contracts, access to distributed talent, etc.

- *Measure and monitor.* Such technologies provide humans and connected processes with the ability to evaluate different aspects of the work activities and outcomes. Such aspects might be the quality of the work product, or predicting the speed of finishing the task, optimizing the match between work and work doer. They can also include monitoring of patterns in work orchestration and finding ways to minimize risks such as likelihood of missing a deadline, running out of budget, or even cyber-theft.

Goal 2: Enable the Workforce

The technology supporting this goal enables workers in the following ways:

- *Do your work better.* These are technologies that enable the workforce to do their work better and easier. This category includes productivity tools including those supporting team communication and collaboration, time tracking, file hosting and synchronizing across collaborators, content change detection, social media maintenance, note taking, safely storing passwords, project management, creation of shortcuts, and even blocking distractions.

- *Be better at your work.* These include solutions that amplify human abilities through intelligent automation and augmentation such as RPAs, which are a form of business process automation using automation agents such as software robots (bots) or artificial intelligence (AI). The beauty of RPAs is that they "watch" the user perform a specific task in the application's interface then automatically build a list of actions to then be repeated by the bot. It makes the automation process easy while simplifying the workflow too. Other technologies included in this category are voice recognition, machine vision, and chatbots.

- *Do the work for you.* These technologies take over activities that might be unsafe, routine, or require a high level of effort from a human. These solutions include the use of robotics, bionic augmentation, autonomous mobility, synthetic media, synthetic voice, and writing.

Goal 3: Optimize Workplace

The technology supporting this goal enables the physical and digital workplace and the ability to create an optimal integration between the two in the following ways:

- *Enable your digital work environment.* Technologies in this category are solutions that enable the digital workspace. These include the devices used to perform the work such as laptop or mobile device, technologies that integrate the physical ambient environment with the digital world through sensors, location data, and fast access to networks (5G and 6G), as well as technologies enabling storage and processing capacity via cloud, edge computing, and quantum computing.

- *Expand the work environment.* Solutions in this category fall under the umbrella term extended reality, used to describe immersive technologies that can merge the physical and virtual worlds. Such technologies digitally expand the work environment through the use of augmented reality devices and experiences where virtual information and objects are overlaid on the real world (eg Pokémon GO); virtual reality where users are fully immersed in a simulated digital environment via a VR headset or head-mounted display to get a 360-degree view of an artificial world; mixed reality (also referred to as hybrid reality) where an MR headset and a lot more processing power enable the digital and real-world objects to co-exist and interact with one another in real time; technologies that diminish reality by soundproofing or creating invisibility cloaks; and haptic technologies, also referred to as technologies that enable kinesthetic communications or 3D touch. These use forces, motions, and vibrations to enable the users to create a *touch* experience.

- *Improve human/machine/workplace collaboration.* Such technologies are aiming to reduce the friction between humans at work, technologies involved in performing the work, and the actual workplace. Such solutions include a variety of interfaces (multipoint capacity touch, voice interface, touchless gesture interactions, bionic limbs, brain-to-text interface) and recognition, which is an advanced computing system that uses our unique features (face, voice, iris, bone structure, posture, emotional state, WiFi) to recognize who we are and the frame of mind we're likely in. It also includes ambient intelligence (wayfinding) technologies, which are navigation apps that help discover and navigate the physical and digital workplaces (think Waze for the workplace). Technologies involved are beacons that act like satellites for outdoors, accelerometers and compasses installed on the phone, WiFi signal or Bluetooth to communicate between phone and beacons, location data, and voice integration (to give directions).

Goal 4: Maximize Value/Worth

Technologies supporting this goal enable work entities to maximize value creation in the following ways:

- *Reward and build trust.* These are technologies that ensure transparency of interactions and transactions in the work environment. Through the reciprocal transfer or exchange of value between work requester and work doer, these technologies enable a sense of trust between involved parties. Direct trade and execution are enabled to transcend traditional organizational constructs. Social behavior and social media tools supplement existing employment models with transparent and equal access to the best work and skills on offer, thereby creating a trust-based work environment. This environment is supported by elements such as referrals to strengthen the verification of authenticity and reputation, blockchain, which is a decentralized, distributed, and oftentimes public digital ledger that is used to record transactions across many computers so that any involved record cannot be altered retroactively without the alteration of all subsequent blocks, and smart payment solutions to bring a frictionless experience for work requesters, work doers, and any other entities intermediating the transaction between the two.

- *Empower, delight, and improve your work experience.* The technologies in this category aim to bring a seamless experience to the work entities. These might include solutions that simplify the workflow through smart automation, reminders and nudges, and assessments; biometric and haptic activations that allow workers to trigger an event or a process by simply waving; sentiment analysis techniques using text mining, natural language processing and understanding, rare event detection and so on, to gauge the most optimal intervention point to improve the worker's perception of their work environment; and gamification techniques to motivate and reward behaviors and ensure there is a bit of fun in all that work.

- *Grow your reputation.* The technologies in this category enable work entities to quantify, track, and grow their reputation and provide a smart way to manage social/digital identity. These include tools, techniques, and services to manage online reputation, digital badges (validated indicators that certain criteria have been met such as task performed, skill acquired, deliverable built to quality), credentials, and certifications all bringing validated evidence of certain capabilities and qualifications possessed. It also includes the organizational rank and level of influence through organizational network analysis, and analysis of online behavior such as number of mentions, retweets, replies, and virality of posts and engagements.

How Can This Framework Help?

- *Adoption.* Consider the goals to make an impact on, or the experience to be created, and then select the appropriate technologies to adopt, implement, and integrate.

- *Governance.* It is important to have a governance framework for the adoption of any WorkTech. It must start with a common definition of what technologies and processes fall into the categories above. It also includes the actual list of approved tools (based on the security requirements and data management principles), security standards, level of access to the system (importance given to the sensitivity of workforce data), system controls and standards required for regulatory compliance, processes for how to manage configuration, testing, deployment of updates and upgrades, backup and recovery, and ongoing maintenance. It might also describe ways to validate the code and define what needs to be retained for compliance and auditing purposes.

- *Oversight.* Adoption of WorkTech technologies requires a process or management solution to monitor the systems, apps, and infrastructure to ensure they are, in most cases, always up and running. This is also referred to as "uptime" and the standard goal for applications is to provide 99.999 percent availability, which means less than six minutes of downtime over a year. It also includes network diagnostic, auto-detection of events, anomalies, breaches and patterns in how the solutions perform, and either dynamically responds to changes or escalates the issues to human agents. For example, during the benefits enrollment period, the system will automatically increase the network capacity to accommodate increased traffic.

- *Omni-channel access.* It is important to enable the automation agents or services to be available across different access channels and devices. This will provide a seamless experience to workers regardless of how they engage with it—be that from a mobile device, laptop at home, office computers, kiosks, shopfloor, and so on.

- *Easy integration.* Ease of adoption, implementation, and integration within the current infrastructure is very important when choosing the platforms. There is a new generation of low-code or no-code solutions that allow users to drag-and-drop integrations and workflow automation functions. This makes it easy for business users to build their own and execute workflows without expert coding knowledge.

- *End-of-life.* When we think about the lifecycle of any technology, app, or service there are several statuses to consider. "Active" status describes the most current offering of that solution. "Active Mature" describes a product that is supported by the provider, but newer products exist, and the organization could benefit from migrating or upgrading. "Discontinued" describes a product that is no longer available or maintained by the provider. The stage that is critical to keep an eye on is "End of Life" when the provider announces that the offering will be discontinued, or the contractual agreement expires. The organization must actively migrate to a replacement or termination of those services. In this case the organization must consider a whole slew of implications: communications to the end user, identifying how the data will be handled (if it requires data retention, where the data will be backed up and for how long, how the security around the data will be handled), and identifying the upstream and downstream systems that are serving up or receiving data to ensure the workflow is not broken.

- *Business case is not about cost savings.* When considering investments in WorkTech solutions it is critical to not consider automation as a way to save costs. It might be possible to automate specific activities, giving the worker an extra few minutes in their schedule. That time efficiency, however, will not translate into a 0.1 FTE of time saving. The case for WorkTech must be about efficiency and eliminating routine and unsafe activities with the intent to create more time and space for humans to do things that machines are not able to. For example, spending more time with the customer or thinking about new products or markets to expand into, or researching novel solutions to problems, or just simply feeling less stressed and gaining some balance, are more productive justifications for automation.

- *Automate the doing not the thinking.* Careful consideration should be given to the risks that are emerging because of delegating increasingly complex activities to technologies, digital agents, and automations. First, the complacency that comes with knowing that you no longer need to worry about specific steps might limit interest in changing the broader process that includes a particular automation, and as a result minimize the opportunities for innovation. Likewise, an "automate and forget" mentality can get really frustrating for the end users ("chatbots" can easily become the new "Interactive Voice Response").

- *Secure yourself.* As compelling as it is to move the work and workforce-related data to the cloud and take advantage of cheaper, scalable infrastructure and frequent upgrades/updates, sizeable data security and privacy risks emerge. As cybercrimes and data breaches are becoming more frequent, significant investment should be made not only in technical solutions to protect organizational data but also in the workers' understanding of their role in preventing hacks, leaks, and threats in the cyberworld.

Endnotes

1 Kerr, W and Robert-Nicoud, F (2019) Tech clusters, Harvard Business School, https://www.hbs.edu/ris/Publication%20Files/20-063_97e5ef89-c027-4e95-a462-21238104e0c8.pdf (archived at https://perma.cc/E38H-DQXJ)

2 PEGA (2020) Remote work done right, https://www.pega.com/remote-work-done-right (archived at https://perma.cc/TWB4-ZTJN)

3 https://www.merriam-webster.com/dictionary/wetware (archived at https://perma.cc/3ASS-APQR)

4 Dery, K and Sebastian, IM (2017) Building business value with employee experience, MIT Center for Information Systems Research, https://cisr.mit.edu/publication/2017_0601_EmployeeExperience_DerySebastian (archived at https://perma.cc/FRZ5-NXZH)

GLOSSARY

Affective computing: The study and development of systems and devices that can recognize, interpret, process, and simulate human affects. It is an interdisciplinary field spanning computer science, psychology, and cognitive science.

AI: See Artificial intelligence.

Ambient data: The information in computer storage that is not referenced in file allocation tables and is generally not viewable through the operating system (OS) or standard applications.

Analytics: The systematic computational analysis of data or statistics.

Android: A robot or other artificial being designed to resemble a human, and often made from a flesh-like material.

Anthropomorphism: The attribution of human traits, emotions, and intentions by humans to their surroundings.

App: A computer program or software application designed to run on a mobile device such as a phone, tablet, or watch.

Artificial intelligence: The theory and development of computer systems able to perform tasks that normally require human intelligence.

Bias: Prejudice in favor of or against one thing, person, or group compared with another, usually in a way considered to be unfair.

Biometrics: Body measurements and calculations related to human characteristics used in computer science as a form of identification.

Career pathways: Workforce development strategy to support workers' transitions from education into and through the workforce.

Co-working: The use of an office or other working environment by people who are self-employed or working for different employers, typically so as to share equipment, ideas, and knowledge.

Computational anthropology: The holistic study of humankind for the understanding of human behavior, culture, and evolution using computational methods.

Computational mathematics: A field concerned with the study of algorithms (or numerical methods) for the solution of computational problems in science and engineering.

Computing: Any goal-oriented activity requiring, benefiting from, or creating computing machinery.

Conspicuous consumption: A term used to describe and explain the consumer practice of purchasing or using goods of a higher quality or in greater quantity than might be considered necessary in practical terms.

Contractor: A person or company that undertakes a contract to provide materials or labor to perform a service or do a job.

Cryptocurrency: A digital currency in which transactions are verified and records maintained by a decentralized system using cryptography, rather than by a centralized authority.

Customer experience: A totality of cognitive, affective, sensory, and behavioral consumer responses during all stages of the consumption process including pre-purchase, consumption, and post-purchase stages.

Cyber security: The practice to protect internet-connected systems such as hardware, software, and data from cyberthreats.

Data: Facts and statistics collected together for reference or analysis.

Digital health passport: A verified digital repository for a traveler's health records including negative virus test results and/or inoculation records.

Digital healthcare technology: A broad, multidisciplinary concept that includes concepts from an intersection between technology and healthcare.

Digital workplace: A network of one or several workplaces that is not located in any one physical space and is technologically connected.

Essential workers: Essential (critical infrastructure) workers include healthcare personnel and employees in other essential workplaces (eg first responders and grocery store workers).

Ethical technology: A sub-field of ethics addressing the ethical questions specific to the Technology Age.

Evolutionary biology: A subfield of biology that studies the evolutionary processes (natural selection, common descent, speciation) that produced the diversity of life on Earth.

Facial recognition: A technology capable of matching a human face from a digital image or a video frame against a database of faces, typically employed to authenticate users through ID verification services; works by pinpointing and measuring facial features from a given image.

Human–computer interactions: The field of research in the design and the use of computer technology, which focuses on the interfaces between people and computers.

Industrial Revolution: The transition to new manufacturing processes in Europe and the United States, in the period from 1760 to 1820 and 1840.

Intelligent automation: The use of automation technologies—artificial intelligence (AI), business process management (BPM), and robotic process automation (RPA)—to streamline and scale decision making across organizations.

Jobs automation: The practice of substituting technology for human labor to perform specific tasks or jobs.

Keynesian economics: A macroeconomic economic theory of total spending in the economy and its effects on output, employment, and inflation.

Keystroke monitoring: A software that captures all keyboard activity and every individual keystroke entered, recording all information to comprehensive logs which can be used to formulate a base of user-based behavior analytics.

Knowledge worker: A person whose job involves handling or using information.

Metaverse: A general term that refers to shared virtual world environments that people can access via the internet.

Mindfulness: The quality or state of being conscious or aware of something.

Neoclassical economics: An approach to economics in which the production, consumption, and valuation of goods and services are driven by the supply and demand model.

Neuroaesthetics: A sub-discipline of empirical aesthetics. Empirical aesthetics takes a scientific approach to the study of aesthetic perceptions of art, music, or any object that can give rise to aesthetic judgments.

Performance management or appraisal: The process of ensuring that a set of activities and outputs meets an organization's goals in an effective and efficient manner.

Platform: An environment for building and running applications, systems, and processes.

Quantum computing: A type of computation that harnesses the collective properties of quantum states, such as superposition, interference, and entanglement, to perform calculations.

Racial audit: A voluntary, evaluative measure designed to identify the sources of persistent racial inequality that can be productively deployed by localities.

Responsible tech: Useful technology that interoperates with other things as far as possible and is designed for real people and situations.

Robot: A machine resembling a human being, able to replicate certain human movements and functions automatically.

Robotic Process Automation: A software technology that makes it easy to build, deploy, and manage software robots that emulate human actions interacting with digital systems and software.

Shareholder capitalism: An economic system in which the dominant corporate form is legally independent companies that can pool capital from many shareholders with limited liability, complemented by an open stock market to trade these shares freely.

Smart performance clothing: A new category of apparel, enhanced with innovative technology designed to provide extra functionality beyond traditional use.

Smart textiles technology: Electronic textiles, e-textiles, smart garments, and fabrics that have a digital component embedded in them.

Social compact: An implicit agreement among the members of a society to cooperate for social benefits, for example by sacrificing some individual freedom for state protection.

Subreddit: A forum dedicated to a specific topic on the website Reddit.

Succession management: A process and strategy for replacement planning or passing on leadership roles. It is used to identify and develop new potential leaders who can move into leadership roles when they become vacant.

Talent marketplace: A technical platform that allows work requesters to post and engage workers in opportunities for open positions, temporary assignments, short- and long-term part-time projects, and other initiatives.

Urbanization: The population shift from rural to urban areas, the corresponding decrease in the proportion of people living in rural areas, and the ways in which societies adapt to this change.

Video assessments: The systematic basis for making inferences about the abilities and aptitudes of job candidates based on the analysis of video recordings of them answering specific interview questions.

Workleisure: Work-appropriate looks like blazers, dresses, and pants made of technical and breathable fabrics usually associated with sportswear.

INDEX

Note: bold indicates glossary items and italic indicates figures

(4+3) Ws Framework 1–4, 165–66 *see also* Work;
    Workforce; Workplace; Worth; Worker Journey;
    Work Experience Design (WXD); WorkTech
365Talents 120

affective computing **221**
aging
    case study (MIT AgeLab) 80–81
    inclusion and 80–81
AGNES body suit 81
AI *see* artificial intelligence
air travel, IATA digital health passports 15
Airbnb 50–51, 117, 140, 142
    case study (Employee experience) 136–37
Alexa digital assistant 60
Alibaba 117
always-on culture, effects on humans 11, 12
Amazon 117, 123, 124
    case study (Empathy deficit) 74–75
    case study (Will technology fail
        humans?) 32–33, 35–36
ambient data 43–44, **221**
analytics **221**
ancient Greece 149
androids 60, **221**
anthropodenial 59
anthropomorphism 58–60, **221**
app-based employers 98
Apple 11, 95, 135
Apple iPhone 116–18
Apple Stores 89–90, 91
apps **221**
Ardern, Jacinda 71–72
Aristotle 14
    on the nature of work and leisure 11–12
artificial empathy (AE) 82–83
artificial intelligence (AI) 20, 31, 42, 45, 57, **221**
    anthropomorphism 58–60
artisanal (pre-industrial) economy 103–05
Atlassian 121–22
    case study (How Atlassian does things) 124–25
    case study (Leadership lessons from the
        Atlassian summit) 123–24
ATSs (Applicant Tracking Systems) 117–18
augmented reality (AR) 31, 156
automation 30, **223**
    impact on blue-collar jobs 9
Autor, David 61
AvalonBay Properties 112

Baron-Cohen, Simon 74
Barra, Mary 107
Behavioral Economics 13
Ben & Jerry's, case study (Journey to impact) 48

Benefit Corporations (B-Corps) 49
Benioff, Marc 18
Bersin, Josh 138
Best Buy 95
    case study (Treating employees as people) 96
BetterHelp platform 17
BetterUp coaching service 20
Bezos, Jeff 33, 74–75, 123
bias **221**
Bible 149
Biden, Joe 73, 97
Biggs, Joanna 27
biometrics **221**
BlackRock 50, 61
Blackstone, William xxi
Bloom, Paul 73–74
blue-collar jobs, transformation by automation and
    robotics 9
blue-collar workers 8, 9
boundaries of work 10–11
Box, George 28
branding, selling the brand to employees 95
Branson, Richard 89
Bravely coaching service 20
Bridgewater 18
burnout 12–13
Business Roundtable 61–62
Butterfield, Stewart 121–22, 123–24

Cannon-Brookes, Mike 121–22, 123–24
career motivation 141–42
career pathways 8, **221**
Carroll, Lewis 58–59
Carter, Dean 33
case studies
    Airbnb (Employee experience) 136–37
    Amazon (Empathy deficit) 74–75
    Amazon (Will technology fail humans?) 32–33,
        35–36
    Atlassian (How Atlassian does things) 124–25
    Atlassian (Leadership lessons from the
        Atlassian summit) 123–24
    Ben & Jerry's (Journey to impact) 48
    Best Buy (Treating employees as people) 96
    Headspace 19
    Microsoft (Can empathy save technology from
        itself?) 76–77
    MIT AgeLab (Inclusion) 80–81
    Patagonia (A cause disguised as a company)
        33–36
    Patagonia (Journey to impact) 47–48
    Ritz-Carlton Hotels (Employee
        empowerment) 89–91
    We Work comes back 110–11

Chambers, Doug 111
Chesky, Brian 136–37
chief medical officer (CMO) role 15
children, setting boundaries on their use of
       devices 11
choice architecture 13–14
Chouinard, Yvon 33
Citi 131
Clear app 15–16
coaching 19–21
Codi 111–12
Cogito voice recognition tool 82
Color of Change 50–51
computational anthropology 221
computational mathematics 221
computing 222
conspicuous consumption 222
consumerism 140–41
contractors 222
Cook, Tim 11
Coughlin, Joseph F. 80–81
Covid-19 pandemic 7
       adjusting to working from home 10–11
       demise of the white-collar economy 9
       detrimental effects of lockdown
              working 12–13
       driver of technology innovation 46–47
       essential role of the blue-collar economy 9
       exponential growth bias 30–31
       focus on employee health and wellbeing 95
       fragility of the gig work model 66–67
       impact on attitudes to work 132–33
       impact on employment culture 97–98
       mental health crisis 16–17
       new approaches to work 13–14
co-working 221
co-working spaces 109–12
cryptocurrencies 156, 222
CtW Investment Group 51
customer experience 94–95, 222
       reflected in workforce experience 91–95
       Ritz-Carlton hospitality model 89–91
Customer Relationship Management (CRM) 93, 94
customer satisfaction
       product development related to 93
       SERVQUAL measurement tool 94
cyber-physical systems xvii–xviii
cyber security 222

Dalio, Ray 18
Damon, Matt 147
Darwin, Charles 59
data 222
Daybase 111
de Waal, Frans 59
Decentraland 156
decision making, nudge concept 13–14
DelBene, Kurt 108
Deming, W. Edwards 39
Design Thinking movement 63–64
       empathy as a decision-making tool 80–81
       empathy by design 77–79
digital health passports 15–16, 222
digital healthcare technology 222
digital workplace 222

Dimon, Jamie 62
Disney, Walt 59
disruptive platforms 115–16
diversity at work 20–21
       racial audits 50–52
DoorDash 98, 117
dress codes 107
Drucker, Peter 39–40, 87–88, 94, 95, 96, 97, 98

Eberstadt, Nicholas 30
Ebrahim, Alnoor 49
economic man (homo economicus) 70–71
Edelman Annual Trust Barometer report
       (2021) 62–63, 97
Eightfold.ai 120
Einstein, Albert 41
emotional intelligence 71
empathy
       anti-empathy backlash 72–74
       artificial empathy (AE) 82–83
       case study (Can empathy save technology from
              itself at Microsoft?) 76–77
       case study (Empathy deficit at Amazon) 74–75
       design thinking and 77–79
       discovering 69–72
       driver of inclusion 80–81
       effects of lack of 74–75
       future of 83
       inclusion and 69–83
       soft skills 83
Empathy Map 79
employee-centric culture, Patagonia case
       study 33–36
employee-centric focus 61–63
employee-centric service model 95
employee experience (EX)
       about more than the technology 137–40
       case study (Airbnb) 136–37
       case study (Amazon) 32–33, 35–36
       case study (Microsoft) 120–21
       changing attitudes to work 132–33
       defining work 133–34
       emergence as a management practice 134–37
       loss of satisfaction with work 140–42
       pay and other motivations 131–33
       rise of the concept 131–42
       turnover tsunami 131–33
       types of motivation for work 141–42
employees
       as the new customers 95–96
       case study (Best Buy treating employees as
              people) 96
       case study (Employee empowerment at the
              Ritz-Carlton) 89–91
       collection of data on 42–44
       customer experience reflects workforce
              experience 91–95
       importance of taking care of 87–88
       monitoring of 42–44
       selling the company brand to 95
       Talent Management approach 87–88
       towards the worker-centered economy 97–98
       viewed as people first 87–88
employers
       concern with workers' health 14–16

hypocrisy of the gig employment
concept 66–67
mental health support services for
employees 17
environmental, social, and governance
reporting 52
Epic Games 156
Epictetus 10, 16, 18, 19
Equity Residential 112
Erlinger, Joe 132
essential workers **222**
ethical technology **222**
Everwise mentoring service 20
evolution of work 7
evolutionary biology **222**
Experience Economy 135
exponential growth bias 30–35
extended reality (XR) 156
externalities xvii–xviii
extrinsic motivation 141
Ezra coaching service 20

Facebook 51
Horizon Workrooms 155–56, 157
facial recognition **222**
Fink, Larry 61–63
Fiverr 118
flexible working arrangements 66–67
Floyd, George 50
Ford, Henry 70
Fourth Industrial Revolution xvii–xviii
freedom, setting boundaries 10–11
Friedman, Milton 96
Fuel50 120

game theory 71
GameStop 115
Gates, Bill 18, 76
Gates, Melinda 76
Gebbia, Joe 136–37
General Electric (GE) 118, 122
Gherson, Diane 64–65
gig economy 118
hypocrisy of the gig employment
concept 66–67
gig workers 27
fragility of the gig business model 66–67, 97–98
Gilbreath, Mark 112
GitHub 118
GitLab 124
Glassdoor 154
Gloat 119
GM 107
Gödel, Kurt 41
Goldman Sachs 131
junior analysts' revolt 105–07
Goleman, Daniel 71
Goodall, Jane 59
Google 10
Goulding, John 21
Grant, Adam 124
Grubhub 98

Hackl, Cathy 158
Hanson, David 60

hard skills 83
Hawking, Stephen 45, 134
Headspace
app 18–19
case study 19
health, work and 14–16
healthy decision making 13–14
Heraclitus 21
HERE Technologies 119
Hervey, Tony 20
HireVue video assessment tool 82–83
Hitch Works 119
Holder, Eric 51
home working *see* work from home (WFH)
HRIS (Human Resource Information Systems) 120
human-centered approach 7
business turns to human-centric
solutions 61–63
evolutionary case for 57
hypocrisy of the gig employment
concept 66–67
institutional resistance to 60–61
new relationship with technology 58–60
performance management battleground 64–66
stakeholder focus 61–63
human-centered design (HCD)
methodology 63–64
fragility of the gig work model 66–67
how humans reclaim the workplace 66–67
performance management battleground
64–66
human-computer interactions **222**
Human Relations movement xxi
Human Resources Management (HRM) 122
Human Revolution 21
humanity of work, reclaiming 21
humanoid robots 60
Humans at Work Manifesto 161–64
components of the manifesto 162–64
definition of a manifesto 161
need for a manifesto 162
Humans at Work Revolution xvii–xix
hybrid workplace 107–09
stages of 108–09
Hyman, Louis 57, 66

IBM 64–65, 118, 120
ibn Dahir, Sissa 31
IDEO consultancy 63–64, 77–78
impact, as a measure of work 45–48
Imperative mentoring service 20
inclusion, empathy and 69–83
Industrial Revolution 104, **223**
information technology 46
intelligent automation **223**
Isaacson, Walter 18
ISO 9241-210:2019 (HCD standard) 64

job holders 141
Jobs, Steve 18, 89–90, 91
jobs automation **223**
jobs vs work 27–36
Joly, Hubert 96
JPMorgan Chase & Co 62, 131
Jung, C.G. 36

Kahneman, Daniel 13
Kano, Noriaki 93
Kelley, David 63–64, 77–79
Kelley, Tom 78–79
Kennedy, Robert F. 134
Keynesian economics 223
keystroke monitoring 223
Kipling, Rudyard 59
knowledge workers 223
Kurzweil, Ray 45

labor market externalities xvii–xviii
leadership
    case study (Lessons from the Atlassian
        summit) 123–24
    why industrial leadership no longer
        works 122–25
leadership development, coaching and
    mentoring 19–20
lean management approach 88
Leavitt, Harold J. 46
leisure, work and 11–14
Leonardo da Vinci 151
Levi Strauss 10
life calling 142
LinkedIn 18, 152–53
LiquidSpace 103, 112

Marcus Aurelius 7
marketing mix (4Ps and 7Ps) 94
Mayer, John D. 71
McCracken, Grant 78
McDonald's 131–32
McGregor, Douglas xxi–xxii
McNealy, Scott 123
measuring work 39–52
    effects of the Covid-19 pandemic 46–47
    environmental, social, and governance
        reporting 52
    history of 39–42
    impact 45–48
    impact as an alternative measure to
        productivity 49–50
    impact audit 50–52
    monitoring of workers 42–44
    racial audit 50–52
    relevance of productivity measures 44–45
    why measurements matter 39–42
meditation practice 18–19
mental health
    detrimental effects of pandemic home
        working 12–13
    impact of the Covid-19 pandemic 16–17
    support services for employees 17
    WHO definition 16
mentoring 19–21
meta identity (MI) 172–73
Metaverse 155–58, 223
Microsoft 18, 107–09, 120, 156
    case study (Can empathy save technology from
        itself?) 76–77
    case study (Employee experience (EX)
        solutions) 120–21
    inequity of the experience of working from
        home 106–07

mindfulness 223
    role in the future of work 18–19
Mintzberg, Henry 39
MIT AgeLab (case study) 80–81
Mitchell, Colin 95
mixed reality workplaces, Metaverse 155–58
monitoring of workers 42–44
Moore's law 42
moral hazard xvii–xviii
Morgan Stanley 51, 131
motivations for working 131–42
Musonius Rufus 19

Nadella, Satya 76–77, 120–21, 156
NASA 134
neoclassical economics 70–71, 223
neuroaethetics 70, 223
Newton, Isaac 105, 106–07
no-collar economy, rise of 8–10
non-fungible tokens (NFTs) 156
Norman, Donald A. 134–35
not-for-profit organizations 49–50
nudge concept 13–14

Obama, Barack 69, 73
online coaching and mentoring services 20–21
online workers, use of the Zoom shirt 9
organizations as platforms 115–27
    case study (Microsoft enters employee
        experience (EX) relay) 120–21
    changing people practices 121–22
    considerations for implementing
        platforms 126–27
    differences from traditional organization
        designs 121–22
    orchestration of work 126
    organizational implications for
        implementing 126–27
    permeability of organizational boundaries 126–27
    transparency and its risks 127
    why industrial leadership no longer works
        122–25

Patagonia
    case study (A cause disguised as a
        company) 33–36
    case study (Journey to impact) 47–48
performance management or appraisal 223
    battleground for HCD 64–66
Pfeffer, Jeffrey 12
Picasso, Pablo 89
Pierson, Richard 19
platform strategy 116–19
platforms 223
    advance of 115–16
    disruptive effects of 115–16
    key talent marketplace players 119–21
    talent platforms 116–19
    transition to 117
platforms, organizations as 115–27
    case study (Microsoft enters employee
        experience (EX) relay) 120–21
    changing people practices 121–22
    differences from traditional organization
        designs 121–22

orchestration of work 126
organizational implications for
      implementing 126–27
permeability of organizational boundaries 126–27
redesign of organizational structures 117–19
transparency and its risks 127
why industrial leadership no longer works 122–25
post-work society 35–36
Procter & Gamble 118
productivity
      impact as an alternative measure of success 49–50
      relevance as a work measurement 44–45
Puddicombe, Andy 19
Pymetrics 120

Qatar Airways 124
quantum computing **223**

racial audits 50–52, 80, **223**
Reif, Rafael 60–61
reputation 145–58
      and its discontents 146–48
      as an asset 145–46, 150–52
      as currency 145–46, **152–55**
      as experience 145–46, 155–58
      as honor 145–46, 148–50
      corporate reputations 153–55
      digital reputations 152–55
      disassociation from work 158
      faking it 147–48
      historical stages of work reputation 145–46
      in the Metaverse 157–58
      internet and 146–48
      professional reputation building 151–55
      reputation management 155
      use of résumés and CVs 151–52
responsible tech **224**
Ridgway, V.F. 39
Rifkin, Jeremy 72
Ritz-Carlton Hotels 95
      case study (Employee-centric hospitality) 89–91
Robinhood platform 115
Robotic Process Automation (RPA) 9, **224**
robotics, impact on blue-collar jobs 9
robots **224**
Rometty, Ginni 8

sales, pivot to customer experience 94–95
Salesforce 18, 94
Salovey, Peter 71
SAP 120
Schneider Electric 118
Schulze, Horst 91
Schwab, Klaus xvii
scientific management xxi
Seagate 119
secular spirituality 18
self-employment, fragility of the gig business
      model 97–98
Sesame Street 59
Shakespeare, William 149
shareholder capitalism **224**
shareholder-first business focus 61–62
Sinclair, Upton 8

Sinek, Simon 89
Six Sigma approach 88, 93
skills-based model of work 28–30
Slack 121–22, 123–24
smart performance clothing **224**
smart textiles technology 9–10, **224**
Smith, Adam 70, 150
social compact **224**
soft skills 83
Solomon, David 131
Sophia android 60
stakeholders, business focus on 61–63
Standard Chartered 118
Stanford University d-School (Design School) 77–78
Starbucks 51, 60, 110, 135
Steiner, Peter 146, *147*
Steinhaus, Joel 111
Stoics 7, 10, 19
subreddits 115, **224**
substance abuse, detrimental effects of pandemic
      home working 12–13
succession management **224**
Sun Microsystems 123, 124
Sunday Blues phenomenon 12
Super Mario Brothers 59

Talent Management approach 87–88, 118–19
talent marketplace **224**
      key players 119–21
      platforms 116–19
Talkspace platform 17
technology
      anthropomorphism 58–60
      changes in workplace clothing 9–10
      changing definitions of 46
      collection of data on employees 42–44
      dealing with the always-on culture 11, 12
      digital healthcare tools 15–16
      new collar jobs 8
      new relationship with 58–60
      online coaching and mentoring services
            20–21
      smart textiles 9–10
      see also WorkTech
technomorphia 60
Thaler, Richard 13
The Nudge, healthy decision making tool 14
Theory X and Theory Y (McGregor) xxi–xxii
TopTal 118
Total Quality Management (TQM) 88, 93
Toyota Motor Company 93
Tversky, Amos 13

Uber 66, 117
Uber Eats 98
unemployment 29–30
Unilever 48, 118
United States
      Declaration of Independence 150
      Securities and Exchange Commission (SEC) 51
      view of employment xxi–xxiii
Upwork 118
urbanization **224**
user experience (UX) 60

Venture L 124
video assessment in job interviews 82–83, **224**
virtual reality (VR) 31
    Metaverse 155–58

WallStreetBets group 115
Walsh, Marty 97–98
Walton, Richard xxii
WearableX 10
Weick, Karl 124
Weiner, Jeff 18
Welch, Jack 122
WeWork, case study 110–11
Whisler, Thomas L. 46
white-collar workers 8–9
women workers, disproportionate effects of the
    pandemic 13, 29–30
Wooden, John 123
Work 1–4, 165–66
    automation of 30
    boundaries of 10–11
    centrality in people's lives 27–28
    coaching and mentoring 19–21
    construct 167
    deconstruction of 167–70
    defining 7–21, 133–34
    divergent views on the nature and purpose of 32–36
    evolution of 7
    exponential rates of change 30–35
    future-of-work theories 29–30
    health and 14–16
    how this framework can help 170
    human relationship with 11–14
    jobs vs work 27–36
    labor market externalities xvii–xviii
    leisure and 11–14
    loss of satisfaction with 140–42
    measuring work 39–52
    mental health issues during the pandemic 16–17
    need for new approaches to 27–28
    new approaches driven by the pandemic 13–14
    post-work society 35–36
    putting humans at the center of 7
    reclaiming the humanity of 21
    relentless tyranny of 12–13
    rise of the no-collar economy 8–10
    role of mindfulness 18–19
    search for the meaning of 140–42
    skills-based model 28–30
    societal evolutional challenge 30
    toxic aspect of the work ethic 27–28
    types of motivation for 141–42
    view of employment in the United States xxi–xxiii
    Work Without Jobs approach 29
work at scale, organizations as platforms 115–27
work design, human-centered approach 57–67
Work Experience Design (WXD) 1–4, 165–66
    construct 201–05
    how this framework can help 205–08
work from anywhere (WFA) 103, 111–12
    talent platforms 119–20
work from home (WFH) 103
    adjusting to 10–11

dealing with the always-on culture 11, 12
detrimental effects on mental health 12–13
different experiences of 105–07
why it is not the answer 105–07
Workday 120
Worker Journey 1–4, 165–66
    construct 191
    focus on the 'in between' moments 191
    good experience is contagious 192–99
    how this framework can help 199–200
    not only HR's responsibility 192
workers
    blue collar 8, 9
    new collar 8
    white collar 8–9
Workforce 1–4, 165–66
    construct 171
    how this framework can help 174–76
    human-centered work design 57–67
    loss of people from 29–30
    meta identity (MI) 172–73
    reputation 173–74
workism 27
workleisure (clothing) 9, **224**
Workplace 1–4, 165–66
    adjusting to working from home 10–11
    alternatives to traditional workplaces 109–12
    artisanal (pre-industrial) economy 103–05
    case study (WeWork comes back) 110–11
    changes in the workplace community 21
    construct 177–80
    co-working spaces 109–12
    evolution of workplace clothing 8–10
    future of work is hybrid 107–09
    how this framework can help 180–81
    Metaverse 155–58
    mixed reality workplaces 155–58
    return of the hybrid workplace 103–05
    return to work decision-making
        process 107–12
    taking work to people rather than people to
        work 110–12
    where work happens 103–12
    why working from home is not the answer 105–07
WorkTech 1–4, 165–66
    construct 209–11
    how this framework can help 216–18
    supporting workplace experience goals
        211–16
    technology clusters 209–11
Workvivo 21
Worth 1–4, 165–66
    employment values 185–88
    how this framework can help 188–89
    motivations for working 131–42
    worth/value exchange construct 183–85

Yuan, Eric 121–22, 123–24

Zalando 124
Zoom 121–22, 123–24
Zoom shirt used by online workers 9
Zuckerberg, Mark 155–56, 157